Women
and the
Public Interest

Aldine Treatises
in Social Psychology
edited by M. Brewster Smith

Women
and the
Public Interest

An Essay on Policy and Protest

JESSIE BERNARD

Research Scholar, Honoris Causa
The Pennsylvania State University

Aldine·Atherton
Chicago/New York

ABOUT THE AUTHOR

DR. JESSIE BERNARD is Research Scholar, Honoris Causa, at The Pennsylvania State University. Her many books include *Remarriage, The Sex Game, The Future of Marriage, American Community Behavior,* and *Social Problems at Midcentury;* and she has contributed more than 50 articles to professional journals. Dr. Bernard, who was educated at the University of Minnesota and Washington University, has had a distinguished professional career that includes a term as president of the Society for the Study of Social Problems. She was also co-chairman of the program for the Groves Conference on Marriage and the Family in San Juan, Puerto Rico in May, 1971.

First published 1971 by
Aldine · Atherton, Inc.
529 South Wabash Avenue
Chicago, Illinois 60605

Library of Congress Catalog Number 79–140005
ISBN 202–25024–5, cloth; 202–25071–7, paper

Printed in the United States of America

The only real justification of any social science is the degree to which it can creatively influence social policy and be one of the sources of constructive social action.

—ROBERT A. NISBET, *The Social Bond*

Contents

*Women
and the
Public Interest*

Introduction

Public policy with respect to women as wives and mothers, as consumers, as sex objects, or as workers, whether embedded in ukase or legislation, or implicit in the mores, has an ancient if not always an honorable history. King Ahasueras, long before Paul, promulgated a law to the effect that wives should subordinate themselves to their husbands. As mothers, women have occupied policy makers concerned with population control. As consumers, wealthy Roman ladies were forbidden to wear more than a certain amount of gold; sumptuary laws in the middle ages specified the nature of women's garments. Then there is the whole inconsistent array of legislation with respect to women as sex objects dealing with prostitution and the sexual obligations of wives. With the advent of industrialization there was added to the common law a large corpus of legislation presumably in the public interest dealing with women as workers. Whether truly in the public interest or in the interest of the male part of the public, policy has thus been concerned with women from time immemorial.

Old as policy problems dealing with women are, they take on new salience in this age. Women are different; the public interest is different; norms are becoming different too. A new policy with respect to marriage is in process of crystallization in the form, for example, of the nonpunitive, no-fault divorce. A permissive policy with respect to family planning, except in regard to abor-

1

tion, is no longer controversial. A nondiscriminatory policy with respect to women's work is formulated in Title VII of the Civil Rights Act of 1964. The implications for the public interest of these policies with respect to marriage, motherhood, and work, as well as the implications for women themselves, are only now being traced and evaluated.

Such evaluation is not easy. Policies dealing with women have always been complicated by the fact that there is sometimes a conflict between their interests and those of men, which has usually been resolvable in favor of men. But today they are also complicated, especially since the decline of the domestic system of organizing production, by a conflict between and among women's functions; especially their maternal functions and their industrial functions as defined in their family roles and their work roles. These conflicts are not easy to negotiate. In addition, policies are complicated also by the fact that there are conflicts among women themselves. Individuation is permitted to more women today, options are available to more of them. Women who show up on tests as having the interests of housewives see policies that foster careers for women as a threat to themselves directly or indirectly through their husbands; and the women Alice Rossi has denominated "pioneers" view policies tailored for the interests of housewives as obstacles to their own interests. Only very recently has the isolation of women from one another been breached enough to make solidarity among them feasible.

This essay is an attempt to bring into focus, from a wide variety of research sources in quite different research traditions, some of the issues that policy makers are going to have to wrestle with in relation to the functions of women in modern society. Not merely such issues as jobs, rights, and discrimination but also even more important ones such as functions, issues that would have arisen even if there had been no protesting women to dramatize them.

The most revolutionary of all the changes involving the public interest which now demand a re-examination of policy dealing with women are those concerned with the declining salience of the reproductive function of women and the technology that makes possible for an increasing proportion of women a divorce of reproduction from sexual relations. These changes call for a thorough reformulation of all our ideas about the sexual differentiation of functions.

This book is not an attempt to cover the whole waterfront, but just one small, though very significant, inlet. It addresses itself to some of the current paradoxes of policy as related to women and the processes now involved in dealing with them. It is an elaboration and up-dating of a position paper originally written for an agency of the executive branch of the government, and it is a sister-volume to a book on the future of marriage.

Although psychological variables are intrinsic to any study of women, the approach here is primarily sociological. After an introductory review in Part I, Parts II and III marshal the analyses and research findings that deal with the sexual differentiation of functions and the sexual division of labor respectively. Part IV reports attempts to adjust the lives of women to the Establishment and Part V the demands of protesting women that the Establishment be adjusted to the lives of women. These protesting women translate the conventional tables of researchers into a different language, perhaps adumbrating, as shown in Part VI, a revolution in the not-too-distant future, if not signaling one already upon us today, for it is a great deal later than we thought it was yesterday.

I

Coming to Terms

No thoroughgoing coverage of all the possible meanings of the several terms in the title of this book is intended in Part One, but only enough to orient the discussion. A great deal of the confusion that arises in discussions about *women* arises because women are not all alike and few generalizations can be made that include all of them. It is to this diversity and the problems it poses for policy makers that Chapter 1 addresses itself.

The *public interest,* or the general welfare, is not always self evident, nor is there even unanimity on its validity as a concept. Thus at least a nod of recognition is due to the complexity of the idea itself. No more than this is claimed. If, as the quotation from Robert Nisbet, the epigraph of this book, says, the only justification for the social sciences is to influence social *policy,* some recognition has also to be given to the nature of policy and, in the case of our own country at least, to the *paradoxes* (Chapter 3) it has to contend with. The "constructive social action" in the present context includes the *protests* of modern women.

1

Women

The Mark of Eve

No one is likely to cavil seriously at the first term in the title
of this book. Despite universal recognition of differences among
women, whatever their causes, women as everyone knows, are
women.[1] Still, Ruth Useem, a sociologist, once commented on the
inadequacy of the single mark she had to make on all documents
asking for "sex." All she could do was check the F box. But she
knew that this "mark of Eve" told the reader very little about
her. There were so many kinds of F: F_1, F_2, . . . F_n, and yet
there was no way to let the reader know which one she was.[2]

Her comment was by no means trivial, facetious, or irrelevant
to policy, for the "mark of Eve" a woman makes in the F box

1. There is, interestingly, less consensus with respect to the term *lady*.
In Victorian times a lady was a special kind of person, refined, circumspect,
noble, virtuous, sexless, well behaved, and well mannered. Both the term
and the concept went out of fashion in the twentieth century. Modern women
did not want to be ladies; to be called "ladylike" came to be something to
be resented. It has been with some surprise, therefore, that I have noted a
return to the use of this term, even by fellow social scientists in research
conferences. They speak of research subjects as "ladies," as though at a loss
of what else to call women.

2. In my book, *The Sex Game,* I used the concept of subsexes as a ploy
to emphasize the importance of such intrasex differences among both women
and men.

ascribes a status to her that is quite independent of her qualities as an individual. Every other mark she makes on that or any other documents will be evaluated in terms of that mark. Assumptions will be made about her on the basis of it. Privileges, responsibilities, prerogatives, obligations will be assigned on the basis of it also. Policy will rest on it. A great deal rides on that one mark, for it refers to the most fundamental differentiation among human beings. But it leaves out differences among the Fs themselves, as important as the similarities. Yet, though there are few bodies of lore and literature more extensive than that on the nature of differences between men and women, there are few less extensive than those on the nature of differences among women themselves.

The Visibility Gap

In the age of innocence, moving picture producers made it very clear to us at the very outset of a picture who were the good guys and who the bad. The good guys wore white hats. In nineteenth-century melodramas the villain wore an identifying mustache so that we knew he was going to foreclose the mortgage unless the beautiful daughter capitulated to his advances. In Greek drama there were appropriate masks to inform us about the characters.

Despite our dependence on visual cues, however, there is always a visibility gap. The outer mark does not tell us all there is to know about the person inside. The same mark stamps a wide variety of people. Not all the farmers who bore the mark of Cain killed grazers and herders. A wide variety of men bore that mark. A wide variety of people inhabit the bodies of women (as also, of course, the bodies of men as well). For women are not interchangeable parts.

$F_1, F_2, \ldots F_n$

Whatever the differences may be between M and F, and whatever the origin of these differences may be, they are matched and in some cases exceeded by differences among women themselves.

A woman may in many ways be more like the average man than she is like another women. A very considerable research literature undergirds the fact that there are extensive differences among women in such sociologically relevant variables as interests, values, and goals. These differences have to be taken into account when dealing with programs or policies involving women.

Two polar types turn up with singular consistency in the research literature on women, whether the point of view is sociological or psychological.[3] Alice Rossi assigned the terms "pioneer" and "housewife" to these types, using the term "traditional" for those who feel in between (Rossi, 1965, pp. 79–80). Another team of researchers called the polar types "homemaking-oriented" and "career-oriented" (Hoyt and Kennedy, 1958). Another researcher spoke of "creative intellectual" when referring to a type that corresponded to pioneer or career-oriented (Drews, 1965). Eli Ginzberg and his associates found women they called "supportive," who corresponded roughly to the housewife or home-oriented subjects in the other studies, and "influential" women who resembled the pioneer type (Ginzberg, 1966). The existence of such types can scarcely be challenged.

The exact numerical population size of these several types is not important, for it doubtless changes over time and is certainly changing today. In the recent past, however, one of the striking facts that emerged from the studies was the agreement they showed with respect to the incidence of the several types in different samples. At the high school senior level, 7 to 8 per cent of the "creative intellectuals" had the drive to achieve the life style they desired. Among college freshmen, 8 per cent fell into the career-oriented category. Among college graduates, 7 per cent were pioneers. Among women who had done graduate work, 10 per cent were living an influential life style. At Cornell, 8 per cent of a sample of women in 1950 and 6 per cent of a sample in 1952 showed high career orientation (Goldsen, 1960, p. 136). At Vassar, however, also in the 1950's, two-thirds answered "true"

3. It is important always to note the date of any research on women. The era of the feminine mystique, from the end of the war through the 1950's, exerted a powerful influence on what women thought and felt.

to the statement "I would like a career" (Freedman, 1967, p. 136). In context, this answer was interpreted by Caroline Bird to mean "career" in a secondary sense. Perhaps more indicative of a pioneer orientation was the answer to the statement "I enjoy children," which elicited a negative in 8 per cent of the women. That the Vassar women were changing rapidly was suggested by Caroline Bird, who noted that the classes of 1964 to 1966 voted for "career with as little time out for family as possible" and that there was even a notable rise in the number of girls who said they were pursuing a "career period" (Bird, 1968, p. 184). The proportion in all the samples who fell into the housewife or home-making or supportive category was consistently about a fifth or a fourth. It is interesting to compare this figure with the proportion, about 18 per cent, of college women who, a generation ago, were reported by Lewis M. Terman to be greatly interested in the domestic arts (Terman and Miles, 1936, pp. 209–210).

It would require considerably more focused research to pinpoint with greater accuracy and precision the relative incidence of the several types and the reasons that explain these proportions. Equally important would be research to document trends in such incidence. My own reading of current trends is that one of the most drastic shake-ups in the social order today is the breaking up of old blocs and their re-forming into new configurations. Yesterday's data no longer reflect the current scene. In 1969 a national sample of youth showed 10 per cent of the young women to be radical reformers and 17.1 per cent moderate reformers (Yankelovich, 1969).

The characterization of the pioneer (or career-oriented or creative intellectual or influential) type varied with the interests of the researchers; but here, too, there was notable convergence. Among the high-school girls, the creative intellectuals tended to be more receptive than other girls to the new, to growth, and to change; they were less conventional and conforming. Among college students, those who fell into the pioneer or career-oriented category tended to show up in all the studies as different from other college women. The Kansas State career-oriented freshmen were higher on "endurance" and "achievement" than the home-making-oriented women and lower on "succorance" and "heterosexuality"—in the sense of being interested in attracting young men, not as contrasted with homosexuality (Hoyt and Kennedy, 1968). Rossi's housewives characterized themselves as dependent; they showed strong nurturance toward the young; they were socially rather than occupationally competitive. In contrast, the pioneers were less dependent, less nururant, more egalitarian; they valued the world of ideas more. They characterized themselves as dominant and occupationally competitive (the married less so than the single). Ginzberg's women with the influential life style were characterized by a striving for autonomy; they found their major sources of gratification in the social significance of their work and the personal relations involved in it. In both the Rossi and the Ginzberg samples, the women in the pioneer or influential category were far more likely to be working (70 per cent in both samples) and less likely to be married; the reverse was true for the housewives and supportive women. At Cornell, it was found that the career-oriented women were more likely than the family-oriented women to be nonconformists with "a certain irreverence for rules and conventions" (Freedman, 1967, p. 140). At Vassar, years of careful research yielded this picture of career-oriented students:

> Students who say "true" to "I would like a career" are somewhat more intellectual, unconventional, independent (perhaps rebellious), and flexible in thinking and outlook. They are also somewhat more alienated or isolated socially. [At Cornell, career women engaged in just as many extracurricular activities as other women and were just as likely to associate with men (Goldsen, 1960, p. 54).] It is interesting to observe that these differences are most pronounced [among seniors]. Results for the Ethnocentrism Scale . . . are in line with findings of other studies which demonstrate that attitudes toward the role and behavior of women are likely to accord with attitudes toward members of outgroups or "underprivileged" groups. Individuals, including women themselves, who hold somewhat stereotyped views of Negroes or foreigners, for example, are likely to adhere to traditional or rather fixed notions of what is appropriate activity for women (Freedman, 1967, p. 140).

The explanations of such differences among women also vary according to the researchers' predilections. One team of psychologists is satisfied by a pattern of "needs." Career-oriented women, they believe, are motivated by one or more of four such needs: to establish one's worth through competitive behavior or achievement, to know intellectually and understand ("intraception"), to accomplish concrete goals (endurance), and to avoid relations with men (heterosexuality). The homemaking women are motivated by needs for affection and acceptance (succorance) (Hoyt and Kennedy, 1958). But another psychologist is quite agnostic: "Psychology has nothing to say about what women are really like, what they need and what they want, essentially, because psychology does not know" (Weisstein, 1969, p. 78).[4] Sociologists and social psychologists tend to look to socialization variables to interpret the differences. (See Chapters 4 and 6 for further elaboration.) Since career orientation may change with age and experience, it is hazardous to put too much credence in any analysis that makes it depend on personality variables, which are presumably quite stable. Such an approach, in any event, still leaves the genesis of the needs themselves to be explained.

Whatever the incidence and whatever the explanation, telescoping all these women into the single F box blots out a great deal of sociologically important diversity. In many situations F_1 may have more in common with M_1 than with any of the other Fs. Rank, for example, is more important than sex in many situations. A princess has more in common with a prince than with a domestic; a professional woman often has more in common with a colleague than with a cleaning woman; an heiress with an heir than with a woman receiving welfare payments. Sometimes F_i and F_j have not only different but opposing points of view, each seeing the other as a threat either to a vested interest or to opportunity for achievement. The wife of a workingman may not agree with the woman worker on the principle of equal pay for equal work; she believes her husband should get more because he has to support his family. (Perhaps the only thing that all Fs have in common as yet is the concern that adequate gynecological, ob-

4. The data and the argument for Dr. Weisstein's agnosticism are presented in Chapter 13.

stetrical, and pediatric services be widely available, and that public toilet facilities be supplied with emergency equipment.)

It would, then, be more in line with the facts of life if, instead of compressing all women into the single F category, the diversity among them could be recognized by allowing for F_1, F_2, . . . F_n. Thus the woman who says she is content to devote her life to the traditional pattern of homemaking could be differentiated from the woman who is willing to settle for nothing less than the complete gamut—marriage, children, and a career.

In the past there has been a tendency to play up the differences between pioneers and housewives, and until very recently the pioneers—active, nonconformist, achievement-oriented women— were the villains, the "bad guys." Career women were stereo- typed as castrating females, horrendous creatures, and the sweet, passive little housewife was seen as needing protection against them. There was a conflict between them: F_p F_h.

But intuitive observers noted that it was the pioneers who needed to be defended and encouraged and protected from the unmotivated, rather than the other way round. David Riesman, for example, noted "a fair amount of evidence . . . that women are their own worst enemies. The evidence lies in the tacit league of educated housewives accusing working mothers of neglecting their families, or the preference of women college students for men teachers or the dislike of women to be 'bossed' by other women" (Riesman, 1964, pp. xvi-xvii). An extraordinarily strong articulation of the women-against-women point of view was made by John S. Eells, Jr., who said that he thought "the greatest threat to the talented women is the untalented women," and he concluded that "we should devise honorable and ethical means of protecting our talented women from untalented women" (Eells, 1964, p. 37).

The isolation of women in the past tended to prevent solidarity from developing among them. But it should be noted in passing— it is discussed in more detail in Chapter 6—that women at the present time are trying hard to minimize such rifts. They do not like to see any woman put down—housewives any more than pioneers. Or vice versa.

Sex

If both the layman and the scientist have underplayed the differences among women, they have tended to overplay the differences between females and males. A great deal of the work of running the world rests on making simple classificatory decisions. Into which category does X fall? Y? or Z? Which rules apply? Anything, therefore, that simplifies this process by predecision is welcomed by administrators and executives and copers in general. Sex is such a predecision-maker. F goes here, M there: so much easier than having to study each case individually to decide on its merits where it belongs, which rule to apply. It is such a simple, straightforward, ineffable, easily applied criterion that it has rarely been challenged.

But new research issuing from clinic and laboratory is beginning to shake our old naiveté about sex. We now know that, far from being a simple, straightforward, genetically determined phenomenon, sex has at least three components—chromosomal, hormonal, anatomical—and conceivably more. Although for most people these three components are matched to produce a clearcut male or female individual, such is not always the case. There can be mistakes. These "errors of the body" have alerted us to some of the anomalies possible in the sphere of sexuality. When all goes normally, as it usually does, the M and F boxes fit very well to distinguish males and females. They can accomodate almost everyone. But things do not always go normally. Sometimes a genetic F is masculinized hormonally *in utero* with the result that anatomical anomalies confuse gender assignment at birth; or a genetic M is not masculinized *in utero,* making gender equivocal. Such errors are rare and turn up so infrequently that relatively little is yet known about them; they are so rare that, once they are recognized, we can disregard them in any analysis of large-scale sociological phenomena.[5] Their major relevance for

5. Female anomalies are especially rare, being only one-third to one-eighth as common as male anomalies (Stoller, 1968, p. 197).

our discussion here is the lesson they teach with respect to the relative contribution of biological, social, cultural, and sociological factors to gender.

With the exception of those who are victims of "errors of the body" there is no overlap between male and female populations. They are categorically different (Figure 1.1). Still it is interesting to note that, different though the equipment at their disposal may

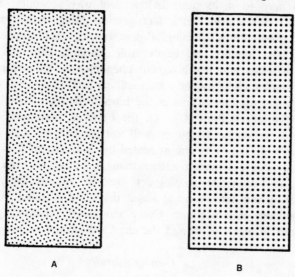

A   B

Figure 1.1. The Sexes Are Categorically Different.

be, they respond quite similarly to the same stimuli. Estrogens and androgens, for example, have the same effect on both sexes, making for greater or less sexual motivation, greater or less aggressiveness (Hamber and Lunde, 1966). This suggests that the two sexes also respond about the same way to other kinds of stimuli—psychological and social. What is important are the kinds of stimuli they are subjected to. Interesting also is the finding that creative personalities, whether housed in female or in male bodies, have similar personality characteristics.

Gender

Gender refers to the complex of traits that determine whether one checks the M or the F box. It is, to be sure, inextricably related to sex, but "the two realms, sex and gender, are not at all inevitably bound in anything like a one-to-one relationship, but each may go in its quite independent way" (Stoller, 1968, pp. viii-ix). Sex is a biological fact; gender, though based on biology, is a social-cultural-sociological-psychological fact. Gender consists of gender identity and gender role (Stoller, 1968, p. 92): the first a social and psychological phenomenon; the second, a cultural and sociological and interactional one.

Gender identity begins in the hospital delivery room. As soon as an infant is born it is, on the basis of anatomical cues, assigned a gender which is well established by age two. The infant's life course is almost sealed by that act; for it is primarily this gender assignment rather than anatomy, or even heredity, that, in Freud's terminology, is destiny. Almost every decision made by the outside world about this child is going to take this assignment into account. Every structured relationship will be defined in terms of it, and the child will accept it in most cases.

Gender Identity

Scarcely a woman alive would have any hesitation about marking the proper F or M box. A woman knows she is a female. The whole matter of gender identity would probably never have occurred to a woman; it looks to her like a man-made problem manufactured by male psychoanalysts, illustrating the sexism that modern women are protesting against. This sexism of psychoanalysts is nowhere better portrayed than in their inability to understand how women could possibly have any sense of femaleness without something like a phallus to prove to themselves that they were women. An inverted phallus or vagina was invoked to solve the riddle. It has been a major contribution of recent gender research to show that it does not take a vagina, notoriously lacking in sensitivity, to confer gender identity on females. Breasts and menstruation serve quite adequately to remind them that they are female, strange as it may seem to a breastless nonmenstruating individual. To psychoanalysts, the muscle that daily (and, in youth, hourly) reminds males of their sex seemed the sine qua non of gender identity; a creature lacking it must be only a defective male. The results of this thinking showed up in therapy; "It is possible that the analyst's view of a successful analysis may be skewed if he feels that he has reached the core of a woman's femininity when he has been able to get her to share with equanimity his belief that she is really an inferior form of male" (Stoller, 1968, p. 63).

Actually a woman's gender identity is firm, even, in some cases, if her heredity or anatomy is not. In Table 1.1 for example, three women are discussed who would unhesitatingly mark the F box; they have female gender identity (numbers 2, 3, and 5). But both their heredities and their anatomies differ. One (number 3) has female heredity and external anatomy but no vagina. One (number 2) has female heredity but, as a result of masculinization *in utero,* male-appearing genitalia; female gender was assigned to her at birth and despite the anatomical anomaly she finds the F box acceptable. A third woman (number 5) has neuter heredity and anomalous anatomy; but, assigned female gender at birth, she, too, has no problem with the F box. Such women may be unhappy about their inadequate or flawed sexuality, but their gender identity is unimpaired; they feel like women and unequivocally check the F box. All are F even though either their heredity or their anatomy does not conform to F specifications.

Such cases show the independence of gender identity from either heredity or anatomy. They illustrate its social nature: "those aspects of sexuality that are called gender are . . . learned postnatally" (Stoller, 1968, p. xiii) primarily from the mother but also from the father, siblings, and friends.

Cases number 1 and 2 also illustrate the social nature of gender identity or the acceptance of the gender assigned at birth. In both cases the infants were genetically females but in both cases the external genitalia, according to which gender is assigned, had been masculinized *in utero* and were therefore anomalous. In the case of one of the children (number 2), the diagnosis of sex was

*Table 1.1. Deviances Illustrating the Equivocal Relation of Gender
Identity to Heredity and Anatomy*

	Genetic Sex	Internal Anatomy	External Anatomy	Gender Assignment	Gender Identity
1.	Female	Female	Equivocal	Male	Male
2.	Female	Female	Equivocal	Female	Female
3.	Female	Defective	Female	Female	Female
4.	Female	Female	Female	Female	Male
5.	Neuter (XO)	Defective	Female	Female	Female
6.	Equivocal (XXY)	Female	Male	Male	Female
7.	Male	Male	Equivocal	Female	Male
8.	Male	Male	Equivocal	Male	Female

SOURCE: Data from Robert J. Stoller, *Sex and Gender, on the Development
of Masculinity and Femininity* (Science House, New York, 1968).

1. "Money and the Hampsons . . . describe two children masculinized *in
utero* by excessive adrenal androgens, both biologically normal females,
genetically and in their internal sexual anatomy and physiology, but with
masculinized external genitalia. The proper diagnosis having been made, one
child was raised unequivocally as a female . . . ; she turned out to be as
feminine as other little girls" (p. 57).

2. "The other, not recognized to be female, was raised without question as
a male . . . and became an unremarkably masculine little boy" (p. 57).

3. "The patient is a 17-year-old, feminine, attractive, intelligent girl who
appeared anatomically completely normal at birth, but behind whose external
genitalia there was no vagina or uterus. Her parents, having no doubts, raised
her as a girl, and female and feminine is what she feels she is" (p. 56).

4. "These people, living permanently as unremarkably masculine men, are
biologically normal females and were so recognized as children . . . Among
those I know one is an expert machine tool operator, another an engineering
draftsman, another a research chemist. Their jobs are quiet, steady, and un-
spectacular; their work records as men are excellent. They are sociable, not
recluses, and have friendships with both men and women. Neither their
friends nor their colleagues at work know they are biologically female. They
are not clinically psychotic" (pp. 194, 196).

5. "[She] is a person as biologically neuter as a human can be, chromosomally XO . . . And yet when she was first seen at age 18 . . . she was quite
unremarkably feminine in her behavior, dress, social and sexual desires, and
fantasies, indistinguishable in these regards from other girls . . . Her gender
identity is not based on some simple biological given, such as endocrine state.
It comes from the fact that she looked like a girl . . . Given the anatomical
prerequisites to the development of her femininity, it set in motion the complicated process that results in gender identity" (p. 22).

6. ". . . born an apparently normal male, . . . the boy's body became feminized" (p. 77).

7. "A child . . . at birth was found to be an apparently normal female and
so was brought up as a girl for fourteen years . . . A physical examination
[at adolescence] raised doubts shortly to be confirmed . . . . The inquiry . . .
revealed that although the external genitalia looked the same as those of a

correct and the child was assigned female gender and reared as a female. In the other (number 1), the diagnosis was incorrect and the child was assigned male gender and reared as a male. The first became as feminine as other little girls, the other a masculine little boy. Same sex heredity, same prenatal "error," but different gender assignment and hence different gender identity.

Gender is so thoroughly bred into the infant by the world around it and becomes so much a part of its identity that even if the assignment is later discovered to be an error, it is almost impossible to change. Despite the discovery that the individual is genetically a male, he continues to have female gender identity.

All these findings warn us against taking the M and F boxes too much for granted. Gender identity does not apparently always just come naturally. It has to be learned. And there is no one-to-one relationship between it and sex.

The emphasis on the social and acquired nature of gender identity does not rule out a biological component, for "if the first main finding of [recent research] is that gender identity is primarily learned, the second is that there are biological forces that contribute to this" (Stoller, 1968, p. xiii). Sometimes, for reasons not yet clear, gender assignment does not "take," as in cases 4, 6, 7, and 8. The resulting phenomena curb any dogmatism we may show with respect to our knowledge of sex and gender. The nature of the biological component involved in gender is still an open question. Beach calls it an unresolved issue (Beach, 1965, p. 565) and Stoller confesses that the evidence is equivocal, "so we must leave this subject without any sense of its having been settled" (Stoller, 1968, p. 85). For this reason as well as for the reason that sexual anomalies are so rare, the strictly biological factors in gender are given no further attention here. Although they teach us a great deal about the normal aspects of sex and gender, they cannot be invoked in sociological analyses. Further

---

normal girl of her age, she was in fact a chromosomally normal male" (pp. 67, 69).

8. "This patient . . . was male in anatomical appearance. However, as far back as memory goes, he was extremely feminine . . . . Hospitalized as a result of hepatitis, he was discovered to be genetically and anatomically male" (p. 75).

discussion would distort the picture by overemphasizing rare exceptions.

Although the etiological contribution of biological factors to gender identity may be equivocal and often irrelevant, the indirect or derivative contribution of biological factors cannot be denied. In the crucial years when both F and M are working out their mature identities, they are producing different reactions in one another. She produces an erection in him; another boy does not. His touch on her breasts thrills her; another girl's does not. She wants him to caress her; she does not want another girl to. Being reacted to by others as F is different from being reacted to by them as M. And the reaction to F is different from the reaction to M. She can receive him, he cannot receive her. It does not take a sophisticated analysis in terms of symbolic interactionism to see that the different effect each has *on* the other and the different reaction each has *to* the other will produce different conceptions of the self in both M and F. These differences are ultimately biological but, like the functional basis for differences (to be discussed later), in a derived rather than in a direct sense.

Gender Role

Along with gender assignment goes a constellation of traits suitable for characterizing the gender. When illustrating or demonstrating the gender identity of patients, Stoller gives such evidence of feminine gender identity as wanting babies and having a great interest in clothes, cooking, sewing, make-up, ornamentation, and the like (Stoller, 1968, pp. 21–22). These are clearly not all the product of heredity nor of anatomy. They are traits that our society labels feminine.

Some of the specific contents or traits that constitute masculine or feminine gender may vary from place to place and time to time. In Iran, for example, some of the traits that we develop as parts of feminine gender are included in the pattern for masculine gender and vice versa:

> In Iran . . . men are expected to show their emotions. . . . If they don't, Iranians suspect they are lacking a vital human trait and are

not dependable. Iranian men read poetry; they are sensitive and have well-developed intuition and in many cases are not expected to be too logical. They are often seen embracing and holding hands. Women, on the other hand, are considered to be coldly practical. They exhibit many of the characteristics we associate with men in the United States. A very perceptive Foreign Service officer who had spent a number of years in Iran once observed, "If you think of the emotional and intellectual sex roles reversed from ours, you will do much better out here." . . . Fundamental beliefs like our concepts of masculinity and femininity are shown to vary widely from one culture to the next (Hall, 1963, p. 10).[6]

The specific contents of masculinity and feminity vary with time also; people worry over the "masculinization of women" and the "feminization of men." The Victorian contents of feminine gender included weakness, helplessness, fragility, delicacy, and even ill health. Clark Vincent has pointed out how ill-fitting the traditional contents of gender roles are today for both F and M. On tradition-oriented tests, modern middle-class women tend to test low; middle-class men, on the other hand, "tend to score high on femininity when items are included which formerly described the more dependent, intuitive, sensitive, 'peacemaking' role of the female in a tradition-oriented society" (Vincent, 1966, p. 199).

Gender specifications vary not only with time and place but also with the researcher or scientist who reports them. One survey of the literature on the feminine character concluded that "there is hardly any common basis to the different views. The difficulty is not only that there is disagreement on specific characteristics [of feminine gender] and their origin, but that even when there is agreement the emphasis is laid on absolutely different attributes" (Klein, 1946, p. 164).

The most widely recurrent traits attributed to women in western societies have been passivity, emotionality, lack of abstract interests, greater intensity of personal relationships, and an instinctive tenderness for babies (Klein, 1946, p. 164). The test of masculinity-femininity includes such items as passivity, disinclination for physical violence, sensitivity to personal slights and to

6. Margaret Mead also made a great deal of the cultural contents of gender, which she labeled *temperament* (Mead, 1925).

interpersonal relations, lack of concern for abstractions, and a positive attitude toward culturally defined esthetic experience.

If femaleness and maleness are categorical, nonoverlapping, the same cannot be said with respect to femininity and masculinity. Here the overlap can be considerable (Figure 1.2). Traits

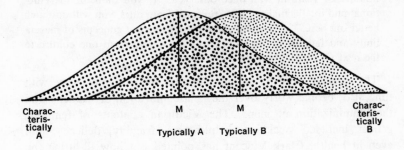

Figure 1.2. Masculine and Feminine Gender Traits Overlap.

Figure 1.2a. The Range of Overlap between A and B Can Vary Widely.

denominated as feminine show up in men and those denominated as masculine show up in women.[7] Here the distinction between *typical* and *characteristic* is important. The typical is the average or the modal. And for many traits, where the overlap is great, the average woman and the average man may not be very different. But when women and men do differ, they differ in characteristic ways, women "characteristically" in one direction, men in another. By and large, women tend to differ in the direction of pas-

7. In a sample of 604 men and 696 women in the general population Terman found both men and women in the range of scores on masculinity-femininity from −80 to +60; but above 60 there were no women and below −99 there were no men (Terman, 1936, p. 72).

sivity, nurturance, nonviolence, and men in the direction of aggression, dominance, and violence. The tendency of most societies is to pull women in one direction and men in the other, so that very often the distributions are skewed (Figure 1.3). For

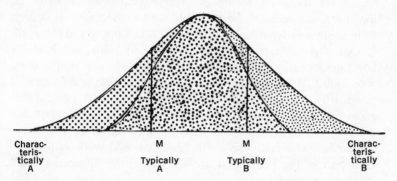

| Charac-
teris-
tically
A | M

Typically
A | M

Typically
B | Charac-
teris-
tically
B |

The socialization process has pulled A and B in different directions, so that the distributions are skewed in a desired direction.

Figure 1.3. Skewed Distributions of Gender Traits.

the convenience of managers and copers, it would be ideal if femininity and masculinity were as categorically clear-cut as femaleness and maleness; it would save them a great deal of trouble if all females were characteristically feminine and all males were characteristically masculine. But the fact is that they aren't. The important thing is not, therefore, whether or not "women" are z-er than "men," or "men" v-er than "women," but whether Mary is z-er than John, or John v-er than Mary.

Viola Klein has traced the conceptualization of sex differences through three stages, beginning with Aristotle's category of feminine traits which led him to conclude that femininity was a "kind of natural defectiveness." According to this conceptualization, women were underdeveloped beings with the external attributes of human beings but lacking individuality, intellectual ability, or character. A second stage granted that women were not inferior men but simply different, complementary, inverse. This point of view flourished at the end of the nineteenth and beginning of the twentieth centuries. The third, current, conceptualization sees personality traits as products of functional roles (Klein, 1946, pp. 169–170).

Despite the enormous amount of ink that has been spilled in clearly specifying the nature of psychological gender differences, the conclusion seems to be that it is not so much *what* is defined as masculine or feminine as that such distinctions are made at all. It makes no difference whether pink is for girls and blue for boys, emotionality for girls and rationality for boys, or the other way round. What does make a difference is that a difference is made. It is not the explanations offered for the existence of differences (inherent, acquired, functional, structural) but the fact that there is something to explain. It is the bifurcation by sex that is the fundamental fact. The traits, functions, and work assigned to each part of the bifurcation are secondary; the bifurcation itself is what is primary.

Sex has inevitable structural concomitants and consequences. The structural components that operate differentially on the sexes are both horizontal and vertical; the world women live in tends to be different, and it is usually secondary to the world of men.

The Sphere of Women

Once an individual has been assigned a gender, he (or she) is thereafter relegated to the world or sphere designed for those with his (or her) gender. Even when the work of both women and men was in the home, they lived in different worlds: there was a sphere for men and a sphere for women. Even today there is a woman's world recognized by almost everyone and thoroughly exploited by the mass media. It has quite a different structure from the world of men.

These worlds can be described in terms of several dimensions or variables that those sociologists who follow Talcott Parsons have found useful in describing social systems. Five such dimensions have been encapsulated in terms of five pairs of variables. A community can, first of all, make one's position rest on what one *does* or on what one *is;* it can be the result of achievement or of ascription. Second, the expectations that parties in any relationship share may be specific or diffuse. Duties, obligations, and responsibilities may be defined specifically and contractually or they may be left unspecified. If they are specified, each party knows precisely what is expected of him and of others; nothing more can be demanded than what is specified and nothing less can be supplied. The accountant may not be asked to run the computer, the lawyer to run the elevator. If they are left diffuse, there is a rather amorphous, blurred set of expectations that leave precise limits undefined. A friend may be expected to lend money, arrange a date, or share a record collection. Third, a community can require that all relationships be governed by general universalistic principles or it can permit them to be governed by particularistic personal loyalties and obligations tailored to the particular individuals involved. Fourth, it can permit behavior to be oriented toward furthering one's own interests or it can require that actions be oriented toward a larger group or the collectivity as a whole, regardless of individual wishes. Finally, the community can admit a wide range of relationships in which there is a minimum of affect or emotional gratification (in which relationships are neutral) or it can allow a wide range of relationships in which affectivity or emotional gratification plays a large part. It is clear that a society in which the first of each of these five pairs of variables prevails will be quite different from one in which the second of each does.

These dimensions or ways of patterning the variables have been used to describe communities or societies of different kinds. For example, ascription, diffuseness, particularism, collectivity-orientation, and affectivity have been used to describe preliterate societies. The first three pairs of dimensions have been used to characterize developing countries as contrasted with modern ones; the degree to which they approachd achievement, specificity, and universalistic characteristics has been taken as a measure of modernization (Hoselitz, 1964).

It is not too fanciful to view the gender world or sphere in which women live as characterized, like a preliterate society, by ascription, diffuseness, particularism, collectivity-orientation, and affectivity. In effect, to view women as inhabiting an underdeveloped, if not a primitive, world.

The first step has been taken when feminine gender is ascribed to the female infant. A lifelong train of consequences then ensues. She is thereafter dealt with on the basis of what she is—a woman—rather than on what she does, on her (feminine) qualities rather than on her performance, just as reported for preliterate cultures.

Once this assignment and consequent ascription have been made, a woman is consigned to a world or "sphere" in which her relationships are diffuse rather than specific or contractual. Even in a work situation where, presumably relations are contractual and specific, the secretary has diffuse expectations to live up to, such as the variegated services expected of an "office wife" or "girl Friday." The sphere of women is expected to be characterized by particularistic morality more than by universalistic morality, by intense personal loyalty more than by principles. Women are to protect their children even when the children are delinquents or criminals, to do everything they can for those near and dear to them rather than be blindly just or impartial. On the job, women, as part of their supportive function, are expected to be more loyal to their employers than are men. One reads from time to time that men have reported wrongdoing on the part of their employers, one rarely reads that women have. The "developed" country that men inhabit almost forces them to undercut one another to get ahead. In the women's sphere, women are expected to be oriented toward the larger group or the collectivity and to make sacrifices for it. We know that in marriage it is wives who make more of the adjustments; it is taken for granted that mothers make sacrifices for their children; it is expectable that if necessary, the daughter rather than the son will sacrifice marriage to take care of elderly parents. Yet the pursuit of self-interest is almost a virtue in the world men inhabit.

In using this form of "pattern-variable" analysis it is essential to make perfectly clear that the personal characteristics of the individuals involved are not the focus of attention; it is rather the shared expectations built into the situation. A social system leads to certain kinds of behavior on the part of its members regardless of their personal qualities or traits. We tend thereafter to attribute to the individuals the qualities expected in them by the system. For example, Freud tells us that the superego of women "is never as inexorable, as impersonal, as independent of its emotional origins as we require it to be in men [affectivity]. Character-traits which critics of every epoch have brought up against women—that they show less sense of justice than men . . . that they are more often influenced in their judgments by their feelings of affection or hostility [particularism]—all these would be amply accounted for by the modification in the formation of their super-ego" (Freud, 1925, pp. 257–258). In terms of the pattern-variable frame of reference, Freud is saying that in women's world affectivity rather than affective neutrality is the expectation, and particularistic rather than universalistic morality. The expectation of this particular pattern in the world of women imposes it on them.

Spock offers specific examples of how such expectations are realized in the modal personality types of men and women. Women, he tells us, become indignant when legal logic results in an unfair decision. "Her husband says, 'Don't you see that the law *has* to take this position, even if it occasionally causes injustice?' " (Spock, 1970). The feminine modal personality type does not. That is not the logic of her (particularistic) world. Her perch is in a particularistic world, his in a universalistic one. They do not see the same things.

There are those who bemoan the passing of the ascriptive, diffusely defined, particularistic, collectivity-oriented, and affective pattern, who believe that a great loss was suffered when it gave way to an achievement-oriented, contractual, specifically defined, universalistic, and affectively neutral pattern. This judgment may have some validity. Still, so long as half of the population inhabits a world patterned one way and the other half another world, the first is at a disadvantage, as indicated in Chapter 6.[8]

8. See "Status, Contract, and the Pay for Women's Work" in Chapter 6.

A Subordinate World

There have been attempts to interpret gender differences in terms of structural factors, in hierarchical terms, and in terms of positions of super- and subordination, some of them credible, some more fanciful.

Mathilde and Mathias Vaerting explained all gender differences in terms of power relationships built into the social structure. They scoured history, especially the histories of Egypt, Libya, and Sparta, to prove that so-called sex traits were in reality the gender traits of superordinates and subordinates, whatever their sex or gender. What we consider to be archetypically feminine—passivity in love-making, obedience, submissiveness to commands and rules, dependence on spouse, fearfulness, modesty, chastity, bashfulness, maidenly reserve, love of home, restricted outside interests, tender care for babies, monogamic inclination, interest in bodily adornment, and love of finery— were merely the qualities of subordinates, wherever, whenever, male or female (Vaerting and Vaerting, 1923). Alfred Adler in a similar vein interpreted so-called femininity in terms of the inferior social position of women (Adler, 1924).

Viola Klein sees many of the characteristics of modern women as consequences of her marginal position. Basing her analysis on E. V. Stonequist's presentation of the marginal man, she points out that "while the marginal person resents criticism by others and is extremely sensitive to the fact of being indiscriminately 'put all in one class' he, at the same time, unconsciously adopts the majority standards" (Klein, 1946, p. 174). Taking over majority group standards leads to increased effort to equal or surpass the superior group's achievement, as well as willingness to undercut it in the labor market. Helen Hacker has interpreted women in terms of their minority group status (Hacker, 1951), an approach that has become increasingly popular among young protesting women.

There are numerous explanations—economic, political, physical—for the structurally inferior position of women. They are discussed in Chaper 7, where the brute impact of sheer male physical superiority in size, weight, and muscular strength is examined.

The term *women* in the title of this essay is not, then, as simple as it might seem. Women are less than completely differentiated from men and at the same time greatly differentiated among themselves—facts that are by no means irrelevant for policy.

REFERENCES

Adler, Alfred, *The Practice and Theory of Individual Psychology* (London: Kegan Paul, 1924).

Beach, Frank, "Retrospect and Prospect," *Sex and Behavior* (New York: Wiley, 1965).

Bernard, Jessie, "Observation and Generalization in Cultural Anthropology," *American Journal of Sociology,* 50 (1945), pp. 284–291.

———. *The Sex Game* (Englewood Cliffs, N.J.: Prentice-Hall, 1968).

Bird, Caroline, *Born Female: The High Cost of Keeping Women Down* (New York: McKay, 1968).

Drews, Elizabeth Monroe, "Counseling for Self-Actualization in Gifted Girls and Young Women," *Journal of Counseling Psychology,* 12 (Summer 1965), pp. 167 ff.

Eells, John S., Jr., "Women in Honors Programs: Winthrop College," in Philip I. Mitterling (ed.), *Needed Research on Able Women in Honors Programs, College, and Society* (New York: Columbia University Press, 1964).

Freedman, Mervin, *The College Experience* (San Francisco: Jossey-Bass, 1967).

Freud, Sigmund, "Some Psychological Consequences of the Anatomical Distinction between the Sexes," *Collected Works,* Standard edition, Vol. 19 (London: Hogarth Press, 1961). This paper was originally published in 1925.

Ginzberg, Eli, et al., *Life Styles of Educated Women* (New York: Columbia University Press, 1966).

Goldsen, Rose K., et. al., *What College Students Think* (New York: Van Nostrand, 1960).

Hacker, Helen, "Women as a Minority Group," *Social Forces,* 30 (Sept. 1951), pp. 60–66.

Hall, Edward T., *The Silent Language* (Greenwich: Premier Books, 1963).

Hamberg, David A., and Donald T. Lunde, "Sex Hormones in the Development of Sex Differences in Human Behavior," in Maccoby,

Eleanor (ed.), *The Development of Sex Differences* (Stanford, Calif.: Stanford University Press, 1966), Chapter 1.

Hoselitz, Bert F., "Social Stratification and Economic Development," *International Social Science Journal,* 16 (2) (1964); also "Social Structure and Economic Growth," *Economia Internationale,* 6 (Aug. 1953).

Hoyt, Donald P. and Carroll E. Kennedy, "Interest and Personality Correlates of Career-Motivated and Homemaking-Motivated College Women," *Journal of Counseling Psychology,* 5 (Spring 1958), 44–49.

Klein, Viola, *The Feminine Character* (New York: International Universities Press, 1946).

Mead, Margaret, *Sex and Temperament in Three Primitive Societies* (New York: Morrow, 1935).

Riesman, David, "Introduction," in Jessie Bernard, *Academic Women* (University Park: Pennsylvania State University Press, 1964).

Rossi, Alice, "Who Wants Women in the Scientific Professions?" in Jacqueline A. Mattfeld and Carol G. Van Aken (eds.), *Women and the Scientific Professions* (Cambridge: M. I. T. Press, 1965).

Spock, Benjamin, "Decent and Indecent" (*McCall,* 1970). This citation from *Washington Post,* Feb. 5, 1970.

Stoller, Robert J., *Sex and Gender* (New York: Science House, 1968).

Terman, Lewis M. and C. C. Miles, *Sex and Personality: Studies in Masculinity and Femininity* (New York: McGraw-Hill, 1936).

Vaerting, Mathilde, and Mathias Vaerting, *The Dominant Sex, A Study in the Sociology of Sex Differences* (London: Allen and Unwin, 1923).

Vincent, Clark, "Implications of Change in Male-Female Role Expectations for Interpreting M-F Scores," *Journal of Marriage and the Family,* 28 (May 1966), 196–199.

Weisstein, Naomi, "Kinder, Kuche, Kirche as Scientific Law: Psychology Constructs the Female," *Motive,* 19 (March-April 1969), 78–85.

Yankelovich, Daniel, *Generations Apart* (Columbia Broadcasting Company, 1969).

2

The Public Interest, Policy, Protest

The Public Interest

There is no more consensus about the second term in the title of this book, *the public interest,* than there is about the first. Thorough explication would involve an almost encyclopedic exegesis of a vast literature in political science, sociology, psychology, and economics. At least half a dozen conceptions would have to be scrutinized in detail.

As some conceptualize the term, it would have to be scrapped; there is no such thing as "the public interest," but only the special and vested interests of congeries of different and often conflicting groups "which maneuver to obtain the greatest amount of public influence and public power, and each of which discerns 'the public interest' in its own image" (Bell and Kristol, 1965, p. 5). The resulting "public interest" is, therefore, only the interest of the part of the public that wields power. Young radicals today tend to espouse this point of view, arguing for or against policies not on the basis of how well or how poorly they contribute to a consensually defined public interest, but either on absolutistic moral grounds or on the basis of how they affect specific segments of the public.

31

It can even be argued, we are told, that the concept is not only fallacious but even dangerous, for "it is probable that as much mischief has been perpetrated upon the human race in the name of 'the public interest' as in the name of anything else" (Bell and Kristol, 1965, p. 4). The term, it is concluded, should therefore be discarded, along with such synonyms or equivalents as "the common good," "the common weal," "the public welfare," and the "national interest."

The concept of conflicting and competing interest groups being preferable to the concept of the public interest is not very suitable in the present context. It might sometimes, conceivably, be applicable to militant women as opposed to antifeministic women, for example, or perhaps in some cases to women versus men, as it was in the old suffrage movement. But it is hard to think of women and children as interest groups maneuvering "to obtain the greatest amount of public influence and public power . . . each of which discerns 'the public interest' in its own image." It is hard, too, to think of women in this kind of conflict relationship with families or "the family." Not other "interest groups" but structural arrangements that get in the way of good relationships seem to be more suitable concepts. And this approach assumes some concept of a public interest.

Even among those who accept the validity of the concept itself, there can be an endless variety of opinions about what specific criteria to apply in determining the substantive content of the public interest. There was a time when we could naively accept Jeremy Bentham's evocative criterion of the public interest: "the greatest good for the greatest number." But recent theorists engaged in studying what they call "social-welfare functions" or group decisions have refined the problem, as stated in those terms, beyond solution, in what has been labeled the "impossibility theorem" (Luce and Raiffa, 1957). Although some students have proposed theoretical ways to by-pass this roadblock, so far as practical applications are concerned, we are still far from securing guidance from these discussions.

Another criterion for determining or measuring the public interest can be stated in terms of optimizing returns in terms of investments, of "costs" and "benefits." The public interest is best served, according to this criterion, when each unit of investment or "input" of any type brings in an optimum return or "output." This criterion raises one of the most basic questions every society has to face: How much is it willing to pay for what? Next, how can it assess these costs? Where does one unit of investment bring the greatest return? What are the best "trade-offs"? Is the public willing to pay for cheaper goods with air and water pollution? To pay for racism with crime? Is the public willing to pay for law-and-order with more restrictions on individual rights? To pay for equality with liberty? And who is going to be charged with the bill: old or young, black or white, men or women?

These questions concerning the balancing of societal costs and benefits are especially sensitive in the area of the relations between the sexes. How is the public interest affected by improving the status of women? Do the interests of men suffer when women become economically independent? Is the present functional sexual differentiation optimal in terms of the happiness of men, women, and children? What are the costs and benefits of such functional specialization? What would the costs of change be vis-à-vis husbands and children? Could change be brought about without depriving anyone of anything? If not, what would be the probable costs? Would they outweigh the benefits? To whom? As related to the topic of this book, policy must take into account not only the possible differences in costs and benefits as between men and women, but also as among women themselves; these latter costs call for as much attention as those between men and women.

In the past the answers to this kind of question have been arrived at blindly, they have just emerged without purposive planning; costs were discovered after they have been incurred. The anthropological way of describing cultures has given the misleading impression that the logic of costs and benefits shown by societies is somehow or other planned and consciously arrived at rather than being discovered by the researchers. Such naiveté is no longer permissible. We are alerted to the balance sheet. We find that we must think about the costs as well as the benefits of whatever we do.

Difficult and vulnerable as the concept of the public interest may be, in one form or another, it persists. We need it. "There has never been a society which has not, in some way, and to some extent, been guided by this ideal . . . no matter how perverse its application, in our eyes" (Bell and Kristol, 1965, p. 5). In our own society the Constitution itself prescribes that government provide for "the general welfare." It is up to the policy makers to deal with special interests in a way to optimize the change to achieve this idea, however conceived.

Policy

The dictionary recognizes both good and bad implications of the term *policy*. Thus it may mean "political sagacity" or "statecraft" or "diplomacy," but also "political cunning." The weight of the definition, however, implies a favorable, though not necessarily benevolent, direction. The term applies to a course of action adopted and pursued not only by a government but also by any other organization that has to make decisions. Thus, the definition reads, "in reference to conduct or action generally: prudent, expedient, or advantageous," although it does not specify expedient or advantageous to whom.

Though policy is usually assumed to be benign or eucratic, it can easily be deflected by noise. Students of decision making have shown that strength of preferences plays a big part in the variables with which policy must deal. If any particular segment of the public does not feel strongly about its interests, policy will not have to give it much weight. Theorists have shown precisely why it is that the creaking axle gets the greasing (Luce and Raiffa, 1957); why, so long as women accepted their lot quietly, they could be ignored by policy makers.

Policies that affect women are not, of course, limited to those of the government. Nongovernmental bureaucracies have policies of their own, sometimes specified in charters and minutes of board meetings; but equally often, if not more so, in the form of unwritten, even unarticulated customs and traditions, far more inaccessible to challenge than the formal ones. And the formal, articulated statement of policy does not always coincide with the actual, operational policy that impinges on people in the day-by-day business of living. The protest of women in the nineteenth century and first half of the twentieth century was directed primarily against formal policies; those of the last third of the twentieth century against the informal ones as well (Bernard, 1968).

Protest

In 1961, a prescient observer of the social scene was trying to prepare us for democracy:

> For many generations, with only a few dissents or protests usually ignored or suppressed, many have been sacrificed, exploited, humiliated and sometimes destroyed by the operation of our established laws, institutions and relations. We have explained and justified these practices by a variety of social, economic, legal, political and theological beliefs and sanctions. These beliefs have been accepted, with little or no protest, by those who have been thus misused and exploited, until recently. Now those who formerly accepted their unhappy lot in life as inevitable, are becoming restless, sometimes resentful and increasingly are protesting against their inferior status and mis-treatment. But this protest comes . . . as they begin to develop a new image of themselves, a sense of their own worth and dignity, a belief in themselves as personalities who should not be so mistreated. This new aspiration of people who have long accepted inferiority and offered submissive obedience to those who dominated them is of immense significance for our democratic aspiration toward a free social order (Frank, 1961).

Women were among these protesters.

For in the last third of the twentieth century there was a great efflorescence of activism among women. A burgeoning upsurge of resentment proliferated a wide variety of forms of protest. One took the conventional form of protest by way of lobbying, strikes, appeals to public opinion, political pressure, and court action. Representative of this approach were NOW, the National Organization for Women, founded by Betty Friedan in 1966, and WEAL, the Women's Equity Action League, which specialized in court action. Another variety of protest, originally a spin-off from the peace movement on the New Left, took a more nonconventional approach, relying on direct-action techniques learned originally in the radical student movement. It came to be called the Women's or Female Liberation Movement. (In this book, its members are called Movement Women in order to include the host of new recruits who were attracted to it after it "seceded" or became "liberated" in 1968 from the male-dominated student, civil rights, and peace movements). Both the conventional and the nonconventional women are here denominated radical women.

A major difference between the conventional and the nonconventional forms of protest lay in the definition of "the conditions that now prevent women from enjoying the equality of opportunity and freedom of choice which is their right as individual Americans and as human beings" (NOW, 1966). NOW defined these conditions in terms of prejudice and discrimination; their chosen field of battle was therefore in the area of legislation, court decisions, and administrative guidelines to eliminate discrimination and promote equality. The nonconventional women had a different definition of the conditions that prevented women from achieving the equality of opportunity and freedom of choice that were their rights as individual Americans and human beings. While they went along with programs for ending discriminatory practices, they probed deeper for more fundamental targets. Their diagnosis led them even beyond NOW's "silken curtain of prejudice and discrimination against women." They zeroed in on the phenomena that, by analogy with racism, they labelled *sexism*. There would always be discrimination against women and inequality of opportunity until they were liberated from sexism.

The term *sexism* was brilliant. The word racism had begun to appear in the dictionaries only in the late 1960's. Until then the word *prejudice* had seemed adequate for analysis of most racial situations. Only by the late 1960's did it appear that a new concept was needed to refer to a situation in which quite unprejudiced people were, willy-nilly, engaged in discriminatory practices. More than prejudice alone had been responsible for discrimination in the past and its continuance into the present. Adverse discrimination was found to be built in to all the institutions (Bernard, 1970).[1] Now young women were protesting that in the same way, discrimination against women—*oppression* was the term they frequently used—was also built in to all our institutions. The term became essential in the study of sex relations as it had in race relations, because adverse discrimination was surviving legal banning.

Racism was the kind of naive assumption that white standards, values, and arts were the best, if not the only, ones. The history of civilization was the history of the civilization of the white races. It was a Greek looking at African sculpture and dismissing it: it wasn't Praxiteles. Or a medieval builder looking at a pagoda and dismissing it: it wasn't Gothic. The new peoples seeking their own identity were infuriated by the insistence of tradition-distorted whites on judging everything as though it ought to conform to white standards; if it did not, it did not warrant attention.

In the case of sexism it was the assumption that male standards, values, and arts were the best, if not the only worthwhile, ones. Like racism, sexism was the unconscious, taken-for-granted, unquestioned, unexamined, and unchallenged acceptance of the belief that the world as it looked to men was the only world, that the way of dealing with it that men had created was the only way, that the values men had evolved were the only ones, that the way sex looked to men was the only way it could look to anyone, that what men thought women were like was the only way to think about women.

Critics of sexism asked about sex the same kinds of questions that critics of racism had asked about race: What is so sacred about the standards and values of males? Why should everyone's

---

1. I recognize that the emphasis on sexism rather than on men as the target (see also Chapter 12) robs the discussion of excitement and color and lowers the decibal count significantly. If this book were designed as a polemic, the full weight of the argument might well be addressed against men. As a social scientist, however, "programmed" for almost half a century to see processes, social forms, structures, and related constructs, I find it difficult to concentrate on the individuals who are the referents. Women can be as sexist as men, and sexism in women is as contrary to the public interest as it is in men.

contribution be judged by the standards and values of men? What's so great about a culture whose priorities put war above education, profit above quality of life, violence above love, aggression above nurturance? Why should female values and contributions be judged inferior because they are not male? The new critics did not feel that the male world was the only worthwhile world. They did not feel that women should be viewed as deviant men or be judged by male values of what was worthy. They protested the constant put-down to which women were subject; they minded the "ignore-ance" of their contribution in discussions.

Movement Women were giving formal expression to their objection to, dissent from, or disapproval of this nonlegal, even unconstitutional, form of discrimination. They withdrew the "consent of the governed." They used whatever tactics were available. They took research from the past that had been used to perpetuate sexism and polemicized it. They used conversion techniques, helping the public see the profile in the psychology textbook's experimental figure as well as the cornice, the hollow cube as well as the solid cube. Descriptions of the status of women that had seemed to imply that this status was the way it had to be looked quite different restated in polemic form; they appeared far less intrinsic and immutable than they did in the now-dated form of the original authors. Most insistently they used tactics as incompatible with the feminine gender role (and hence with the greatest shock value) as they could devise, direct action in the form of confrontations, disruptions, and demonstrations. It was as though the experimental animal on the dissecting table had sat up and said to the scientist, "Look, I'm more than just a specimen!" In the past we did not expect the subjects we studied and researched to do such things, but that was precisely what students, black militants, and NOW women, too, were doing. The research worms were turning.

The conventional and the nonconventional women differed also in their conceptions of equality. Alice Rossi distinguished three models of equality. The pluralist model accepts the present sexual differentiation of functions, which puts women at a great disadvantage, but seeks to mitigate their handicap by stop-gap plans of one sort or another. The assimilation model looks forward to a 50–50 distribution of the prestigious occupations and political positions of society, ignoring the fact that so long as the present sexual differentiation of functions persists, such equality is impossible. The hybrid model of equality seeks a radical reassignment of functions, so that men as well as women would share functions now exclusively assigned to women, as well as the other way round (Rossi, 1969). In general, conventional women accept the first two models of equality (Part IV), Movement Women insist on the third (Part VI).

By sexist standards, the style of NOW, its rhetoric and its historical manner of organization made sense; its modus operandi fit traditional models. It dealt with policy in ways that those in power, pro or con, could deal with; they knew the ropes. Both NOW and they were operating according to the same ground rules. Not so the style, rhetoric, manner of organization, or modus operandi of Movement Women. Their style was personal, their rhetoric emotional, their manner of operating antihierarchical, antileadership, resting on autonomous small groups. Their style was one of direct action rather than lobbying. Policy makers had a hard time dealing with them, first because Movement Women dealt with topics that embarrassed them and also because Movement Women were less interested in formal policy per se than in its underlying sexist preconceptions.

All protestors disturb policy makers; Movement Women more than others. They challenged the sexism-tainted scientific facts on which policy makers have traditionally had to rely. They refused to see our society through establishment eyes. Was the family as now structured actually a benign institution? Was marriage all that sacred. Were all those "happy housewives" *really* all that happy? If so, why did they present such an unfavorable mental-health profile (Bernard, 1971)? Was the present rigid specialization of functions by sex good for men? for women? for children? Movement Women were, in brief, troublemakers for the status quo. And they meant to be.

There was in the beginning some tendency for members or adherents of the two types of protest to denigrate one another. NOW dissociated itself from Movement Women, and Movement

Women condemned the "capitalist militancy of middle-aged NOW members," which they likened to NAACP in its soft liberalism. But the dangers of such factionalism were soon recognized, and efforts were made to arrive at some kind of accommodation, at least to prevent public displays of disagreement. The importance of solidarity became recognized by all, however difficult achieving it might be—not only solidarity among the many organizations themselves but also among the many kinds of women—$F_1 \ldots F_n$. No more talk of "women are their own worst enemies." Women were no longer to put women down.

Essay

"Essay" may be the term in the title of this book that is the most difficult for some, especially academic, readers to accept. It was selected because, although it is based squarely on research findings culled from a wide variety of research traditions,[2] this book is basically a personal, albeit disciplined, statement—neither, I hope, an inert, disinterested treatise nor a passionate polemic, however much I recognize the importance of both of these forms of expression and communication.

My own position on women and the public interest has been greatly influenced by the protests of Movement Women. I have been sensitized to the phenomena of sexism that they have so dramatically forced upon our consciousness. It had never before been made so clear to me how dominated by male standards and values all our thinking has been in the past.[3]

I accept the research evidence documenting the existence of

2. The diversity of the several research strands brought together here has made it difficult to weave a seamless web. The research traditions do not always mesh, even when they are preoccupied with the same phenomena. Hopefully the result of trying to weave them together is not too patchy.

3. This sexism was vividly brought home to me at a conference on the subject, "Are Women Different?" Why, it struck me, should it be assumed that men constituted the standard and that women had to be measured against the male standard, explained as "different" or "not different" from that male norm? Why not, "Are Men Different?"

sex differences, inevitable whether or not intrinsic. Efforts to deny them seem to me a capitulation to sexism, an effort to show that differences somehow or other prove the inferiority of women, that they must therefore be denied. What I object to is the unexamined assumption that the measures, standards, and evaluations of differences should be in male terms. What I reject is the overvaluation of the contribution of men and the undervaluation of the actual and potential contribution of women.

I view, for example, with the same horror as others the raped and ravished earth that has been the natural and inevitable outcome of unbraked male values. The mentality of men created the technology that has made lunar exploration possible, affluence feasible, and the masterpieces in the several arts creatable. But it has also led to the violated earth. With David Riesman, I wonder what would have been the outcome for science if women had had more influence on the direction our culture has taken?

> Competitiveness is so very American or more broadly Western in its style that I am led to wonder whether it bears some relation to our progress in scientific work, or rather whether, if women had a larger influence on that work, other sorts of discoveries might not be made, other "laws" emphasized, and altered patterns of scientific and academic organization preferred and discovered. . . . It could be argued that it took a particular set of sex-role attitudes as well as specific religious and cultural values for Western science and technology to develop initially, although to *continue* the work, one might speculate as to whether a different pattern of attitudes might not be productive (Riesman, 1964).[4]

Viewed from this perspective, sexism, which exalts male values, can be seen as the most serious threat to the public interest today, and the Movement Women who attack it as the most serious defenders of the public interest. I tend to go along with Roxanne Dunbar who notes that since women have been "programmed" for the nurturance of children, a function that allows "the female principle to take ascendance over the male principle," their world

4. The statement refers to the discussion in my book, *Academic Women*, of the part played by sex in the creation, recognition, and transmission of knowledge.

view has tended to be peaceful and noncompetitive (Dunbar, 1969, p. 14). If men were also subject to this schooling in nurturance the public interest might greatly profit. In their assaults on sexism, therefore, I believe that Movement Women are performing one of the most important functions called for in our society today.

In addition, it seems to me that they are also performing another major function, not deliberately or purposively, but, in my opinion, no less basic for all that, namely, preparing us for a world in which reproduction will take only a small part of a woman's life, for a world in which women will have to be redefined in far broader terms than in the past, a world in which all relationships will be modified by the attrition of the core function, reproduction, which up to now has been almost determinative of the whole social structure.

Although I have long known—and said—practically everything the radical woman are now saying, I have learned a great deal from them. To the sober, objective statements of sociological and psychological researchers who have been teaching us about women for such a long time, the radical / women have added punctuation, primarily exclamation points and question marks, thus directing our attention to meanings that escape us when punctuated only by uncommunicative periods. And they have convinced me as a sociologist of the validity of their protest. As the black militants and the campus radical have, these women have made a strong case. They have taught me to readjust the lens through which I observe the current scene. I have not shared the experiences that so anger them, any more than I have shared those of black militants or young radicals. But I do not believe one has to be a black man in order to understand the rage of black men nor a campus radical to understand a student protester. I regret that these protesting women have had to resort to disruption and violence to reach me and other favored members of the Establishment. But I try not to judge their message by the means they have had to resort to to convey it. I hope that because I am not part of the solution—an activist, that is, or a polemicist —I am not therefore a part of the problem.

REFERENCES

Bell, Daniel and Irving Kristol, editorial, *The Public Interest*, 1 (1) (Fall, 1965).

Bernard, Jessie, "The Status of Women in Modern Patterns of Culture," *Annals Amer. Acad. Pol. & Soc. Sci.*, 375 (Jan. 1968), 3–14.

———, "Sexism and Discrimination," *The American Sociologist*, 5 (Nov. 1970), 374–375.

———, "The Paradox of the Happy Housewife," in Vivian Gornick and Barbara Moran (eds.), *51 Percent* (New York: Basic Books, 1971).

Dunbar, Roxanne, "Female Liberation as the Basis for Social Revolution," *Jour. Female Liberation* 1 (2) (Feb. 1969), 103–115.

Luce, R. Duncan and Howard Raiffa, *Games and Decisions* (New York: Wiley, 1957), Chapter 14.

National Organization for Women (NOW), "Statement of Purpose," adopted Oct. 29, 1966.

Riesman, David "Introduction" in Jessie Bernard, *Academic Women*, (University Park: Pennsylvania State University Press, 1964), pp. xix–xx.

Rossi, Alice, "Alternate Models of Sex Equality," *The Humanist* (Fall, 1969).

3

The Paradoxes of Policy

General Welfare and Pursuit of Happiness

It is not only the formal definition or conceptualization of policy that invites attention but also the substantive contents included in it. In the case of policy in the United States two-guidelines have been laid down. The Constitution directs the government to "provide for the general welfare;" and an equally hallowed document declares the inalienable right of individuals, all born equal, to pursue happiness. The two objectives of policy are not always compatible. The resulting conflicts have plagued and continue to plague those responsible for formulating and implementing policy.

Dealing with these conflicts is hard enough in the area of economic policy: "How much 'happiness' may be permitted to the rugged individualist without damage to the general economic welfare?" We have invented clues for measuring the gross national product to help answer the first question. It is now argued that we also need social indicators or indexes of other dimensions of the general welfare if we want to know how well off we really are (Committee on Education of the President's Commission on the Status of Women, Report, 1963). It should be possible, it is argued, with adequate social indicators, to rationalize an accommodation of the demands of the general welfare when they conflict with the pursuit of happiness of either individuals or groups of individuals.

44

In the case of women, what is the relationship between their interests and the public interest in terms of both the general-welfare directive of the Constitution and the pursuit-of-happiness doctrine of the Declaration of Independence? What should be the policy when women's pursuit of happiness conflicts with men's? Or when the pursuit of happiness by some women conflicts with that of other women?

The distinction between the general-welfare and the pursuit-of-happiness points of view is by no means merely academic, for the point of view one espouses will influence the policy he favors. So far as the worker roles of women are concerned, the general-welfare orientation will tend to a policy of "optimum utilization of human resources;" the pursuit-of-happiness orientation will tend to one of self-actualization or self-realization. Both have found expression in the relevant literature and in public documents.

The General Welfare and the Optimum-Utilization-of-Human-Resources Policy

The talents of women, according to the optimum-utilization-of-human-resources policy, may be viewed as a resource to be exploited for the benefit of the economy as a whole, a reservoir to supply services our society needs and will increasingly need. And, in fact, they are. For the skills, talents, and gifts of any population are indeed the major resources of nations anywhere, as those attempting to modernize underdeveloped areas of the world have long since found out. In fact, the utilization-of-human-resources point of view has been proposed as a basis of policy for the whole world. A world-wide inventory of human resources in engineering, medicine, and the natural sciences carried out under the supervision of the United Nations was recently suggested. There would also be a survey of the needs for these resources throughout the world. Charts of supply and demand like those for coffee, wheat, and cocoa would be drawn up. A formula would be devised for international coordination of the uses of such talent "in accordance with the best interests of the world community." It would operate much as tariff agreements do. Planning would take the place of the free market in determining the supply, eliminating overproduction in some areas and underproduction in others (Eren, 1969 pp. 32–33). One does not have to envision such a 1984 mechanism to recognize the principle that the general welfare does call for judicious use of human resources. What constitutes optimum use, however, is by no means obvious; it may even vary from place to place and time to time.

In the United States, the optimum-utilization-of-human-resources orientation currently tends to dwell on the enormous functional shortages that students of the labor force see about us and looming ominously ahead. At the beginning of the last third of the twentieth century, for example, President Lyndon B. Johnson catalogued the anticipated deficits as they looked to him then:

> In the next decade alone we will need 900,000 additional school teachers and college instructors; one million additional specialists in the health services; 800,000 additional science and engineering technicians; 700,000 additional scientists and engineers, and 4½ million additional state and local employees, exclusive of our teachers.
>
> The requirements in these fields alone will be 110,000 additional trained specialists every month for the next 10 years. That requirement cannot be met by men alone, and unless we begin now to open more and more professions to our women and unless we begin now to train our women to enter those professions, then the needs of our Nation just are not going to be met (Johnson, 1966).[1]

And he concluded that "the underutilization of American women continues to be the most tragic and the most senseless waste of this century" (Johnson, 1966).

Making the same point, a sociologist quoted the President's Science Advisory Committee to the effect that "impending shortages of talented, highly trained scientists and engineers threaten the successful fulfillment of vital national commitments" (Com-

---

1. It was not altogether clear whether these workers were going to be needed in addition to those then in the labor force or in addition to the normal increase expectable as the labor force expanded.

mittee on Education of the President's Commission on the Status of Women, Report, 1963). In the late 1960's we were importing enough such engineers and scientists to amount to an annual saving of about four billion dollars invested in their training (Porter, 1968, p. 6). Many of our medical services would have had to be even more drastically curtailed than they were if we had not been similarly importing 1,500 physicians every year. This so-called "brain-drain" had produced a considerable amount of resentment in countries that lost talented workers to the United States (Porter, 1968, pp. 6–7).[2] The general welfare was clearly involved. Implication: make more effective use of women.

Since President Johnson's statement, the *market* demand for a variety of skills has receded. But recessions—mini, midi, or maxi—do not reduce the functional need of students for teachers, of sick people for medical care, of laboratories for technicians, or of poor people for goods, however much they may reduce the market for them. Nor do they reduce the need for biomedical engineers, however much they may reduce the market demand for aerospace engineers. In response to the talk of a market "glut," one editor asked in 1971, "Is there really a *surplus,* even temporary, of skills and brainpower today? Are we really doing all we can afford in fields requiring professional expertise? In the language of the bureaucrat, are we 'allocating our human resources toward a viable input-output system?' " (*Washington Post,* Feb. 26, 1971). His answer was a resounding No!

This point is important, for there were those who were using the "glut" of highly trained personnel of the early 1970's as an argument against encouraging women to train for and enter the higher professions. Alice Rossi was warning women to expect precisely such a contingency. When we have all the professional services we need, rather than only those we can "afford," there will be time to talk of "surpluses."

---

2. The deputy ambassador from Turkey to the United Nations noted that immigrants had furnished 21 per cent of the United States' need for physicians and that between 1967 and 1969, thirteen per cent of our annual supply of scientists came from abroad. He estimated the annual benefit from such imported talent to be about $45 million, amounting to a billion dollars since World War II (Eren, 1969, p. 11). A subcommittee of the House Government Operating Committee published a report on this problem in 1968.

Figure 3.1, based on Table 3.1, shows actual trends in labor-force participation by women since 1890 and the increases that would be required if women were to supply half (B) or all (C) of the anticipated deficit in personnel. Figure 3.2, also based on Table 3.1, shows what proportion of the labor force has been contributed by women since 1890 and the rate of increase that would be necessary to equalize the labor-force participation of both sexes. Table 3.2, showing the so-called dependency ratio, highlights the importance of women in the labor force, a result of the relatively larger load of young and old people that has to be carried by the working population.

Proponents of the optimum-utilization-of-human-resources policy orientation have in mind all those hospitals crying for nurses and technicians, all those clinics calling for therapists, all those laboratories calling for technicians and imaginative scientists. They see a seller's market; they see women as potential suppliers of a wanted product. They feel charged, therefore, with encouraging, enticing, cajoling, or even coercing women to enter the labor market, and certainly with removing barriers to their equal opportunities for entering it.

With the passage of the Civil Rights Acts of 1964, it did in fact become an unlawful employment practice for an employer:

1. To fail or refuse to hire or to discharge any individual, or otherwise to discriminate against any individual with respect to his compensation, terms, conditions, or privileges of employment, because of such individual's race, color, religion, sex, or national origin; or
2. To limit, segregate, or classify his employees in any way which would deprive or tend to deprive any individual of employment opportunities or otherwise adversely affect his status as an employee, because of such individuals' race, color, religion, sex, or national origin (Civil Rights Act of 1964).

The general-welfare approach does not denigrate or minimize the pursuit-of-happiness approach, for such pursuit can itself contribute to the general welfare. Thus the National Manpower Council, established in 1951 by the Ford Foundation at Columbia University, in a statement made in the late 1950's, found itself "troubled by the waste of human abilities . . . and . . . dissatisfied

Table 3.1. Proportion of Labor Force Composed of Women and Proportion of Women in the Labor Force, 1890–1969

	Proportion of Labor Force Composed of Women	Proportion of Women in Labor Force
1969	37.6	42.0
1965	35.0	37.3
1960	33.3	36.3
1955	31.2	33.8
1950	29.0	32.1
1945	36.1	37.0
1940	25.4	27.6
1930	21.9	23.6
1920	20.4	22.7
1910	—	—
1900	18.1	20.0
1890	17.0	18.2

SOURCE: Data for 1890–1965, Women's Bureau, *1965 Handbook on Women Workers*, bul. 290, (1965), p. 6; 1969 data from Women's Bureau, *Monthly Statistics on the Woman Labor Force* (July 1, 1969).

with traditional ways of utilizing manpower," especially womanpower, which constituted "not only an essential, but also a distinctive part of our manpower resources." It realized "how vital to the development of our manpower resources is each individual's freedom to choose his or her occupation and work," and concluded that there should be a more determined effort to make that freedom effective (National Manpower Council, 1957). Guaranteeing freedom to choose one's occupation and work was good policy because it was "vital to the development of our manpower resources," a means to an end, not an end in itself.

Table 3.2 Dependency Ratio, United States, 1940–1968

	Total	Youth	Old Age
1968	93.1	74.8	18.3
1960	89.7	73.0	16.7
1950	72.5	58.5	14.0
1940	70.4	56.8	11.8

SOURCE: For 1940, 1950, and 1960, Donald J. Bogue, *The Population of the United States* (Free Press, 1959), p. 771; for 1968, Census Bureau estimate (February 17, 1969).

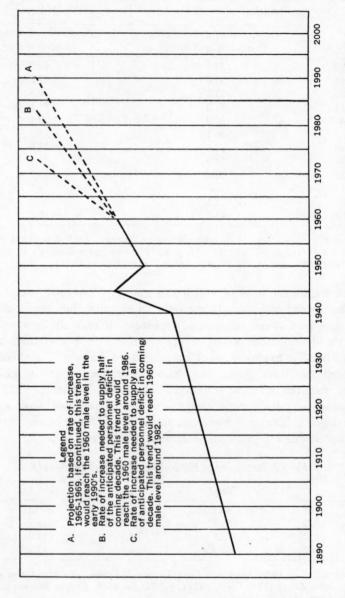

Legend

A. Projection based on rate of increase, 1965-1969. If continued, this trend would reach the 1960 male level in the early 1990's.

B. Rate of increase needed to supply half of the anticipated personnel deficit in coming decade. This trend would reach the 1960 male level around 1986.

C. Rate of increase needed to supply all of anticipated personnel deficit in coming decade. This trend would reach 1960 male level around 1982.

Figure 3.1. Proportion of Women 16 Years of Age and Over in the Labor Force, 1890 to 1969. Source: Table 3.1.

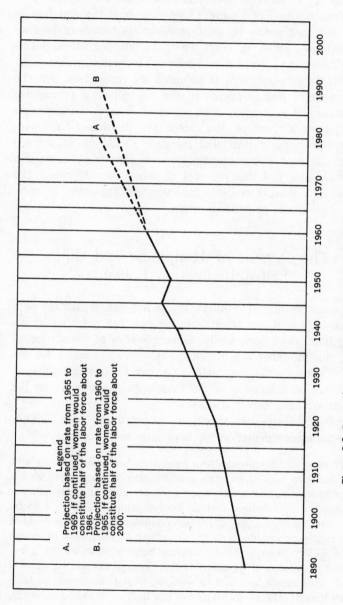

Legend

A. Projection based on rate from 1965 to 1969. If continued, women would constitute half of the labor force about 1986.

B. Projection based on rate from 1960 to 1965. If continued, women would constitute half of the labor force about 2000.

Figure 3.2. Proportion of Labor Force Composed of Women. Source: Table 3.1.

Others argue, however, that this general-welfare way of viewing human beings has a sinister overtone, implying that human beings may legitimately be used, in effect, as factors of production (Bernard, 1964, p. viii). To them this orientation seems manipulative and nonhumane, even when well-intentioned or ostensibly benign, unless it is balanced by recognition that the development of human talents is also an individual prerogative to be cherished in its own right, an intrinsic part of the pursuit of happiness. Critics of this optimum-utilization-of-human-resources view argue further that everyone should be encouraged to make the most of his talents, whatever they may be, women along with men, and that the goal of policy should be to make such self-actualization possible for everyone, regardless of race, color, religion, sex, or national origin.

The Pursuit of Happiness and the Self-Actualization Policy

Emphasis on the pursuit-of-happiness orientation calls for policies that help men and women realize their full potential by removing barriers to opportunity. Government is at the service of people, not the other way round. In this view, "concern for the status of women is fundamentally a concern for human fulfillment (Committee on Education of the President's Commission on the Status of Women, Report, 1963).

Bruno Bettelheim has specifically rejected the utilization-of-human-resources orientation for both men and women.

My ideas of commitment to a profession has nothing to do with considerations such as society's need for trained manpower. Such a necessity may or may not exist for a country at a particular moment in history. . . . I believe that all human beings, if they are to be committed to their work, need the conviction that what they do is intrinsically important to them, regardless of the needs of others or of society, though this also enters because what we do is enhanced in our eyes if we also feel that through our job we make a significant contribution. But to work at what is important to us— rather than to others—forms part of our finding personal fulfillment, as women if we are women, as men if we are men. My concern is with the human aspects of the problem of commitment to one's life work, and not at all with particular skills or what is asserted are the needs of society (Bettelheim, 1965, pp. 8–9).

John Gardner's thinking has run along similar lines. As Secretary of Health, Education, and Welfare in the Kennedy Cabinet, he was so convinced that he argued in behalf of an aggressive, even a compensatory, policy in behalf of women, for "if we really mean what we say about equality of opportunity and the work of the individual—if we are really committed to the belief that all our citizens should have a chance to go as far as their abilities will carry them—then we have to create special opportunities for women. We have to expand their choices. That is another way of expanding freedom.[3]

Insofar as specific policies are concerned, the self-actualization point of view as related to work implies a buyer's market. Women are to be free, like everyone else, to "buy" whatever they wish to. If they choose a career, public policy must remove the obstacles of one kind or another that may stand in their way. These include not only the obstacles resulting from conflicts with the traditional sexual division of labor, primarily discriminatory practices, but also the major roadblock, the conflicting demands of family roles. Policy must, that is, somehow or other help women meet such demands by providing whatever services, including child care, are necessary.

A Combined Point of View

It is characteristic of Americans to see non-zero-sum rather than zero-sum games, to seek solutions that accommodate all parties, to conclude that what's good for General Motors is good for the country. Thus there are those who see no conflict between an

3. John W. Gardner in a release announcing the formation of a Professional and Executive Corps, December, 1967. The Corps was designed to provide part-time work for high-level professionals, the time to be tailored to their wishes.

optimum-utilization-of-human-resources and a self-actualization point of view. Bruno Bettelheim writes:

> Since I believe that what is best for women is also best for the society in which they happen to live, I can forget the claimed needs of society and in my thinking be guided only by what I believe to be in the best interest of this particular group of college educated women, convinced that what is best for them is also in the long run best for society. . . . It is immaterial how many professional women our society seems to need, how many industry, government, research and education are able and willing to absorb. The important problem is not how many of them can and do attain professional and occupational positions akin to those of men but what constitutes women's self-realization. . . . Unfortunately all too much of the discussion of women's role in society concentrates on externals as how many women go to graduate school, to the detriment of our recognizing that the essential problem is self-realization (Bettelheim, 1964).

Official recognition of the compatibility of the two orientations found expression in the Act establishing a Commission on the Status of Women in 1961. In a statement establishing the Commission, President John F. Kennedy said:

> Whereas prejudices and outmoded customs act as barriers to the full realization of women's basic rights which should be respected and fostered as part of our Nation's commitment to human dignity, freedom, and democracy, and
>
> Whereas measures that contribute to family security and strengthen home life will advance the general welfare; and
>
> Whereas it is in the national interest to promote the economy, security, and national defense through the most efficient and effective utilization of the skills of all persons; and
>
> Whereas in every period of national emergency women have served with distinction in widely varied capacities but thereafter have been subject to treatment as a marginal group whose skills have been inadequately utilized; and
>
> Whereas women should be assured the opportunity to develop their capacities and fulfill their aspirations on a continuing basis irrespective of national exigencies; and
>
> Whereas a Government Commission should be charged with the responsibility for developing recommendations for overcoming discriminations in government and private employment on the basis of

sex and for developing recommendations for services which will enable women to continue their role as wives and mothers while making a maximum contribution to the world around them:

Now, therefore, by virtue of the authority vested in me as President of the United States by the Constitution and statutes of the United States, it is ordered as follows: Part I. Establishment of the President's Commission on the Status of Women. . . .

Official recognition of the compatibility of the two approaches also came from HEW Secretary John Gardner, who stated candidly that his Professional and Executive Corps, consisting of workers who wanted less than full time employment, was designed not only for the benefit of women but also for the well-being of his department: "We are not without self-interest in offering these opportunities made available in the professional and executive Corps. . . . I expect the Department to profit immensely from the talents and energies of the members of this Corps" (Gardner, 1967). What was good for these women was good for the department also.

Any number could play, and win. But it isn't always easy to convince people. When the two orientations cannot be combined and a choice has to be made, the public welfare has tended to supply the rationale for policies that fostered self-actualization rather than self-actualization supplying the rationale for policies designed in behalf of the general welfare. Acts of Congress are obliged to justify themselves on the grounds that they provide for the general welfare, not that they provide for the pursuit of any special interest's happiness.

As an interesting if parenthetical note, it may be pointed out that there have been many theoretical attempts to accommodate the general-welfare and the pursuit-of-happiness policy orientations. Thus, for example, Bernard de Mandeville found that private vices led to public good. Adam Smith found that individual men all pursuing their own private gains would, without necessarily planning to, best contribute to the wealth of nations. But, conversely, the conservative tradition, embedded in the Durkheim school of thought and distorted almost beyond recognition in the Germanic *Volk* myth, taught that the individual achieved greatest fulfillment by subordinating himself to the community. A long tradition of scholarship buttresses both approaches, the general welfare via individual pursuit of happiness and the individual pursuit of happiness via serving the general welfare.

A kind of unacknowledged, unrecognized, perhaps even unwitting equilibrium has been achieved by viewing the world of men in terms of the first—say, the Adam Smith—paradigm, and the world of women in terms of the second, the Durkheim paradigm. Men can best serve the general welfare by competing, pursuing their aggressive goals; women can find fulfillment by subordinating themselves to community needs. A recent book argues that since hunting and warfare required so much organization, men learned how to work together, while the work of women, not requiring much common endeavor, left them "unbonded" (Tiger, 1969). The precise opposite could be argued equally well: men have been taught to be individuated, competitive, striving for the individual rewards; women to be protectors of the community.

It is less important to clarify exactly the nature and the rationale of the several approaches to policy with respect to women —either or both the general-welfare and/or pursuit-of-happiness by way of work—than it is to recognize that all have been explicitly affirmed by our government to be official policy. No one has to argue that the general welfare is helped by correct policies vis-à-vis women or that the pursuit of happiness by women is a proper goal of policy. There is official documentation stating these points. This, at least, is settled.

Implementing these policies is another matter. For the paradoxes implicit in the several approaches are not easily resolved. It is not always clear what specific programs contribute best to the general welfare, or how women can best pursue happiness, or how, if there is a conflict between the general welfare and the pursuit of happiness by women, it should be resolved. These, as Hamlet might say, are the questions.

Where Does the Public Interest Lie?

Even if there is agreement on a general-welfare orientation, it is by no means always easy to determine what is best for the general welfare. Applied to economic policy the problem is difficult enough, but at least there are measures to help solve it. It can be demonstrated in terms of productivity and efficiency—by no means trivial criteria, however subject to dispute—that it is demonstrably better to have the best qualified person for any job selected to perform it than to have the best qualified person rejected because of some extraneous factor. One might argue about the use of efficiency and productivity as criteria and the use of gross national product as an index of the public interest, but not about the validity of rejecting discrimination. In terms of the general welfare it was, therefore, wholly consistent for the Civil Rights Act of 1964 to forbid the sexual division of labor and to specify that the best qualified person get the job, no matter what it was, regardless of sex.

It could be argued in a similar way that some distributions of the national income are better than others, that too great inequalities of income are counterproductive, that our economy cannot afford discrimination or poverty or preventable defects and ill health. Thus even so paradoxical an Act as that establishing the Office of Economic Opportunity in 1964 noted that "the United States can achieve its fullest economic and social potential as a nation only if every individual has the opportunity to contribute to the full extent of his capabilities and to participate in the working of our society. It is therefore the policy of the United States to . . . [open] to everyone the opportunity for education and training, the opportunity to work and the opportunity to live in decency and dignity (Economic Opportunity Act of 1964).

But how about the pursuit of happiness and the public interest? Until very recently the concern of policy with the individual's pursuit of happiness could be limited to economic pursuits. And even there it was primarily criminal economic pursuits that engaged policy makers. Interdiction of the pursuit of happiness in the noneconomic areas of sex and "crimes without victims" was left to long-established laws, traditionally sanctioned by the mores, thus eliminating the need for policy directives, for policy is only called for when norms do not exist or have broken down.

Policy has been especially diffident in the area of the relations of the sexes. Alvin Schorr reminds us, for example, that the national government "has tended to avoid deliberate influence of any sort on family patterns." He quotes Arthur W. Calhoun to the effect that it has followed a "democratic disposition to deal with individuals, not families." Policy with respect to the family, as with respect to population, has been derivative, indirect. Thus "we take for granted that public policies affect family patterns and values in a wide variety of unintended and undetected ways. For example, Social Security has encouraged old people to live separately from their children and Old Age Assistance has pressured some old people into living with their children and others into living separately from them. But none of these effects is deliberate. . . . On the whole, we have avoided understanding the profound effect of government on our private lives, possibly because ignorance serves our sense of privacy" (Schorr, 1970).

But now, suddenly, policy has to tangle with pursuits of happiness, in areas it has been loathe to deal with and is still squeamish about.

Something New Has Been Added

The concern of policy with women's pursuit of happiness has now outgrown placing its emphasis primarily on their work roles. In a new and unexpected turn of events, the attention of policy makers is being drawn toward a potential conflict between the public interest and women's pursuit of happiness by way of motherhood. Now the reconciliation of the public interest and the pursuit-of-happiness policy guidelines is not at all susceptible to Bettelheim's cheerful solution. If the happiness of some women means that they are to have the 3.4 children they say they want, the public interest is as much involved as it is in the case of women whose pursuit of happiness means career opportunities. Other ways of pursuing happiness have to be provided for them.

The United States, unlike many European countries, has never had an avowed pronatalist policy. It has, in fact, never had a specific, official population policy at all. But it has had a covert or unofficial pronatalist policy. Judith Blake Davis has summarized its contents as follows:

> [The provisions of this policy] weave throughout the structure of our entire society. . . . These policies relate directly to family roles and family behavior. Generally speaking, they involve a re-

markable standardization of both male and female sexual roles in terms of reproductive functions, obligations, and activities; and, in addition, they involve the standardization of the occupational role of women—half of the population—in terms of childbearing, child-rearing, and complementary activities. Such policies insure that just about everyone will be propelled into reproductive unions and that half of the population will enter such unions as a career, as the principal focus of their lives (Davis, pp. 67–68).

Concern about population growth has lead to demands for policies to control and even reduce the birth rate. Since direct controls did not seem feasible, all that policy could do was influence the choices that individual families made, and "one way to influence them is to make alternative careers available for women, careers other than parenthood, other than the domestic pattern which is the norm of American life. . . . We will never persuade women to play their full role in society, let alone to have fewer children, unless we give them opportunities for something else to do—something meaningful and important to do" (Revelle).

The argument had come full circle, back to the optimum utilization of human resources, but with a new twist. Judith Blake Davis reminds us that it is more important to use women in the professions than in childbearing and childrearing: "We need the services of the adults whose intelligence and motivation we are now squandering in an absorbing concern with childbearing and rearing. In effect, not only is population growth independently creating environmental and social problems for us, but the organization of human activities that produces this growth is itself wasteful of human talents and resources that our society requires for other purposes" (Davis, p. 69).

The Paradoxes of Policy: Case in Point

It is usually easier to see sociological processes operating in another culture than it is to see them in one's own. The history of policy vis-à-vis women in the marriage and divorce laws in the Soviet Union as related to policy makers' conception of the public interest is an illuminating case in point (Vorozheikin, 1969).

The 1918 code was designed, at least so later commentators insisted, to clear the ground of old obstacles to individual freedom, especially of women:

> One of the main aims of the Communists was the emancipation of women. In pre-revolutionary Russia, not only did a woman have no freedom to choose a trade or profession; she could not even decide her own place of residence. Her rights in regard to her children's education and the disposal of property were restricted. In the family she was subordinate to the men. . . . In the marriage laws of the Russian empire it was plainly laid down: "A wife must defer to her husband as the head of the family, must live with him in love, respect and infinite obedience, and must give him every satisfaction and affection." The first piece of "State interference in personal life" was the rebuilding of family relations on a more progressive basis.

The 1918 code made divorce very easy; marriage could be dissolved on the demand of either party. It established also the equality of men and women with respect to property.

By 1926 a change was called for by the public interest; the permissiveness of the 1918 code was having a deleterious effect on the birth rate. "Additional legislative measures became necessary to reinforce the stability of the family and to stimulate the interest of the family in having children and rearing them." The problem was now to reconcile "principles which were each precious in their own way. The choice went to those which were felt to be most acutely necessary—[including] the emancipation of women." There was a conflict between slavery in the family on one side and the ideology of free love on the other. Reformulation of policy was interrupted by World War II and resumed afterwards. In 1944 a new law was passed increasing state aid to mothers. Foreign observers interpreted this as an attempt to force women back into the home, as going counter to the earlier law that had encouraged women to leave the home to enter production. Not so, says the Soviet commentator. The 1944 code had overcome the inequality of the sexes; now there were new problems, among them the encouragement of motherhood. Thus "the

1944 law envisaged a whole series of measures to make things easier for women in the home and in production (the building of more nursery schools and crèches, maternity and child welfare centers, etc.). It raised the social prestige of women, and especially of mothers, strengthening their position in the family and society, their equality with men." Divorce was made more difficult. In 1968, divorce was once again simplified, and paternal responsibility for support of children was increased. The idea was to reduce the number of children "brought up without fathers, which was morally detrimental to the younger generation." A man could not initiate divorce action while his wife was pregnant or within a year after the birth of the child.

Underlying the insistence that "the cornerstone of the law remains the same equality of the sexes," policy dealing with women as expressed in the several Soviet codes was always oriented in the direction of the general welfare as the policy makers saw it, not in the direction of the pursuit of happiness by women. When women were needed primarily in the labor force, marriage was a relaxed kind of bond. When this kind of relationship was seen to be antinatal in effect, policy changed. The goal appeared to be a situation that would maximize both motherhood and industrial productivity. It was for women the worst of both worlds, in effect, for despite the plethora of verbiage about equality of the sexes, nothing was said about the double burden such "equality" imposed on women.

REFERENCES

Bernard, Jessie, *Academic Women* (University Park: Pennsylvania State University Press, 1964).

Bettelheim, Bruno, "The Talented Woman in American Society," in Philip I. Mitterling (ed.), *Needed Research on Able Women in Honors Programs, College, and Society* (New York: Columbia University Press, 1964), pp. 1, 5.

———, "The Commitment Required of a Woman Entering a Scientific Profession in Present-Day American Society," in Jacqueline A. Mattfeld and Carol G. Van Aken (eds.), *Women and the Scientific Professions* (Cambridge: MIT Press, 1965).

Civil Rights Act of 1964, Title VII, Section 703.

Committee on Education of the President's Commission on the Status of Women, Report (October 1964), p. 41.

Davis, Judith Blake, statement at hearing before a subcommittee of the Committee on Government Operations, House of Representatives, 91st Congress.

Economic Opportunity Act of 1964, preamble.

Eren, Nuri, "Supply, Demand, and the Brain Drain," *Saturday Review* (August 2, 1969).

Johnson, President Lyndon B., quoted in *Fact Sheet on Women in Professional and Technical Positions,* Women's Bureau release 67-164 (Nov. 1966), p. 5 (mimeograph).

National Manpower Council, *Womanpower* (New York: Columbia University Press, 1957).

Porter, John, "The Future of Upward Mobility," *American Sociological Review,* 33 (Feb. 1968).

Revelle, Roger, statement at hearings before a subcommittee of the Committee on Government Operations, House of Representatives, 91st Congress, p. 27.

Rivlin, Alice M. and Associates, *Toward a Social Report* (Washington, D. C.: U.S. Government, Department of Health, Education, and Welfare, 1969), p. xii.

Schorr, Alvin L., "Family Values and Public Policy in 1975–2000," paper prepared for Clara Brown Arny Symposium on Family Values, University of Minnesota (March 1970), p. 2.

Tiger, Lionel, *Men in Groups* (New York: Random House, 1969).

Vorozheikin, Yevgeni, "Marriage and Divorce in the Soviet Union," *Sputnik Monthly Digest* (January 1969), 35–45.

II

The Public Interest and the Sexual Specialization of Functions

The public interest is concerned with the optimum uses of human beings in the division of labor and in the performance of all other necessary functions. The sexual division of labor is not the same as the sexual specialization of functions. Nor are the two processes governed by the same principles or factors, or susceptible to the same criteria of evaluation.

Adam Smith, a political economist, thought in terms of the division of labor and the resulting industrial specialization as they contributed to the wealth of nations, and he established the intellectual tradition that has guided labor-market analysis. Emile Durkheim, a sociologist, thought in terms of functional differentiation. The paradigms that deal with the two approaches are different; the collective representations on which they rest are different; policies derived from them are different.

Different, but related—in fact, inextricably bound together. The reproductive and child-care functions of women, for example, may interfere with their labor-force participation and hence influence the sexual division of labor. Homemaking responsibilities assigned to women add to the difficulties of pursuing a career, not only in terms of time and energy, but also in terms of the effect housekeeping as an occupation has on mental abilities. And even more subtle, though no less relevant, is the inherent conflict between the supportive function expected of women (Chapter 5) and the demand for aggression found in the most prestigious jobs, those at the top.

The basic analysis in Part II is in terms of functions rather than in terms of roles. The same function (*e.g.,* the supportive) may be included in a variety of roles; the same role (*e.g.,* the domestic) may comprise a variety of functions. Sociological analyses of the functions of structures have tended to avoid the corollary analyses of functions that were not being performed, with consequent threat or actual threat to the social system. Discussion of the absence or lack of provision for functions felt to be needed especially by minorities has been left to reformers, utopists, and revolutionaries, including radical women. (For strictures on the functionalist approach as applied to women, see Chapter 12.)

Part II deals with the functions assigned to women and Part III with the sexual division of labor. The point of view in both is that of the public interest. The pursuit-of-happiness point of view is reserved for Parts IV, V, and VI.

4

The Functions of Women

Functions and Structures

Few sociological concepts have undergone more tortured exegesis than the concept of function and the related concept of structure, an exegesis approaching metaphysical refinement. Bypassing several decades of semantics and interpretation, we begin simply with the statement that "functional requisites are answers to the question: 'what must be done?' [and] structural requisites are answers to the question, 'how must what must be done, be done?'" (Levy, 1968, p. 23). Among the major components of social structure, "the distribution of authority and prestige" is the most relevant focus of our concerns here.

Some social structures do "what must be done" for a given status quo, but they could be dispensed with if a different one obtained. In a democratic state, for example, parliamentary debate performs the important function of controlling or limiting power. In a dictatorship, it performs a dysfunction. Conversely, censorship of the media performs the important function of controlling access to information in a dictatorship; it is dysfunctional in a democratic state. Functional analysis does not tell us which is preferable, a democratic state or a dictatorship.

More relevant for our interests here is Erik Grønseth's allegation that the way we assign functions to men and women in our society today is functional for "the capitalist industrial societies as well as for their modal personality or character structures in their present authoritarian and repressive forms," but not "for a further development towards democratic social structures and a self-regulating, creative character." He is especially concerned with the exclusive assignment of the provider function to husbands, but this assignment "can probably not be abolished without also abolishing the exploitative and authoritarian socio-political and character elements of capitalist industrialized societies" (Grønseth, 1970).

For some people, therefore, including young radicals and some of the radical women, destroying a status quo may itself have a valuable function in helping to make way for a better one. Functional-structuralism thus emphasizes not only the way functions are structured, but also the functions performed for a social system by given structures. It emphasizes also the reciprocal relationships among the structural components of a social system; it tries to trace how change in one ramifies and changes others.

Fortunately for our purposes here, not much analytic sophistication is required. For no matter what school of functionalism one belongs to, there is never any hesitation, as there is in relation to some functions, in accepting the fact that bearing and rearing children is a correct answer to the first question raised at the beginning of the chapter: "What must be done . . . if the unit is to persist in its setting?" With the exception of minor celibate communities of the nineteenth century, these functions are independent of any particular status quo; they are universal and requisite, however structured. About the other functions, the question "must they be done?" can always be raised. Are they truly requisite to the persistence of the society, or are they requisite only to the persistence of a specific status quo? If they are, indeed functional requisites for the persistence of the society, are there other alternative ways to structure or institutionalize them? Is the prevailing way the optimum way? For everyone concerned?

There is never any question that not only is the bearing of children a requisite function, but that also it is a function of women. All societies fit their structures to this fact; no maternal instinct or other psychological datum is called for. Functionalism "is based on the assumption that the social traits existing in a society at a given time are interrelated in a systematic way and that ordered relationships can be discovered among 'social facts' or social institutions without necessarily bringing in psychological or historical factors" (Levy, 1968, p. 29). Some of the other functions variously allocated to women may be requisite only to one particular system, dysfunctional to another. And even if functionally requisite, they may be differently structured, for example, assigned to men, or assigned on the basis of some nonsex criterion, or shared. But not the childbearing function. As long as this function dominated the lives of women, every other aspect of their lives had to conform to its demands. Only now, in the last third of the twentieth century, is the childbearing function losing its position as the keystone in our society and posing brand new questions for policy makers and demanding new assessments of the public interest.

Compatibility and Incompatibility among the Functions of Women

The manifold functions that women in our society perform, in addition to the reproductive, may be subsumed in no less than five categories: homemaking, childrearing, glamor, emotional support, and industrial production. In the past there was—with the exception of the glamor function that is *sui generis*—relatively little if any incompatibility among the several functions. There was, rather, a certain logic, a basic coherence to them that made sense, at least in terms of the public interest. When the domestic system of production prevailed, for example, there was no hiatus between the productive function and the others. Women could make their industrial contribution and perform the other functions simultaneously without conflict.

But when the first industrial revolution took much productive work out of the home, a bifurcation with which we have become boringly familiar developed. A staggering research and polemical literature has accumulated dealing with the problems arising from the incompatibility between the productive function of women in the new circumstances and their other functions. Most

Table 4.1. *Compatability and Incompatibility
among Functions of Women*

	Produc-tive	Home-making	Child-rearing	Glamor	Stroking	Repro-ductive
Reproductive						
Homemaking	+					
Child rearing	+	+				
Glamor	−	−	−			
Stroking	+	+	+	±		
Productive	−	−	−	−	±	

+ = compatible
− = incompatible

of the attention has been devoted to the rather obvious conflict between the domestic or family functions—reproduction, homemaking, child rearing—and the productive (Table 4.1). Chapters 5 and 7 of this book are devoted to an examination of this conflict and the problem it poses for policy makers concerned with the public interest.

It is only recently that our attention has been attracted to another conflict among these functions, one having to do with the incompatibility between the supportive function and at least some aspects of the productive. It is subtler than the home-related versus the job-related responsibilities assigned to women, less amenable to policy directives, less susceptible to a simple cost-benefit or trade-off analysis in terms of the public interest. The ramifications of this conflict are so pervasive that they are examined in some depth in Chapter 5.

The glamor function raises questions about compatibility with all the others and calls for at least peripheral attention also; but since it has not yet been subject to serious research examination, all its ramifications have not been charted. It is therefore given only peripheral attention here.

Policy is not equally involved with all of these functions. It is perhaps most concerned with the reproductive and the productive, least so with the glamour and the supportive. Homemaking and child rearing involve policy primarily as related to the reconciliation of the reproductive and the productive functions.

Not all women are required to perform all of the functions. All that the public interest demands is that enough of them perform enough functions to maintain the social system. Indeed, there is a rough kind of specialization among women (implicit in the discussion of F_1, F_2, and F_n in Chapter 1), some finding more self-actualization or satisfaction in one function, some in another. The pursuit of happiness for most probably involves some suitable "mix" of functions. How to achieve it in terms either of the public interest or the happiness of women is one of the major problems confronting policy makers today.

The existence of conflict or incompatibility between or among functions means that sometimes policy choices have to be made or priorities assigned. When (or if) there is a conflict, policy makers must ask which function should, in terms of the public interest, take precedence. When, for example, is it better to encourage women to concentrate on the bearing of children and when to enter the labor market and concentrate on the productive function? We saw at the end of Chapter 3 how policy makers in the Soviet Union dealt with this question. Even more difficult are the two antecedent questions: When is the general welfare the most suitable criterion? When the pursuit of happiness? And what to do if the answers are themselves incompatible? In a totalitarian regime, the general welfare would tend to be given priority, at least theoretically. In an affluent democratic society, the happiness criterion would have a better chance. It is a luxury that only affluent societies can afford—possibly. For, confronted with the demonstrable damage to the general welfare to which the happiness criterion in the form of uncontrolled consumption of goods can lead, even affluent societies find it an equivocal guide to policy.

Our concern here is to discuss the several functions currently assigned to women, including their effect on the character of women, and a brief statement on how they affect social structure.

The Reproductive Function

For the present at least, reproduction cannot be shifted or shared. Even if we should learn to use a surrogate womb, unless we were willing to use animals lower than human animals, it would still be a woman who carried the infant. The mechanical womb would probably take so much time and attention from doctors, nurses, and assorted medical technicians that it would be too costly to the public interest as compared with the usual cheap, biological way of gestating infants. So for the present and foreseeable future, this function seems clearly to belong exclusively to women, with all the attendant complexities that go with it. Even if every other function at present assigned primarily to women could be shared by men, this one could not. And until now, it has been almost determinative of all the others. Whether it will continue to be is a question.

Policy, in brief, can never eliminate the sexual specialization of reproduction in the way it attempts to do, for example, with the sexual division of labor (Chapter 6). It can never direct men to share it. All that policy can do is to encourage or discourage the rate of reproduction itself. Thus when a large population was wanted, whether needed or not, the answer to any question about the relative priority of the several functions assigned to women was fairly simple: the reproductive came first. The public interest seemed to be best served by the policy of at least *Kinder* and *Kuche,* if not necessarily *Kirche.*

But today the situation is quite different. The reproductive function does not necessarily take unquestioned precedence over all the others. It is generally conceded by thoughtful policy makers, mindful of world demographic trends, that the reproductive function should at least be moderated. Once a family has two children, the productive function should be accorded precedence over the reproductive. The ramifications and reverberations of this re-ordering of priorities constitute a major revolution.

In the past, women were reconciled to bearing children whether they wanted to or not. The children were needed, and women's own happiness was no issue. Some women—they have been called "nestlings"—find their major satisfactions in the reproductive function; they want more babies than would be consonant with the public interest. In some cases it is just babies they want, that is, small infants to cuddle, not sons and daughters who will grow up to be individuated human beings in their own right, independent, even hostile to them. Thus as soon as a child begins to grow beyond babyhood, they feel they must replace it with another infant. Other women, it is alleged, have children precisely to escape participation in the labor force. (Even among the Alorese some women used child care as an excuse to get out of field work) (Du Bois, 1944, p. 35). Such women feel they ought to be doing something useful; they do not want to be parasites. Having children looks like an appropriate solution to what they want; at least it seems preferable to routine, run-of-mine jobs. Moreover, in the past having children was an honorable occupation. A woman could expect to be respected just for having them. The girl who said she wanted a dozen children was judged to be a truly feminine, womanly girl, deserving kudos.

Childlessness declined drastically after 1940. By 1960 only 11 per cent of white women 35 to 44 years of age living with their husbands were childless, and the proportion childless among younger women when they reached the same age was expected to drop to 8 per cent (Glick, 1965). In the past a major argument in behalf of contraception had been to prevent *unwanted* pregnancies—it was estimated that between a fourth and a third of the increase in population in the United States in the 1960's was contributed by unwanted pregnancies—but now it was coming to be seen by some as prevention of *wanted* pregnancies also. In the past, employment outside the home had been deprecated because it kept women from having babies; now it was being advocated precisely because it would have that effect. In 1969 a young woman expected homage when she announced at graduation that she intended to have no children. Childlessness now earned the encomiums.

For in a world that no longer needs an abundance of babies, however much they may be wanted, a world that, in fact, needs rather a brake on population growth, women who engage too enthusiastically in procreation, for whatever reason, are now more likely to be viewed critically than appreciatively. Ways have to be found for women who achieve self-fulfillment in bearing babies—who would, therefore, be the ones to bear the "cost" of a lowered reproductive rate—to achieve such fulfillment in ways other than reproduction.

This drastic reorientation of attitude toward the reproductive function of women has modified priorities. Now it is the costs of permitting unbridled reproduction that engage attention rather than the other way round. Supplying jobs to women as substitute sources of gratification rather than discouraging women from taking jobs is now seen as a major focus of policy. The policy becomes one of reconciling the reproductive and the productive functions rather than one of favoring the first.

It will take quite some time to get used to the idea that the reproductive function of women is going to become a minor one, calling for a smaller and smaller proportion of their total life span: time, and a lot of emotional readjustment on everyone's part.

With new revolutions being proclaimed almost every day, it is hard to distinguish the important ones from the merely fashionable. But there can be little doubt that the revolution in the salience of the reproductive function of women resulting from the (miscalled) population explosion ranks high among the half-dozen most important. In terms of its impact on everyday human relations, it is undoubtedly the most important, taking priority over the atomic, the computer, and the space-technology revolutions. Or even the revolution going on in race relations or the revolution being fomented by the young. For this revolution, in tandem with the others, adumbrates a shake-up and restructuring of social relations on a scale of magnitude we are only beginning to appreciate.

The Homemaking Function

We sometimes think of homemaking today as analogous to the primitive woman's care of the hearth. Not so. The home as we know it today is a relatively new phenomenon, a place with no industrial (as distinguished from *economic*) function at all, a place where goods are not produced: the home's economic function today is primarily in the field of consumption.

Under the domestic system of organizing production, families lived in the workshop. Women managed small, or even large, domestic enterprises rather than "kept house" as we think of it today. The concept of a place specialized only for family living is relatively recent, something of a luxury, a product of affluence. Before the fifteenth century, homes were so unpleasant and disagreeable that a large part of people's lives was spent in the community, in public (Aries, 1962, p. 405). Among the poor, there were hovels for married couples, children, and animals that were mere shelters for sleeping and sometimes for eating. They performed no social functions. Children left them early to live with spouses or brothers or as apprentices in a big house. The big house, a community in itself, served the public as a meeting place, with general-purpose rooms. The big houses were hardly private homes as we now think of them.

But in the fifteenth century such comforts as chimneys, window glass, and pillows became available even for the poor so that "the home became the center for pleasurable activities." And a wholly new domestic function for women was created, for now "to have a wife a home-maker—one that could change into comforts the necessities that man produced—was so much the more desirable" (Calhoun, 1917). Those who could afford such homes could withdraw from the coarser community life. A process of privitization began which at the same time emphasized the nuclear family as an oasis of morality in a desert of dissoluteness and as a haven, a retreat from threats, moral as well as physical. Homemaking as distinguished from housekeeping came to perform a moral and emotional as well as a protective function.

A parenthetical mention of the "hostessing" aspect of homemaking at the present time deserves at least a moment's attention. W. Lloyd Warner and William Whyte, Jr., showed us how important "social life" was in maintaining a power elite, not only the social life of the male clubs which served as valuable channels of information important for business and industrial decision-makers, but also the social life of the home (Whyte, 1956). The wife skilled in "entertaining" provided a necessary professional service for her husband; "social life" was essential for the kind of organization a power elite needed. C. Wright Mills showed the same processes at work on the national level (Mills, 1956).

Since its emergence in the fifteenth century, the homemaking function has been one of the most undisputed functions assigned to women. The time and energy spent on it has equaled, when it has not surpassed, that spent by industrial workers at the lathe, desk, or bench. Home economists have found on the basis of numerous studies that the amount of time invested by women in homemaking activities has varied from around fifty to not less than thirty hours per week.[1] It has been estimated that if the unpaid work of women had been measured, it would have increased

1. In 1930–31, a study of 693 graduates of six eastern colleges reported an average of 49.5 hours per week devoted to homemaking activities in small cities, 47.1 hours per week in larger cities. None of the women was employed outside the home. A study of 80 white families in three Mississippi towns in the early 1940's reported that women in lower economic levels averaged 50.4 hours per week, and those in higher levels 45.5 hours. In 1951, the housewife function took 31 hours per week for mothers with two to four school-age children in the upper lower class and 34 hours in the upper middle class. In 1965, wives spent an average of 40 hours per week on regular housework; husbands, 4 hours; and other family members, 7 hours. This total of 51 hours spent on housework even with all the modern gadgets at their disposal—a total greater than that reported in earlier studies —seems to confirm Joseph K. Folsom's statement of a generation ago that many labor-saving devices may save energy but they do not save time. In 1952, it was found that nonemployed farm and urban women spent almost twice as many hours daily (7.5) as did employed women (4.1). In 1958–1960, nonemployed women were reported to spend almost a third more time than employed women on food preparation alone. Similar results were reported for rural families. Homemaking services, in brief, were added to the labor-force activities. They were her responsibility, in or out of the labor force (U. S. Department of Agriculture, *Research Time Spent in Homemaking, An Annotated List of References,* Agricultural Research Service 62-15, Sept. 1967).

A similar situation is reported in the Soviet Union. There it has been estimated that such homemaking activities as shopping, cooking, and cleaning absorb 100 billion hours annually, the equivalent of a year of life for 12 million people. Alex Simirenk, "Post-Stalinist Social Science," *Trans-action* (June, 1969), 42.

In Sweden it has been calculated that women spend 2,340 million hours annually in housework as contrasted with 1,290 million in industry. And the Chase Manhattan Bank is quoted as estimating that women's overall working average 99.6 hours. Juliet Mitchell, "Women, The Longest Revolution," *New Left Review* (Nov.–Dec. 1966), 17. Contrasting with the very large amount of time invested in homemaking activities is the average number of hours devoted to professional activities in the labor market. These range from 32.9 in the case of librarians to 39.8 for electrical and electronic technicians. In the case of men the range is from 32.4 for librarians to 43 for biologists (Rossi, 1965, pp. 70–71).

the gross national product by 38 per cent (Morgan, 1966). Another exercise in forensic economics concluded that as of 1969, a 41-year-old housewife with three sons, who had worked as a secretary before she married, had a replacement value, if she died ten years before her youngest child reached 21, of $105,546 (Soo, 1969).

There is no intrinsic reason why homemaking chores cannot be more widely shared by all members of the household and, indeed, such a trend does seem to be in the making. Although W. J. Goode and the radical women do not seem optimistic about men's willingness to help with housework (Goode, 1963; Mainardi, 1969), at least some young husbands do share part of the burden (Bloode and Wolfe, 1970).

Quite aside from the time and effort expended on homemaking chores, there has been a high cost in terms of their effect on women's mentality.[2] A great deal about femininity discussed in Chapter 1 can be interpreted in functional terms, for not only does sex influence functional assignments but so also do functions influence personality and character. Occupational sociologists have long since familiarized us with the "stigmata" of occupations. We know that the occupation one specializes in finally affects one's appearance, stance, manners, behavior, and attitudes. In an analogous way the functions women perform affect their personalities, character, and mentality; they become creatures of their "sphere." A generation ago Terman found that the most "feminine" women were domestic servants (Terman and Miles, 1936).

As long ago as the beginning of the twentieth century, the stultifying effect of domesticity on the minds and characters of women was being commented upon:

> The reaction of an occupation pursued through a lifetime is so tremendous upon the physique and the mental and moral development of men, that its effects are easily recognized everywhere. . . . Many of the minor characteristics set down as peculiarly feminine

2. There has been an equally great cost to women of the domestic role in terms of their mental health. These costs have been documented in great detail in the sister volume of this one, *The Future of Marriage,* (World Book Company, forthcoming), Chapter 3. See also Bernard, 1971.

are, in fact, the product of the universal domestic employment of women in past times. . . . Given a vocation which demanded incessant attention to a thousand small matters, even when the number of these affairs was diminished so as to greatly release the housewife, the average woman would still inevitably pursue trifles until there was both a chance and an incentive to follow larger things. . . . There were thus both negative and positive reasons for woman to become small-minded. On the one hand, the sole occupation of her life consisted of exacting, repetitious, and ephemeral things; on the other, until there was an imperative call to other vocations outside, she could not develop the larger mind and become convinced of the futility of the conventional methods of housekeeping. The more conscientious the housewife was, the more petty she surely became, devoting herself to the elaboration of food, clothes, decoration, and needlework in the effort to be the perfectly correct feminine creature. . . . The cumulative effect of domesticity has been to produce scrappy-mindedness in woman. The average housewife's attention hops from one thing to another, never having been concentrated upon a continuous, homogeneous occupation, but rather upon a succession of miscellaneous details, all of which are about equally unimportant, but none of which must be forgotten (Coolidge, 1912, pp. 78–84, 96–97).

A generation later, another analysis of the nature of housework as an occupation and its effect on women noted that it was noncompetitive and hence nonstimulating, permitted day-dreaming and mind-wandering, was isolating and hence conducive to brooding, erratic judgments, and personalistic ideas (Bernard, 1942). There was also a good deal of talk of "the nervous housewife," whose fatigue and other psychosomatic symptoms were being traced to her occupation (Myerson, 1929).

Mary Roberts Coolidge had predicted that the "strictly domestic" woman would vanish, though it might take several generations "before the effects of domesticity upon the character of women . . . [would] disappear" (Coolidge, 1912, p. 86). But by that time the normal development anticipated by Mrs. Coolidge was intercepted by what Betty Friedan labeled the feminine mystique, the belief that the only way to validate one's sexuality was to return to the home and produce babies. This time, however, domesticity was making girls sick with an illness that had no name (Friedan, 1963). And they were increasingly returning to the labor force.

There is some evidence that the process of privatization, already under attack by communitarian critics in the nineteenth century, after reaching apotheosis in the 1950's, has about run its course. A countertrend seems to be in the offing. The costs of housekeeping as an occupation in terms of its destructive effects on women might well outweigh the benefits of such intense specialization. Radical women are seeking new ways of structuring this important function, both to minimize the costs and to distribute them more evenly.

The Child Rearing Function

Almost as universally sex-typed as the function of child bearing has been that of child rearing. So long as women's work was in or around the home the assignment to them of child rearing seemed all but inevitable. There seemed no better use for the time and energies of women. Policy took it for granted. In fact, at the beginning of the twentieth century the theory of the Mothers' Pension movement, later embodied in the Social Security Act of 1935 providing aid for dependent children, was precisely that the public welfare gained more when the time and energies of women were invested in the care of their children than when they were invested in the labor force.

In trying to assess the public interest in less intuitive, more objective terms, however, one runs up against one of the absurdities of the concept of public interest as measured in terms of the gross national product. For if a woman stays home and looks after her own children, she is making no contribution to the gross national product. If, however, she takes a job outside of the home and hires someone else to take care of her children, both are contributing to GNP. The current discussion of this function does not, however, rest on such a line of argument. It rests in part on the quite nontheoretical necessity to provide child-care services for working mothers, and as such it is well on its way (theoretically if not practically) to becoming institutionalized. But whether the child care is performed by the mother or by some surrogate, it is still assumed to be a woman's function.

Actually, the child-rearing function, like the homemaking function, is relatively new viewed historically. Philippe Aries has shown that the concept of childhood itself is as new as that of the privatized home. Until the end of the middle ages, children entered the adult world at about the age of six or seven. "In medieval society . . . as soon as the child could live without the constant solicitude of his mother, his nanny or his cradle-rocker, he belonged to adult society (Aries, 1962, p. 114). In England in the late fifteenth century, children were sent away as apprentices at about the age of seven, and in France the age of seven was also given as the age when children left the care of women and went to school or entered the adult world (Aries, 1962, p. 365).

By the sixteenth and seventeenth centuries, however, a new idea of childhood began to appear, and child care and education became central family values. Women and nannies still had the care of very small children, but teachers at home or in schools assumed increasing responsibility. Even with the glorification of childhood, the care of children was a denigrated function. It was held in contempt; thinking men felt a repugnance toward children (Aries, 1962, p. 114). But some leaders found "the education of children to be one of the most important things in the world" (Aries, 1962, p. 114) and one woman religious, assigned a boarding school by her order, concluded that "the education of children is so important that we are bound to prefer that duty to all others when obedience imposes it on us" and that it should even yield spiritual pleasure (Aries, 1962, p. 114). This new pro-child point of view waxed so that by the eighteenth century "everything to do with children and family life has become a matter worthy of attention. Not only the child's future but his presence and his very existence are of concern: the child has taken a central place in the family" (Aries, 1962, p. 133). By the end of the nineteenth century, Ellen Key, a great feminist, was proclaiming the twentieth century as the century of the child—especially of the middle-class child, and at the expense, some argued, of women (Slater, 1970).

There are indications that suggest the pattern of child rearing that emerged in the fifteenth and sixteenth centuries and became standard in the seventeenth, eighteenth, and nineteenth centuries is no longer suitable. Increasingly the function of child rearing is seen, especially by radical women, as by no means intrinsically a feminine function exclusively. Cora DuBois, for example, tells us that among the Alorese it is not. She had the impression, though she did not document it quantitatively, that "young men were even more inclined to fondle infants than were young women" and she explained this observation on structural rather than on psychological grounds, as the result of the greater leisure the young men enjoyed (DuBois, 1944, p. 35). Mothers gave precedence to their productive functions; child care was secondary:

> Since women are primarily responsible for garden work and the subsistence economy, mothers return to regular field work ten days to two weeks after the birth of the child. It is not customary for the mother to work with the child on her back or even near her. . . . Instead the infant is left at home in the care of some kin, for example, the father, an older sibling of either sex, or a grandmother whose field labor is less effective or necessary than that of a younger woman. . . . When the mother returns from the field in the late afternoon, she usually takes the child immediately to nurse and fondle. For the rest of the evening the child is either in the mother's carrying shawl or on her lap. . . . At night the child shares a mat with its mother. . . . The child's dependency on the mother is less marked than in our culture (DuBois, 1944, pp. 33–34).

The father's contribution to child rearing was not one that could be depended on, however. As in our own society, his financial and ceremonial occupations came first. Thus "it is definitely the less busy—that is, the less important—father who has time to be a good mother substitute" (DuBois, 1944, p. 38). The father is not the provider, is often absent, and as a result "he plays [only] a sporadic role in the education and rearing of the child" (DuBois, 1944, p. 178).

In our society so far as policy is concerned, the idea of supplying child-care services to encourage women to leave assistance rolls and enter the labor force has been accepted; moneys have even been appropriated for them. But in general such services are still staffed by women, for the care and rearing of children, especially of young children, is still viewed as exclusively—and dysfunctionally—a woman's job (Sexton, 1969).[3]

What new ways for performing the child-rearing and socialization functions will develop to engage men in is as yet a moot question. In the form of urban and rural communes and communities and collectives and assorted other attempts to help others than women share the function, the new ideas are still considered radical, though they do suggest that we may in time learn how to allow men to share more in its performance (Chapter 13).

It must be confessed that despite increasing research on child rearing and the vast research literature that has accumulated on the subject, there has not yet emerged a scientific consensus with respect to the most suitable way to structure it. One school emphasizes the dire results of maternal deprivation, with convincing research support; another emphasizes the dire results of maternal overprotection, with equally convincing research support. In one time and place, the research results confirm one point of view on policy; in a different time and place, another.

Nor, in fact, do we yet know what criteria to apply in judging the several alternative ways to structure the child-rearing function. Although the research results are confusing, this is still a matter that can be subjected to scientific scrutiny, with costs and benefits totted up and the interest of the public weighed.

In the meantime, there is relatively little theoretical difficulty with the more conservative proposal of fathers taking a share in child rearing. An official report of the Swedish government to the United Nations in 1968 stated that "the division of functions as between the sexes must be changed in such a way that both the man and the woman in a family are afforded the same practical opportunities of participating in both active parenthood and gainful employment" (Sweden, Government of, *The Status of Women*

---

3. Freud, however, was of the opinion that the education of boys by male slaves in Greece had encouraged homosexuality.

in Sweden, a report to the United Nations, 1968). Men, women, and children would, it is assumed, all benefit, and therefore the public interest would also be served.

The Glamor Function

The function here labeled "the glamor function" falls into a category all by itself. It is certainly the most vulnerable in terms of functional analysis. The Oxford Dictionary defines *glamor* in these terms: magic, enchantment, a spell; a magical or fictitious beauty attaching to any person or object; a delusive or alluring charm. Glamor resembles *charisma* in the sense that it is easy enough to understand, in the sense of experiencing, what the term refers to, but extremely hard to know intellectually what it is, how it operates, what it does. It is an artifact in the sense that it is "artificial," "delusive," and hence a cultural phenomenon; but because it cannot be achieved by everyone, it must have some intrinsic base, whether in biology, psychology, or what-have-you. There are several ways of structuring this function—theater, the arts, spectacles, opera, ballet—but in the context of the discussion here the appearance of women is the major focus of attention. If one accepts the legitimacy of the glamor function at all—and not everyone does, as we shall note presently—there seems to be no logical reason why it should be specialized and assigned to women. If not abolished, it might well be argued, it should at least be shared. Men performed it in the eighteenth century and seem to do so increasingly today. Gorgeous uniforms richly ornamented with ribbons and medals are still widely used to glamorize certain masculine roles.

It could be argued that glamor in its pristine form, so far from performing any function, is dysfunctional for the public interest. It is incompatible with all the other functions assigned to women and can even subvert them. An Italian study a generation ago concluded that the fertility of the most glamorous women was less than that of other women (Gini, 1938). It is hard to imagine glamor in the kitchen, despite television ads to the contrary. Or in the nursery. Glamorous women are not feminine in the conventional sense. A study of a hundred beautiful women models, whose stock-in-trade is glamor, portrayed an essentially masculine character, which the author labeled the "James Bond syndrome." It involved an aversion to routine and, conversely, a preference for "exciting, adventuresome activities, including those with the abstract feel of danger, . . . the dramatic, . . . the unstructured" (Campbell, 1966). Only certain kinds of jobs are compatible with glamor, such as those in the theater, opera, ballet, fashion. Glamor in the narrow sense is essentially elitist; it is not available for everyone. Jacqueline Kennedy Onassises are not common.

Because it is essentially subversive of the conventional functions assigned to women, glamor has been seen for milennia as the enemy of those in the seats of power. The Church Fathers raged against it, as have their descendants ever since. When the Soviet economy could not afford any trimmings, when its managers felt that it was in the public interest to subordinate all efforts to the production of heavy goods, austerity was a great virtue. Glamor, except in the ballet, was a degenerate vestige of capitalism. The resulting drabness that all observers reported chilled and depressed the scene. And that was not in the public interest.

Though glamor may fly in the face of everything practical, serviceable, and matter-of-fact, it seems to find its way back even when banished. Young cadets at the Soviet naval academy in Sevastopol complained that though "there are many pretty girls . . . the poetic charm of femininity is absent" (*Current Digest of the Soviet Press,* "Where are Sevastopol Cadets to Find Girls with Feminine Charm?" December 1968, p. 11) and girls were not likely to develop feminine glamor in the institutes they were attending. The demand for glamor was so great that the moment the Soviet economy could afford it, the rulers in the Kremlin had to concede. Fashion shows, cosmetics, elegance, chic became possible for at least some. The Parisian House of Dior was invited in to establish the glamor industries, and they found a ready market for their products among the elite. A Washington reporter of the social scene, speaking of Soviet women in the diplomatic corps, noted that it was "as if the Kremlin had sent them all to charm school" (Cheshire, 1968). Make-up, wigs and wiglets or artificial Dynel braids, the cut and fabric of clothes were now flawless; glamor had been restored to the diplomatic scene, for centuries one of its natural habitats.

Glamor in the elitist sense is a luxury that only a relatively small number of people can specialize in. But like other prerogatives it has tended, to use an accurate if unlovely barbarism, to become "massified" in recent decades. A kind of watered-down or ersatz glamor has nowadays become almost a staple. It is anyone's right to be glamorous; numerous industries, especially cosmetics, invest enormous amounts of time and money in creating products for producing the illusions that are the core of glamor. Everyone's eyes can be glamorized, as can everyone's lips, skin, legs, breasts, hair. Glamor in this watered-down form becomes little more than stepped-up sex appeal.

Quite aside from the contribution to self-actualization of such quasi glamor, it might be argued that only an unreconstructed Puritan could view it as trivial, frivolous, or contrary to the public interest, that anything that contributes to the attractiveness of women contributes to the public interest, that feminine attractiveness is itself a valuable "good" and its erosion a net loss. As a corollary, that anything that forces or even leads women to feel hostile, resentful, or in any way victimized, detracts from their attractiveness. That appreciation of women and attentiveness to them are good investments for any society. That however subversive glamor might be of the other functions assigned to women, specialization of some women in that function is not inconsistent with the public interest and that even the popular ersatz forms are at least tolerable. Men in general tend to defend the idea of "an impossibly attractive, charming . . . woman" as an ideal and a Soviet poet urges "a cult of women's charms" (Selvinsky, 1967).

But not all women do. Some deplore the emphasis on glamor in the mass media as denigrating to women (Banning, 1964) and radical women reject it out of hand, especially as it expresses itself in advertising of cosmetics, clothes, and adornment. In its "mass" sex-appeal form it performs merely the latent function of increasing consumption. And there is certainly a kernel of truth in this, as even the most cursory glance at advertisements in the mass media shows: "Sure. You live with him and take care of him and hang up his clothes. But just because you do the things a wife's supposed to, don't forget you're still a woman. One of the nicest things you can do for a man is take good care of your skin. . . . Why don't you do something soft and young and special for him?" (Potomac, 1963). In this sense it is merely part of a cult of consumerism, which they deplore.[4] They are willing to pay for its elimination with a reduced level of living if, as some economists maintain, that would be the price, for they hate consumerism and the system that demands it.[5]

Equally dysfunctional from the point of view of radical women is the tie-up of glamor with sexism. The sex appeal that ersatz glamor is designed to enhance has been standardized for a young woman between eighteen and twenty-five. And because it has enormous value, women of all ages attempt to achieve it. Their efforts, radical women point out, put women at an enormous disadvantage vis-à-vis men. They subject themselves to great indignities to be attractive to men; but, worse still, they hand over to men powerful weapons to be used against them. "You're all ugly, there's not a pretty girl among you," Yale alumni shouted at protesting women at a Homecoming assembly (*Washington Post*, 1970). Worse still, the acceptance of the ersatz glamor ideal makes a woman's whole life after the age of twenty-five downhill all the way. It robs her of self-confidence and denigrates her identity as a human being.

Whether, on balance, glamor in either its elitist or "mass" form contributes to the public interest and the pursuit of happiness of women or whether it performs primarily the latent function of stimulating consumption and is denigrating of women, it is not often that official policy in our society is called upon to deal with the glamor function. Among the first such confrontations was the

4. Opponents argue that there must be more than mere consumerism involved, for even in economies that do not need the stimulus of advertising to increase consumption, in which, as a matter of fact, as in the Soviet Union, the demands of consumers are subordinate to those of producers, the glamor function persists when it can be afforded.

5. Not everyone, opponents point out, would be willing to pay that price. There are still many people, they reminds us, including millions of black people, who want more of the material goods of consumerism that a less productive system would cost.

issue raised in the application of the Civil Rights Act in 1967. If sex were a bona fide occupational requirement for flight attendants, then they were exempt from the provisions of the Act and they could be fired at age 32 or when they married. If sex were not a bona fide occupational requirement, then no such requirements could be imposed on women unless they were also imposed on men.

The argument used by the airlines in stating their case amounted to an apologia for the glamor function. Serving meals, checking seat belts, and relaying messages could be done by men as well as by women. But when one company had replaced women by men, business fell off. The mere presence of pretty young women performing the chores was a plus. Each company invested hundreds of thousands of dollars in the planning and designing of new outfits for its stewardesses, showing how important they judged the glamor function to be. Admittedly a large component of glamor as they conceived it was a euphemism for sex-appeal; but they argued that even women found air travel more appealing when attended by young women trained to be attractively attentive. An advertisement of one airline looking for charm-school teachers also testified to the importance attached to glamor and specified its components as the airline conceived it. The job was called "Appearance Counselor" and the woman sought was "the woman among women who can teach our stewardesses the Secret Art of being beautiful and ladylike . . . the techniques which from time immemorial have passed female-to-female and never been revealed to the opposite sex . . . someone who knows the do's and don'ts—A to Z—of modeling, hairstyling, makeup, poise, manners, voice modulation, everyday psychology of getting along with people" (*Washington Post,* 1967).

REFERENCES

Aries, Philippe, *Centuries of Childhood* (New York: Knopf, 1962).

Banning, Margaret Culkin, "Portrayal of Women by the Mass Media," in Report of the *President's Commission on the Status of Women,* 1964, p. 22.

Bernard, Jessie, *American Family Behavior* (New York: Harper, 1942), pp. 531–534).

————, "The Paradox of a Happy Marriage," in Vivian Gornick and Barbara Moran (eds.), *51 Percent* (New York: Basic Books, 1971).

Bird, Caroline, *Born Female: The High Cost of Keeping Women Down* (New York: McKay, 1968), Chapter 8.

Blood, Robert O., Jr. and Donald M. Wolfe, *Husbands and Wives, The Dynamics of Married Living* (New York: Free Press, 1960), Chapter 3.

Calhoun, Arthur W., *A Social History of the American Family, Vol. 1. Colonial Period* (Cleveland: Arthur H. Clarke, 1917), p. 38.

Campbell, David P., "The Vocational Interests of Beautiful Women," paper given at the Midwestern Psychological Association (May, 1966), mimeographed, p. 5.

Cheshire, Maxine, "Very Interesting People," *Washington Post,* Nov. 9, 1968.

Coolidge, Mary Roberts, *Why Women are So* (New York: Holt, Rhinehart and Winston, 1912).

Current Digest of the Soviet Press, "Where are Sevastopol Cadets to Find Girls with Feminine Charm?" (December 1968), p. 11.

DuBois, Cora, *The People of Alors* (Minneapolis: University of Minnesota Press, 1944).

Friedan, Betty, *The Feminine Mystique* (New York: Norton, 1963), Chapter 1.

Gini, Corrado, "Beauty, Marriage and Fertility," *Human Biology,* 10 (Dec. 1938), pp. 575–576.

Glick, Paul C., "Marriage and Family Variables Related to Fertility," paper prepared for the United Nations World Population Conference, Belgrade (Aug., 1965), p. 2.

Goode, W. J., *World Revolution and Family Patterns* (New York: Free Press, 1963), p. 369.

Grønseth, Erik, "The Dysfunctionality of the Husband-Provider Role in Industrialized Societies," paper prepared for the 7th World Congress of Sociology, Varna, Bulgaria. (Abstract No. E3856 in *Sociological Abstracts,* August, 1970.)

Levy, Marion J., Jr., "Structural-Functional Analysis," *International Encyclopedia of the Social Sciences* (New York: Macmillan, 1968), Vol. 6, p. 23.

Mainardi, Pat, "The Politics of Housework," *Quicksilver Times Supplement* (Oct., 1969), 16–17.

Mills, C. Wright, *The Power Elite* (New York: Oxford University Press, 1956), pp. 58–60.

Morgan, James N., et al., *Productive Americans,* Institute for Social Research, Monograph 43 (Ann Arbor, University of Michigan, 1966).

Myerson, Abraham, *The Nervous Housewife* (New York: Little, Brown, 1929).

Potomac, Nov. 16, 1969, p. 68.

Rossi, Alice, "Who Wants Women in the Scientific Professions?" in Jacqueline A. Mattfeld and Carol G. Van Aken (eds.), *Women and the Scientific Professions* (Cambridge: M. I. T. Press, 1965).

Selvinsky, Ilya, quoted in *Washington Post,* April 13, 1967.

Sexton, Patricia, *Feminized Males: Class Rooms, White Collars, and the Decline of Manliness* (New York: Random House, 1969).

Slater, Philip E., "What Hath Spock Wrought?—Freed Children, Chained Moms," *Washington Post,* March 1, 1970. This article was excerpted from *The Pursuit of Loneliness—American Culture at the Breaking Point* (Boston: Beacon Press, 1970).

Soo, Chong, "The Monetary Value of a Housewife," *Amer. Jour. Ecs. and Sclgy.,* 28 (July 1969), 271–284.

Sweden, Government of, *The Status of Women in Sweden,* a report to the United Nations, 1968.

Terman, Lewis M. and C. C. Miles, *Sex and Personality: Studies in Masculinity and Femininity* (New York: McGraw-Hill, 1936).

Warner, W. Lloyd and Paul S. Lunt, *The Social Life of a Modern Community* (New Haven: Yale University Press, 1941), Chapter 12.

Washington Post, Feb. 2, 1970.

———, Dec. 10, 1967.

Whyte, William H., Jr., *The Organization Man* (New York: Simon Schuster, 1956), pp. 258–261.

5

The All-Pervading Function: Stroking

The Stroking or Supportive Function

The sexual allocation of the function we are here calling the "stroking or supportive function"—to be described presently— is more pivotal than the others, more central, more pervasive in its influence, more subtle, and so more difficult to evaluate in terms of impact on the general welfare or to assess in terms of costs and benefits. It has rarely been formally articulated and has never been the concern of policy. It has been too deeply embedded in the fabric of groups and societies to elicit general comment or public discussion. It is only now surfacing in the laboratories and in the polemics of radical women.

Among the most widely accepted conceptualizations of group functions is the one issuing from R. F. Bales' laboratory at Harvard University, delineating the instrumental function, which keeps a group at work, and the emotional-expressive function, which in its positive form keeps the group at peace. The person performing the positive emotional-expressive function does it in these ways: he shows solidarity, raises the status of others, gives help, rewards, agrees, concurs, complies, understands, passively accepts.[1] The function also includes the converse of all these things, but when the term is used it usually connotes the positive kind of expressiveness just specified. However, to avoid this ambiguity the term *supportive* or stroking instead of emotional-expressive is used here to refer to this function. Whatever it is called, the behavior is archetypically "feminine."

The indispensability of the expressive function in task-oriented groups can be documented in the laboratory. Without it the group is not likely to accomplish its task. Its ubiquity suggests its universal contribution to groups and social systems everywhere. Indeed, a very cogent case can be made for the statement that it supports any status quo. In the form of counseling, it has been charged with being simply a way of "cooling the mark out" (Bernard, 1969). And some radical women claim that the supportive function performed by wives is basically antirevolutionary, minimizing revolutionary ire (Bernard, 1969, Ch. 18). The Marxist phrase, the religion serves as an opiate of the people, is another expression of the same idea. Marx's implication was that capitalism must supply some form of stroking to make acceptance of its injustice palatable. The corollary that some other system would not require such a prop is a more debatable proposition. Still, in addition to the benefits to the status quo of the stroking function, which absorbs revolutionary anger, there are benefits to individual men themselves that are not difficult to discern.

For although both sexes are capable of performing both the instrumental and the supportive functions, there has tended to be in most cultures throughout the world a specialization of women in the supportive or stroking function (Zeldith, 1955). In fact, this assignment of the supportive or stroking function to women can be traced in all their roles throughout the social structure, in

1. Edgar F. Borgatta revised the Bales schema to make provisions for intensity of response, to differentiate, for example, between a simple "Hi," and "You know, that's one of the best ideas I've heard in a long time," both being examples of showing solidarity. The Borgatta schema also distinguishes between active and passive responses. The major category of interest remains, however, the stroking function dealing with the showing of solidarity by raising the status of others, including "buttering up" (Borgatta and Crowther, 1965).

the family, at work, at play, and in social life generally (Bernard, 1968). There are few feminine wiles better documented than the willingness of young women to build up the male ego by underplaying their own talents. Mirra Komarowsky has shown its presence among college women; feminists have been decrying it for decades. A whole literary genre has grown up based on "life with father" or "what every woman knows," portraying the wife as building up the husband's ego even at the cost of self-denigration. A century of guidebooks for working girls has emphasized the importance of ego-support for male employers. Girls are admonished not to win at tennis or other sports. They are taught to be good listeners no matter how bored they may be when talking to men in social situations (Bernard, 1968). No matter what job a woman is doing or what role she is performing, high or low, the supportive function is assumed to be part of it. Indeed, the behaviors that constitute stroking as listed above add up to a description of the ideal-typical woman wherever she is found.

Cases in Point

Stroking in one form or another is expected of all women. It is almost as ineluctably female as reproduction. A woman could drink, swear, and swashbuckle like a trooper, but if she performed the stroking function she would be considered feminine. Stroking is feminine almost by definition, from schoolgirls to Ph.D's. Here at one end of the gamut is John Greenleaf Whittier's little schoolgirl:

> I'm sorry that I spelt the word;
> I hate to go above you,
> Because—the brown eyes lower fell—
> Because, you see, I love you.

She should have raised his status by failing to spell the fatal word.

And at the other end of the scale, here is how it looks to a high-level professional woman, completely aware of what is taking place, able to analyze it objectively—and accepting it. She is talking about behavior at professional conventions:

91

A typical encounter between an anxious, tense, over-stimulated male conventioneer and a female colleague proceeds as follows. The male spots the female at the other end of the main lobby, where like himself hundreds of his fellow sociologists have been milling for hours. He quickly disentangles himself from the colleague whom he meets each year at the convention, greets heartily, checks on whether he is still at the same institution and then finds that the conversation runs dry. Using arms, legs, eyebrows, and voice to attract his [female] colleague's attention, he finally makes his way through the crowd and rushes over, arms extended to renew a casual acquaintance that has lain dormant since the last convention. He quickly gets over the preliminaries. . . . Speaking at his special convention rate of 275 words per minute, he recounts his achievements of the past year. He describes, briefly, the seventeen major articles and six research notes and book reviews that he has completed. Taking a little longer for each of the following, he then goes on to explain the major thesis of the seven monographs that are almost ready to go to the publishers. . . . He suggests they find a place to sit down and have a drink. . . . Having refreshed himself . . . he launches into an account of the nine proposals that he has written for major research projects, each of which he expects to receive immediate foundation support. He then . . . describes the four definite and three "feeler" job offers that he has had to turn down. . . . Just as they are getting up . . . he remembers the really stupendous idea that he has had only ten minutes ago—in the next fifteen minutes he outlines it fully. Each then goes off in his separate direction.

Why does the male conventioneer seek out his female colleague for conversations such as the one described above? [Because] had he had the above discussion with a male colleague there would have been a *quid-pro-quo*. After describing his accomplishments over the past year he would have to listen to and then reward a similar catharsis for his colleague. By that time, his own psychic gains would have been negated. He would leave the situation experiencing as much psychic stress as when he entered it. But, in selecting a female colleague he can have his catharsis, the enjoyment of feminine companionship, and best of all no requirement or even expectation that he reward in kind a similiar recitation of accomplishments from his colleague (Mintz, 1967, p. 158).

As a professional colleague, the woman can give appreciation that is worth more than, say, his wife's would be. The profes-

sional woman "is a task expert who has been trained to participate in the same world of ideas and research as her male counterpart. She can understand and judge the worth of an idea or a
piece of research. She can also reward achievement. But as a
woman, she has learned how to distribute love, support, encouragement, and other expressive verbal rewards" (Mint, 1967, p.
158). Not, however, as we shall presently note, without costs to
herself.

Here is another almost identical incident reported at a different
professional gathering:

> Two top-ranking men and two top-ranking women, all leaders in
> their profession, are having dinner together during a professional
> conference. At the end the two women leave together and one turns
> to the other and laughingly comments: "Did you notice that as we
> fed them questions and comments to draw them out, to give them a
> chance to tell us about their achievements, not once did they do the
> same for you and me?" "Yes," replied her companion. . . . They
> laughed together—too successful, too reconciled, too experienced to
> care (Bernard, 1967).

(Too reconciled by far, radical women would fling at them.)[2]

Nathaniel Hawthorne summed it all up:

> Woman is the most admirable handiwork of God, in her true place
> and character. Her place [where have we heard that before? ask the
> radical women] is at man's side. Her office, that of sympathizer; the
> unreserved, unquestioning believer; the recognition, withheld in
> every other manner [by other men] but given, in pity, through
> woman's heart, lest man should utterly lose faith in himself; the echo
> of God's own voice, pronouncing, "It is well done."

Benefits to Men

The male conventioneer described above reaped a considerable
cathartic bonus from the woman's appreciation without having
to pay anything for it but the price of a cocktail. Nor is there any

2. Compare with the charge by some Movement Women, mentioned
above, that this soaking up of male frustrations is antirevolutionary.

question about the value, not only to men, but to everyone, of the supporting function. We spoke above of its contribution to any status quo; it has a more personal impact also. In a world that generates such meager quantities of friendliness and affection, any minimization of stroking would make living together less tolerable. If women ceased to supply support, even radical women, who most resent the assignment of this function to women, admit that the world would be a less friendly place (Densmore, 1968). Women would no longer suffer fools gladly, be kind to men simply because they were men, shore up their sagging sense of superiority by "echoing God's own voice."

The issue is, then, since both sexes are capable of performing this function, why assign it so preponderantly to women, and always to women in a two-sex setting? Is the benefit to men purchased at the expense of women? Would the public interest be better served if men themselves shared the performance of this function to a greater extent than now? By an equaling upward rather than an equaling down? If men were as appreciative of women as women must be of men, shored up their sense of inferiority rather than adding to it, ceased to put them down? Perhaps just better manners would help? More awareness of what their often insufferable lack of sensitivity "costs" women? For the costs to women can be serious.

Costs to Women: The Woman Who Pays and the Price She Pays

We used to say "the woman pays" when referring to abandoned girls. In the present context the woman pays again, but this time a different woman and in different coin. It is the achieving woman this time who pays; and her coin is achievement. The costs to women of having to perform the supportive function are subtle and difficult to delineate and almost impossible to convey to men. How communicate, for example, the anxiety, the depression, the self-denigration that the young woman conventioneer felt after her tête-à-tête with a male professional peer? Her own achievements of the year—papers, research proposal, and book manuscript—now seemed inconsequential. In one brief encounter he had cut her down way below size and built himself up at her expense. Unlike a male peer, she could not elicit the same support from him. Her achievements were not rewarded by appreciative listening on his part. Now they seemed trivial even to her.

Equally subtle is another kind of cost. A review of the components of the expressive function—showing solidarity, raising the status of others, giving help, rewarding, agreeing, concurring, complying, understanding, passively accepting—reveals how incompatible they are with the kinds of activity demanded by the most prestigious jobs. If women must perform the stroking function they are ipso facto disqualified for jobs that require fighting and competing and challenging. It is difficult to be supportive to a competitor or opponent. Men do not expect support from men; they are nonplussed when it is not forthcoming from women. Support is much easier for someone who is removed from the battle, someone in a protected position, but the protected positions are likely to be the dull, unglamorous ones.

Specialization in the stroking function is probably also incompatible with the kind of aggression called for by creativity (Bernard, 1964). Alice Rossi has shown that if we tailored our training of girls to produce scientists instead of man-pleasing or supportive women, we could increase the number of scientists and promote self-actualization by way of creativity (Rossi, 1965). Both the public interest and self-actualization would be served. Instead, we train women for failure (see Chapter 6).

In and of itself, the stroking–supporting function does not demand inequality. The professional counselor can perform it vis-à-vis a client without losing his superior position in the relationship. But, taken in conjunction with other aspects of the "sphere" of women, it is a recipe for subservience. "Raising the status of others," for example, may mean a denigration of one's own. In extreme form, it is simply fawning.

$F_1, F_2 \ldots F_n$ Again

Many women may be quite willing to accept the sacrifice of their own achievement; they are more interested in men than in careers. Even the achieving woman conventioneer quoted above, after weighing the costs and rewards of her experience, concluded that the gains outweighed the costs. The punch line of her piece was an invitation to her male colleagues not to be deterred by her statement but to continue to "Come ahead."

But not all women are this willing. They can understand why some women are willing to give up their own achievement potential for the sake of men's, but they are not willing to do so themselves. For them the pursuit of happiness calls for the self-actualization that comes from their own achievement, not indirectly from that of a man. They reject a sexual specialization in the supportive function which implies that women should be denied opportunities to make the most of themselves so that they can be available to soothe egos and build other people up so *they* can achieve more! No, thank you! They bitterly resent the sexism that demands such severe sacrifice on their part.

Costs of Change to Men

Erik Erikson has raised questions about the costs to men if women were released from the constraints imposed by their functional responsibilities to them.

[Men are apprehensive about] what might happen if women once released from the restrictions imposed on them really did take part in all of those activities that men have considered their privilege and their preserve and from which most men seek refuge by returning to women. And it is hard to look for refuge in a would-be competitor. In some discussions men otherwise not of a sentimental bent insist so strenuously that children need their mothers at home that one cannot help wondering if it is not the husband himself who is the needy person—the tired husband who wants a ravishing companion free of all connotations of the office and the laboratory (Erikson, 1965, pp. 236–237).

Keep women out of the arena, protected, sequestered, segregated, so that they can bind the wounds of men. If they become competitors of men, it is anomalous to expect them to perform the supportive function.

If women were not specialized to supply support, and if men were unwilling to make up the deficit, there might indeed be a real loss in the total amount of such support that is generated in our society. A loss, some argue, never envisioned in any computation of the gross national product, (or even calculated). Is the admitted need for more scientists and other professionals so compelling, they ask, that we should bend all our efforts to producing them? Might the total cost, not only to men but also to the general welfare, be excessive in terms of the effective gains? Would the increase in scientific productivity or creativity be worth more than the loss in the support contributed by women in their present functional specialization? In brief, they ask: would the public interest be furthered?

Radical women ask a different question: Suppose men *became* as supportive of our careers as we are expected to be of theirs? Or, more radically, suppose we all became more supportive of one another?

THE CICHLID EFFECT

Maleness is harder to achieve than femaleness. We all begin life in a sexually undifferentiated form with undifferentiated genital tracts. In order to achieve maleness, the testes of those with male chromosomes must secrete masculinizing hormones; the growth of the male genital apparatus is therefore more difficult and complex than that of the female (Hamburg and Lunde, 1966). We know on the basis of fetal deaths that it is more difficult for a male to survive prenatally and, on the basis of mortality data, even postnatally. For these reasons a case could be made that males need the handicap imposed on women and the support it makes possible.

More immediate is an argument based on the dependence of male sexuality on the essentially antiaggressive quality of female behavior. I have called this phenomenon, first described by Konrad Lorenz, the Cichlid effect (Bernard, 1968).

Erikson ascribes men's resistance to change in women to the fact that "a clear elaboration of sexual types is always essential for the polarization of the sexes in sexual life in their respective identity formation" (Erikson, 1965, p. 237). Here Erikison is zeroing in on a phenomenon reported by Lorenz in Cichlid fish. Among these fish there are no obvious or apparent sex differences so far as size, coloring, or other characteristics are concerned; nor do they differ in capacity for aggression or fear.

It is in the relationship among these three forms of behavior in this species that sex differences show themselves:

> In these fish, the relation of miscibility of the three great drive sources is different in the male and in the female; in the male, the motivations of flight and of sexuality cannot be mixed. If the male has even the slightest fear of his partner, his sexuality is completely extinguished. In the female, there is the same relation between aggression and sexuality; if she is so little in awe of her partner that her aggression is not entirely suppressed, she does not react to him sexually at all (Lorenz, 1963, p. 103).

All analogies between human beings and animals are suspect, and it would be fallacious to conclude that human beings are identical with Cichlid fish in their sexuality. Still, at least for the older generation the analogy is striking. Among them sexuality did seem to depend on the kind of deaggressing of women that resulted from assigning them a supportive role. In 1948, for example, a psychoanalyst noted the Cichlid effect among his patients; that is, the dependence of male potency and female responsiveness on the nature of their relationship. "Nature has made adequate provision that the animal should not become sexually aroused when his survival is threatened. When self-esteem is involved, the man loses his erection or gets premature ejaculation, and the woman becomes frigid. Where there has to be a state of defense against potential injury or humiliation, the sexual impulse is lost (Sapirstein, 1948, pp. 154–155).

As though to forestall such an outcome in view of the essential equality of the sexes, there seems to be an almost universal institutionalization of hypergamy among women, that is, a tendency for girls to marry "up," within a general tendency toward homogamy. It is not that women are masochistic and want to abase themselves; it is a structural characteristic for woman's "sphere." If a choice has to be made between their own superiority and that of their husbands, the assigned supportive function guarantees that most will prefer their husband's. Hypergamy makes it easier.

Male Backlash or Generation Gap?

If women were no longer disqualified for the competitive positions in our society by the constraints imposed by the stroking function, Erikson gloomily sees the "possibility that when the number of competitive women . . . increases, there may well be something of a male 'backlash' " (Erikson, 1965, p. 237). In this he reflects the attitudes of a generation formed under the influence of Freud who, in turn, had based his theories on Victorian models of human nature, and on the patients who had dredged their unconscious, revealing to him the structure created by that peculiar model. The achieving woman then may well have looked threateningly like a castrating female; for in an age when men were supposed to be superior to women—and women to work hard to convince them that they were—a woman who equaled a man did indeed denigrate him. The costs of the standard of male supremacy were great to men as well as to women. The same kind of psychoanalytic evidence seemed to show that once women were liberated from the Victorian sexual restraints and freed to make sexual demands on men, they could use such demands as weapons of war against men. They could show that male sexual superiority, never tested when the sexual initiative was exclusively a male prerogative, was a myth (Stannard, 1969). In a society that does not demand that men be superior there is less trauma when they are not.

If it were demonstrably true that human male sexual potency does indeed depend on female subservience, then its functional necessity for the general welfare could certainly be established, whatever it meant for anyone's pursuit of happiness. The sacrifice of male sexual potency would be too high a price to pay for releasing women from the supportive function. But the trend of events today seems to show that male sexuality does not have to be ransomed by female servility, that men can live happily without demanding the subservience of women.

A good case could even be made, as Philip Slater has done, that independent women are more attractive as sex partners than dependent women (Slater, 1970), that the subservience traditionally called for in women reduced the excitement, stimulation, and sheer fun of an encounter, that the emphasis on Victorian passivity in women rather than on their responsiveness reduced rather than enhanced male sexuality. Much depends on how independence is handled. If it is associated with arrogance, condescension, rejection, contempt, or other forms of hostility, it's not so likely to turn a man on as if it is associated with more friendly attitudes. (Just as subservience associated with anxiety, fear, clinging, and possessiveness is not likely to be welcome either.) The relevant point is not the subservience but the emotional flavor. And the chances that a subservient woman would be hostile and sullen are greater than the chances that an independent woman would be. Since the independent partner shares the relationship because she wants to, she can be more joyful and exuberant and therefore more exhilarating about it.

If a tradition-oriented man knows only one model of a male-female relationship, any other looks threatening. If a man knows only a dominant male-dependent female pattern, he can only dread the idea of an autonomous female. How would he fare in such a relationship? It would disorganize him. But a man who knows a relationship of equality may wonder how anyone could bear the incubus of subservience.

There is evidence that the generation now entering the scene is in process of working out new relationships between the sexes that should mitigate the remnants of the Cichlid effect. There was a time when if a wife was even gainfully employed, this fact reflected on her husband; he lost face. She was supposed, in Veblen's terminology, to perform vicarious leisure for him. Now it is accepted as commonplace not only that a wife may work but also that she may even support her husband in graduate school. In 1967, 37 per cent of all married women living with their husbands were in the labor force; among the talented, they were pursuing a career. Among Vassar graduates in the class of 1966, "career drive" was found to exceed "mating drive," a rather sharp reversal of previous trends. Caroline Bird (1968), summarizing the relevant literature, concluded that "women will increasingly find themselves living in ways that parallel rather than complement the lives of their husbands." And at least some of the men, she found, welcomed the change.

In the 1960's, ardent support for the feminist revolution came from the new companionable husbands, the new main recruiters of womanpower, the presidents of men's colleges who wanted to get girls on the campus, the political and business leaders who were actively promoting women in policy-making position. Some of the most effective New Feminists were men, and there were more of them than appeared at first glance.

According to the American Institute of Public Opinion, there was a real increase in the proportion of men who would vote for a qualified woman President. This survey organization asked the question in a poll of 1955 and again in 1963. Over that interval of eight years, the percentage of women who would vote for a woman President dropped slightly from 56 per cent to 51 per cent, but the male vote rose from 47 to 58 percent. At the last count, a majority of men saw no objection to the idea of a woman President of the United States.

In brief, generations change; relationships that have not existed in the past emerge; relationships that were standard in the past vanish from the scene. There is more sharing of the supportive function. Relationships that have seemed to be deeply embedded in human nature are discarded without a second thought. They were embedded in Victorian human nature, not in the human nature of the last third of the twentieth century. Relations once viewed as impossible become commonplace.

The subtitle of Caroline Bird's book, "The High Cost of Keeping Women Down," reflects a cost-effectiveness as well as a self-actualization point of view for policy. She does not pretend that there will not be costs in raising women up—such as less unpaid welfare work, increased labor costs, reduced flexibility of the economy, fewer services for executives in the office—but not, if young men are any test, any costs in male sexuality. It is hazardous to take the Cichlid effect as a permanent rule of the game that policy must forever take into account. Young men seem to be learning how to live happily with achieving women, and achieving women with men, without any threat to masculinity. In any event it is hard to see what policy could do, with respect to either the general welfare or the pursuit of happiness.

Not so, however, with respect to the last of the functions of women discussed here, the productive, and the division of labor within which it operates. It has become an increasing preoccupation of policy.

REFERENCES

Bales, R. F., *Interaction Process Analysis: A Method for the Study of Small Groups* (Cambridge: Addison-Wesley, 1950).

Bernard, Jessie, *Academic Women* (University Park: Pennsylvania State University Press, 1964), Chapter 11.

———, "The Second Sex and the Cichlid Effect," *Jour. Natl. Assn. Women Deans and Counselors,* 31 (Fall 1967), 9.

———, *The Sex Game* (Englewood Cliffs, N.J.: Prentice-Hall, 1968).

———, "Functions and Limitations in Counseling and Psychotherapy," in Donald A. Hansen (ed.), *Exploration in Sociology and Counseling* (Boston: Houghton Mifflin, 1969), pp. 369–374.

Berne, Eric, *Games People Play* (New York: Grove Press, 1964) is the source of the term "stroking."

Bird, Caroline, *Born Female, The High Cost of Keeping Women Down* (New York: McKay, 1968), p. 184.

Borgatta, Edgar F., and Betty Crowther, *A Workbook for the Study of Social Interaction Processes* (Chicago: Rand McNally, 1965).

Densmore, Dana, "People Power," *Journal of Female Liberation,* (1) (Nov. 1968), 23.

Erikson, Erik, "Concluding Remarks," in Jacqueline Mattfeld and Carol G. Van Aken (eds.), *Women in the Scientific Professions* (Cambridge: M. I. T. Press, 1965).

Hamburg, David and Donald T. Lunde, "Sex Hormones in the Development of Sex Differences in Human Behavior," in Eleanor Maccoby (ed.), *The Development of Sex Differences* (Stanford: Stanford University Press, 1966), pp. 1–24.

Lorenz, Konrad, *On Aggression* (New York: Harcourt, Brace, 1963).

Mintz, Geraldine R. (pseudonym), "Some Observations on the Function of Women Sociologists at Sociology Conventions," *Amer. Sociologist,* 2 (Aug. 1967).

Rossi, Alice, "Who Wants Women in the Scientific Professions?" in J. A. Mattfeld and C. A. Van Aken (eds.), pp. 112 ff.

Sapirstein, M.R., *Emotional Security* (Crown Press, 1948), pp. 154–155.

Slater, Philip E., "What Hath Spock Wrought?—Freed Children, Chained Moms," *Washington Post,* March 1, 1970.

Stannard, Una, *The New Pamela or Virtue Unrewarded* (New York: Ballantine Books, 1969).

Strodtbeck, Fred L. and Richard D. Marx, "Sex Role Differentiation in Jury Deliberation," *Sociometry,* 19 (March 1956), 9–10.

Zelditch, Morris, "Role Differentiation in the Nuclear Family: A Comparative Study," in Talcott Parsons and Robert F. Bales (eds.), *Family Socialization and Interaction Process* (New York: Free Press, 1955), pp. 307–352.

III

The Public Interest and the Sexual Division of Labor

Both men and women perform productive functions. Since the first industrial revolution much of the productive work of the economy has been performed in the labor force rather than in the home, so that the composition of the labor force reflects the sexual division of labor.

The labor force has become increasingly a concern of policy. "When the utilization of formally free labor occupies a place of central importance in social policy . . . there is . . . special interest in the factors determining working force status" (Jaffe and Stewart, 1951). Until the first industrial revolution there was little need for research and study of the working force or for labor policy dealing with it. Work allocations were made by administrative decision in the light of prevailing custom and authority structures. "During the Mercantilist period, European states in varying degree exercised close control over the working force in the interest of national policy" (Jaffe and Stewart, 1951) as they saw it; but little abstract theory informed their decisions. Under laissez-faire, policy was not formally concerned with the nature of the work force; that was determined by the market. Theoretical economics viewed the situation in terms primarily of wages. Malthus, to be sure, saw that far more was involved than merely economic factors, but his attention was directed more to the dole and its effects than to the allocation of industrial work.

Still, even without the demands of policy to support them, men as diverse as Thomas Jefferson and Timothy Dwight, sensing the importance of the labor force for the general welfare, began to call for the inclusion of occupational statistics when the census was taken. Thus a substantial body of data on the labor force began to accumulate, and its analysis and performance became the focus of interest not only of economists but also of industrial and vocational psychologists and sociologists. By 1961, the optimum utilization of the labor force was being seen as a legitimate concern of national policy: "It is in the national interest to promote the economy, security, and national defense through the most efficient and effective utilization of the skills of all persons" (Kennedy, 1961). Including women. For women were an increasing proportion of the labor force and "the factors determining [their] working force status" ramified widely throughout the whole social system as well as the economic system and therefore called for serious consideration from policy makers.

REFERENCES

Jaffe, A. J. and Charles D. Stewart, *Manpower Resources and Utilization, Principles of Working Force Analysis* (New York: Wiley, 1951), p. 2.

Kennedy, President John F., Statement Establishing a Commission on the Status of Women, 1961.

6

The Jobs of Women

Implementing Labor-Force Policy

If it is, indeed, the policy of our society, as President Kennedy stated it to be, to achieve "the most efficient and effective utilization of the skills of all persons," what criteria should be applied to implement it? How can the skills of all persons be utilized in an optimal way? Given a labor force with a certain sex composition, is the present use being made of it the best possible one?

It is not easy to set up criteria for answering these questions in terms of the public interest. In general, however, two criteria sound logical: one is "the best person for the job," and the other is "the best job for the person." From the point of view of the public interest—ignoring any preference of the individual workers themselves—basing policy on these criteria would presumably lead to at least a rational allocation of jobs. The first criterion is violated when there is sex-typing of jobs and the second when there is underutilization of the talents of workers. And the sex-typing of work often leads to the underutilization of talents.

"Best Person for the Job" and Sex Typing

The division of labor is a universal phenomenon, and sex is universally one of the bases on which it rests. That it does not rest entirely on biological sex differences is shown by the fact that the precise nature of the work specifically assigned to men and to women is not universally the same. In one society the care of cattle, for example, may be woman's work; in another, women may not even be permitted near the cattle. In a study of 324 societies around the world, G. P. Murdock found only one occupation, metalworking, to be universally men's work; weapon-making and the pursuit of sea mammals and hunting were almost so. No work at all was exclusively women's work everywhere. Here and there, men had taken over work usually allocated to women, as making clothing, cooking, carrying water, and grinding grain; but almost nowhere had woman taken over hunting or weapon-making, and nowhere metalworking. Men, in brief, had a wider range of occupations than women did (Murdock, 1937).

Even in modern societies, the work assigned to the sexes varies from place to place. Women clean the streets in the Soviet Union; men do it in the United States. Work allocation by sex varies over time also. Women used to mine coal; now men do. Men used to be schoolmasters; later women took over; now men are returning to the schoolroom. The first secretaries and stenographers were men; most are women today, and so on (Baker, 1964). The "sex" of jobs varies also according to the setting, being "male" if it is done in a factory and "female" if it is done at home. The fact, then, that different kinds of work are assigned to the sexes in different times and places and that the specific kinds of work assigned to them in any one place may change over time indicates that biological sex differences per se are not determinative. And they appear to become less so with industrialization, as mechanical power is substituted for human muscle power and instrumental speed for human speed.

The precise nature of the work assigned to men and to women is not, in fact, important in itself. What is important is that the work, whatever it is, becomes sex-typed and, once sex-typed, tends to attract or be allocated to members of only one sex regardless of the qualifications of individual members of the other sex.

If vocational skills and abilities were completely sex-dominated, as in Figure 6.1 it would be easy to use sex as a major factor in allocating work. Men would simply not have the ability

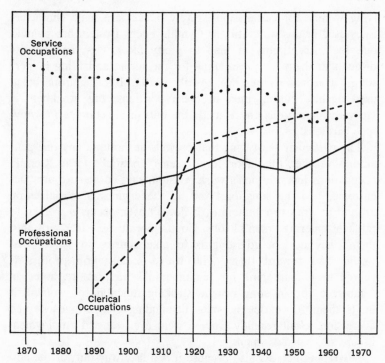

Figure 6.1. Proportion of Employed Women in Three Occupations, 1870-1968 .

Source: For the years 1870 to 1940, A. J. Jaffe and Charles D. Stewart, **Manpower Resources and Utilization, Principles of Working Force Analysis** (Wiley, 1951), p. 502; for 1940 to 1968, **1969 Handbook on Women Workers** (Women's Bureau, 1969), p. 92.

to do certain kinds of work, nor women other kinds. But we know that most human traits, even when their incidence varies by sex, show considerable overlapping between the sexes, as in Figure 1.2. We cannot, therefore, determine qualifications for a job—or lack of them—simply by sex. A woman may be stronger than the average man; a man may be more passive than the average woman. Sex-typing gets in the way of finding the best person for the job. Still, it persists.

Sometimes, in fact, it persists perversely. Some traits are almost as categorically distributed as those in Figure 1.1. But although such female characteristics are often cited as reasons for disquali-

fying women for certain jobs, rarely if ever are male characteristics used in this way. Still, as Cynthia Fuchs Epstein has pointed
out, the susceptibility of men to pretty faces, legs, and breasts
disqualifies them for jobs calling for the hiring and firing of personnel (Groves Conference, April, 1970). But far from being
used against putting men in these positions, this weakness is
viewed as humorous and is made the butt of affectionate *Playboy*-
type cartoons.

The particular sex-typing that prevails at the time any one generation reaches the labor force seems "natural" to it. Certain
occupations just are men's work. Custom says so and we are "accustomed" to the situation. And all the engines of socialization
are put to work to maintain it. It doesn't even occur to women to
think of entering "men's" jobs. Counselors do not steer girls into
them; they do not advise girls to take courses in school that
would lead toward them. The whole socialization process is
geared to prepare girls for feminine jobs and, as we noted in
Chapter 5, by insisting on the stroking function for women, it
unfits them for masculine ones demanding competitiveness and
aggression. Until recently women were even refused employment
in jobs sex-typed for men.

Sex-typing persists also because it is a lazy way out for the employer. It is much more difficult to determine aptitude for a job
by studying the applicants themselves than it is to judge them on
the basis of their sex. It is easier to promote on the basis of sex
than it is on the basis of proved competence. Sex-typing persists
because of inertia.

It persists also because of its potential for exploitative use.
Women are laid off and men hired in their place at women's
wages; or men are laid off and their jobs reclassified. They are
then replaced by women who work for less pay. Or women are
hired as part-time or full-time but temporary workers to avoid
payment of fringe benefits (Jordan, 1968).

Only since the passage of the Civil Rights Act of 1964, designed to eliminate discrimination in employment, have such
practices become illegal. To the extent that it prevents employers
from engaging in practices that discriminate against women it

will certainly serve the public interest according to the criterion of the best person for the job.

Sexism and Sex-Typing of Work

But even when discrimination in hiring becomes illegal, extra-legal pressures remain, for though the law may ban blatant discrimination, it can hardly dent sexism. And if sexism remains, one does not need discrimination; the same result can be achieved differently. For if one can set up the criteria for a job, as sexism permits men to do, certain people are automatically eliminated. Not because they are women, but because they just do not qualify. And the qualifications have been established precisely to see that they do not.

The all-but-complete control of the division of labor by sexism is hard to see precisely because it is so pervasive. Sexism is so "natural," so taken for granted, so accepted, and even so unconscious on the part of many, as to be indignantly denied by them when accused of it. Everyone is sure he can't be guilty of it. As Ruth Tuck reminded us a generation ago, discrimination against Americans of Mexican descent wasn't done with the fist. If the discriminatory practices that she described in a town she called Descanso had been articulated, they would have been repudiated.

If a law read, "All persons of Mexican origin, after 5 years' residence in the United States shall cease to display, in action or manner, recognizable signs of their former culture, under penalty of forfeiting access to equal employment opportunity . . . a tornado of protest would engulf the unfortunate administration . . . over this [insult to] the spirit and letter of our Constitution. But Descanso, having accomplished practically the same ends by indirection, considers its methods, not regimentation, but "common sense." Its practices toward its Mexican group actually constitute a large unwritten body of law. This law, in effect, says: "Those of different culture and/or race, particularly if they lack economic power, are to be treated by standards inferior to those prevailing for residents of the United States at large." . . . The unwritten law, or any intimations of it, never stood a chance of getting on a statute book. Public opinion would not have stood for seeing it in black and white, for Descanso's assertion that it wants to be fair is not an idle one. If the cards had been laid on the table, in the form of crystallization of practice into law, Descanso would have been sickened by the sign of the marked deck it was dealing. This was one folkway it could not have stood seeing embodied in a stateway.

If, however, Descanso could claim that the unwritten law did not exist, or if it could rationalize its practices on the ground that the group concerned was "low" or "different" or "inferior," a bad conscience was thereby eased (Tuck, 1946).

Substitute sex for culture or race, and the picture describes also how sexism works.

Discrimination may not be enforced with the fist, but it is enforced with methods that may be no less psychologically and emotionally violent. Girls who do not conform to customary patterns may be hazed on the job, viewed as oddballs, as peculiar, unfeminine, or unwomanly, made to feel uncomfortable and out of things. A thousand informal sanctions may be brought to bear against them. Men make it very clear that they do not like to work with women (Caplow, 1964). The net effect is to retain extralegal sex-typing of jobs.

Both carrot and stick are used to channel women into such "feminine" jobs as secretaries and out of such "masculine" ones as the professions:

The high recognition given the successful secretary and the satisfaction she derives from being closely identified with the successes of her employer often combine to forestall her desire to move from the clerical to the professional category. The stereotype of the American woman as the helper to the man is perpetuated and, besides, it is both comforting and sage. . . . In contrast, the professional woman in our society must constantly prove herself and, for most, recognition is at best both temporary and elusive. . . . Surely if more women are to be encouraged to make long-range plans for careers in the professions . . . society must accord the professional woman as much opportunity for self-realization and satisfaction of needs, both personal and material, as society makes available for its secretaries (Alpenfels, 1962, pp 80–81).

Some radical women refuse even to accept secretarial positions as supposed openings to higher levels, alleging that if they are good as secretaries every effort will be made to keep them in that position. (The secretary–employer situation is also an interesting illustration of the diffuse-specific dimensions of a relationship referred to in Chapter 1. The employer's obligations are merely contractual; he can be held responsible only for paying her salary, contributing to her Social Security account, providing proper working conditions, and the like. But the secretary's are more diffuse, including not only the contractual ones but also, if asked, shopping for presents, taking his son out for a haircut, watering the plants, or whatever).

The way sexism operates in academia has been reported in terms of a "stag effect." In fast-moving sciences it is important to be in the right communications channels, including face-to-face contacts at professional meetings of one kind and another. It has been estimated that almost half of the contents of such rapidly growing sciences is still in the minds of the creators, not generally available in published form. At scientific meetings it is—or has been—difficult for women to share in the small discussion groups where the most avant-garde thinking is going on. Often such informal gatherings are in bars or hotel rooms to which women are not invited simply because it does not occur to anyone to invite them.

A study of Radcliffe doctors some years ago illustrates the kinds of obstacles that such sexism placed in their paths: "There are still difficulties for a woman in getting the kind of experience that is necessary to be 'tops' in physics"; "in my earlier years . . . we were made to feel not quite 'acceptable' and rather 'de trop' at scientific meetings"; "no doubt there are social arrangements, like clubs and stag dinners, that if they have any value could [by excluding women] be [viewed] as barriers"; "professional societies ignore the women members"; and finally, "men here have an advantage, because . . . there is much to be gained from the easy social contacts possible for men at meetings of learned societies" (Bernard, 1964, pp. 302–303). "Women," another story reported, "were less likely than men to be invited to participate in

situations making for opportunities for informal communication."
By being thus cut off from simple professional contacts, women
are cut off from important channels of scientific communication.
(Surely contrary to the public interest.) We have already noted,
in Chapter 3, that social contacts at meetings of learned societies,
so far from having a helpful impact on women, may have precisely the opposite effect, depressing and denigrating.

Even when women have achieved "formal equality" on their
own campuses, another study of the academic woman noted, the
crucial issue remained "the 'atmosphere' in which she works, her
colleagues' perception of her intrinsic as well as her exchange
value and her acceptance into the club. Perhaps it is among these
factors that there is a basis for complaint and indignation"
(Simon, 1967, pp. 221–36). The authors conclude that "the 'problem' which bothers the woman Ph.D. who is a full time contribu-
tor to her profession is that she is denied many of the informal
signs of belonging and recognition. These women report that
even on such simple daily activities as finding someone with
whom to have lunch or take a coffee break, or with whom she can
talk over an idea, or on larger issues such as finding a partner
with whom she can share a research interest, the woman Ph.D.
has a special and lower status. Perhaps then, it is in matters such
as these that she has achieved less than full membership in the
club, and she is left with a feeling that she belongs to a minority
group which has not gained full acceptance" (Simon, 1967, p.
236). This kind of sexism cannot be dealt with easily by law;
it has to be dealt with by "consciousness raising," a technique
adopted by young radicals for rubbing our noses in matters we
would rather not have called to our attention.

Women in the field of journalism have been handicapped in
the past by policies that excluded them from clubs and informal
groups, or by having more stringent criteria applied to them than
to men. One woman, who disclaimed any interest in the clubbi-
ness aspects of such organizations, complained that exclusion
"closes off easy access to sources [of news] that others, my competitors, have" (Von Hoffman, 1970). Cynthia Fuchs Epstein
has summarized how sexism operates in professional careers in
general (Epstein, 1970).

Blatant discrimination can be reached by law and administrative rules. Universities that have contracts with the federal government are being brought into court for violating the fair employment specifications of such contracts. Attempts are being made to bring educational institutions under the provisions of the Civil Rights Act of 1964. But sexism is more resistant. The law cannot completely get rid of sex-typing of jobs so long as it is so much easier to judge on the basis of sex rather than on more individual criteria. So long as women are discouraged even from considering certain kinds of work because of anticipated hazing or exclusion from the club. Whatever the basis on which sex-typing rests, or how it is implemented, it does interfere with the optimum utilization of the labor force. In Sweden it has been estimated that the national income could be increased 25 per cent if women were given free and equal opportunities in the labor market (Grønseth, 1965).

Occupational Prestige and Sex-Typing

The amount of prestige accorded an occupation depends on a complex variety of factors, including the generality and abstraction of the decisions involved in pursuing it, the amount of education called for, the seriousness of the responsibilities entrusted to it, the amount of pay it can command, and so on. But its prestige depends also on the sex that engages in it.

By and large, occupations assigned to men tend to have more prestige than those assigned to women. Whatever men do, no matter what it is, has more prestige than what women do, even if it involves the same kind of decisions, requires the same amount of education, and deals with equally serious responsibilities. The recruitment of men into the professions of social work and home economics was admittedly a method for improving the professions' prestige level. (The men promptly took over the higher-level positions). This point of view can be corroborated by the example of the comparative prestige of medicine, which in the Soviet Union is predominantly a woman's profession on the prestige level of, say, school teaching, while it is a man's profession in the United States. It is a fairly modest profession in the

Soviet Union, one of the most prestigious in the United States. When only women lawyers went in for jobs in the welfare agencies it was a low-prestige career solution. Today, some of the brightest young lawyers opt for cases involving the public interest (so-called poverty law), and the most prestigious law firms permit a certain number of their young recruits to handle such work as a lure.

Men can exact higher pay for what they do; this also helps to enhance the prestige of their work. When women perform the supportive function as part of their feminine roles, freely and without fees, it is taken for granted, never paid for, at least not in the form of salary or fees for service. When men professionalize support as "counseling" or "therapy," it acquires prestige and can command a high fee. E. Lowell Kelly has, in fact, noted that "the problem of the utilization of talent among women . . . [is] in large part a function of the fact that our culture is not prepared to utilize some of the greatest strengths and talents of women simply because we have not yet been able to equate them with making money" (Kelly, 1964, p. 65). Attach a price to women's ability to perform the supportive function, he suggests, that is, "to contribute [the emotional-expressive function] to groups—whether they be family groups, societal groups, social, community or political groups," and, he implies, it could be marketed (Kelly, 1964, p. 64).

Because the prestige associated with an occupation is conferred and not necessarily intrinsic, it is susceptible to change. During the depression of the 1930's, for example, when white men took over the lowest menial jobs formerly permitted to black men, as in the case of street cleaners, the prestige was enhanced by donning a white coat and labeling the worker a "sanitarian."

In the recent past most of the work of the industrialized world has been done in bureaucracies. Bureaucracies are organized hierarchically, and status in terms of rank tends to determine prestige. But two incipient trends are worth watching. There is a strong, if not yet overwhelming, move to find other than hierarchical forms of organizing work (Bennis and Slater, 1968). Warren G. Bennis looks forward to small institutions centered on the people who develop them. They would be pluralistic and adaptive and would have a far more feminine cast than bureaucracies, which are more impersonal and formal (Bennis, 1970). The other trend is one among young people to reject old bases of prestige. More young men are choosing work formerly assigned to women, such as teaching, and even among those who enter other professions, more now select areas formerly the domain of women. Thus, as just noted, young men lawyers now devote themselves to the poverty law, a specialty formerly sex-typed for women lawyers.

Status, Contract, and the Pay for Women's Work

Since so large a component of the prestige of jobs inheres in the pay they command, equalizing the pay for men and women and upgrading the pay of jobs sex-typed for women would be a first step in equalizing prestige. Paying women at all for their unrecognized contribution to the infrastructure that makes the superstructure work would, as David Riesman has noted, be a further step. He has commented on the narcissism of men who take all the credit for their achievements, disregarding the infrastructure that makes them possible. "There is among . . . American men a kind of rosy individualism which consciously asserts one's self-made status, neglectful of the infrastructure—governmental, societal, and often female—which makes the visible show possible" (Riesman, 1964).

One of the most bemoaned changes that have come with the modern industrial order has been the substitution of a contractual or "cash" nexus for the love-and-duty status nexus that prevailed in the old domestic system. Today almost all kinds of work relationships are contractual, responsibilities and benefits clearly specified and limited. Jobs are minutely described and, in the case of unions, rigidly assigned. Less and less of any kind of productive behavior is based on love and/or duty; more and more on contractual agreements.

Except in the case of women. Women are still expected to do things because of love and/or duty. The very thought of paying women for their housekeeping services is horrifying, anathema. Even in the labor market they are not supposed to be paid very

much for services that are "only natural for women anyway."
Thus the love-or-duty standard was invoked against nurses when
they first asked for suitable pay and working conditions. Hospital
administrators, patients, and the public were all shocked at the
idea that they should make such a demand. It was not only un-
professional, it was unwomanly. It was long a tenet in the social
work profession that paying families for foster-home care of children would denigrate the value of the service. The implicit assumption was that women should perform it for little or nothing.
In general, in all personal service occupations it was considered
unfeminine for women to demand any pay, let alone equal or
suitable pay. "All my friends feel free to call on me for help,"
says one ex-professional woman. "They think I ought to do things
for them as a matter of course. The fact that if I had an office
and a letterhead I would be charging for these services never occurs to them. I am a woman and therefore everyone is entitled to
my help."

It may well be, as critics of the present order insist, quite re-
grettable that these changes "from status to contract" have taken
place. It might have been better to have all functions performed
on a love-or-duty basis. But as long as the cash nexus has come
to one (the male) part of the social order, it leaves at a disadvantage those who are still bound, as wives usually are, by status
bonds. The contributions that women *qua* women make in performing the supportive function do not get paid for at all; those
that they make as housekeepers, usually in kind. This fact makes
a big difference. Ask any wife how it would affect her behavior
if she had an assured independent income equal to her husband's.

If women threatened to stop supplying such support without
pay, the prestige of their contribution, as Kelly suggests, would
tend to rise. The story of Lysistrata's effort to organize a sexual
strike to stop a war is relevant but not prototypical. A sexual strike
would have less impact than a support strike. A stonily compliant
sex partner could be as disconcerting as a rejecting woman, or
even more so.

The achievement of prestige by the use of power is so inconsistent with the supportive function that it is hard to see how it
could be accomplished. Whether it is even theoretically possible

is debatable. The implications are nevertheless instructive to contemplate.

Trends in the Sex-Typing of Jobs

If all sex differences were categorical and mutually exclusive and all occupations sex-typed on the basis of these differences, some occupations would have a zero percentage of women and others 100 per cent. If there were, for example, no women with scientific gifts or no men with language gifts, there would be no problem, as there is never any problem in a marriage as to who should bear the children. Only one sex can do it. Or if men and women were interchangeable parts, with identical distribution of gifts, and if there were no sex-typing of work, then all occupations would have the same sex composition as the over-all labor force. Neither of these extreme limits obtains, although some occupations approach close, such, for example, as private household workers, 97.6 per cent of whom were women in 1968, and craftsmen and foremen, of whom only 3.3 per cent were women (Table 6.1).

Table 6.1. Women as a Percentage of Total Employed in Major Occupations, 1940, 1950, 1968

Total Labor Force	1968	1950	1940
	36.6	29.3	25.9
Professional, technical workers	38.6	41.8	45.4
Managers, officials, proprietors (except farm)	15.4	14.8	11.7
Clerical workers	72.6	59.3	52.6
Sales workers	39.7	39.0	27.9
Craftsmen, foremen	3.3	2.4	2.1
Operatives	29.9	26.9	25.7
Nonfarm laborers	3.5	2.2	3.2
Private household workers	97.6	92.1	93.8
Service workers (except private household)	57.0	45.4	40.1
Farmers, farm managers	4.1	5.5 ⎫	8.0
Farm laborers, foremen	28.0	27.4 ⎭	

SOURCE: *1969 Handbook on Women Workers* (Women's Bureau, 1969), p. 92.

It is the overlap in the distribution of talents that makes dealing with sex differences problematic. But even if it is stipulated at the outset that the two sexes show different distributions of talents, no distribution of intellectual talents and values explains the sexual divisions of labor shown in Tables 6.1, 6.2, and 6.7. There are, clearly, quite extraneous factors at work here; and there is strong evidence that the resulting occupational structure violates the criterion of "best person for the job."

Nor are the trends auspicious. The decline in the proportion of librarians, nurses, and social workers who are women (Table 6.2), however slight, means that sex-typing in at least these occupations is moderating somewhat; and sex-typing has already been diluted in the case of high school teaching. The professions of social work and of home economics have made deliberate attempts to reduce sex-typing by recruitment of men.

On the other side, however, is the situation with a new profession like medical and dental technician. In 1950 it was still not completely sex-typed as a woman's profession, but it moved in the next few years toward a take-over by women. The phenomenon which is known in housing as the "tipping point" may mean that it will soon become sex-typed as a woman's profession.

Nor was there reciprocity in the occupations sex-typed as masculine except in the case of industrial engineering. "Men's increased willingness to abandon time-honored sex labels attached to women's jobs has not been matched by the disappearance of 'men only' tags attached to masculine profession" (Weston, 1969). Sex-typing still fosters underutilization of the talents of women and prevents the best person for the job from getting it.

Especially noteworthy is the decline of the proportion of women in the professional and technical professions. Women were contributing more than one-fifth fewer workers relatively in 1968 than in 1940, holding only 38.6 per cent of such positions in 1968 as compared with 45.4 per cent a generation earlier. This decline is related to the fact that it is the sex-typed male professions that may have been expanding most rapidly, and among them the relative contribution of women has declined most (Table 6.2).

Table 6.2. Women as a Percentage of All Workers in Selected
Professional Occupations, United States, 1900–1967

	1967	1960	1950	1940	1930	1920	1910	1900
Natural scientists	8	9.9	11.4					
Agricultural scientists		5.2	5.3					
Biological scientists		26.7	29.2					
Chemists		8.6	10.0					
Geologists, geophysicists		2.3	5.6					
Mathematicians	10	26.4	38.0					
Physicists	3	4.2	6.5					
Miscellaneous		9.8	15.9					
Engineers	1	0.8	1.2					
Aeronautical		1.6	1.9					
Industrial		2.1	1.2					
Metallurgical		0.9	2.0					
Civil		0.6	1.6					
Other engineering and physical scientists		12.8	18.0					
College professors, presidents, instructors		19.0	23.0	27.0	32.0	30.0	19.0	
Doctors	7	6.8	6.1	4.6	4.0	5.0	6.0	
Dentists		2.1	2.7	1.5	1.8	3.2	3.1	
Medical and dental technicians		62.4	56.7					
Lawyers*	3	3.5	3.5	2.4	2.1	1.4	1.0	
Librarians	80	85.0	89.0	89.0	91.0	88.0	79.0	
Clergy		5.8	8.5	2.2	4.3	2.6	1.0	4.4
Nurses		97.0	98.0	98.0	98.0	96.0	93.0	94.0
Social workers	60	57.0	66.0	68.0	62.0	52.0		

SOURCE: U.S. Bureau of the Census, *Census of Population, 1960*, vol. 1, Table 202; for 1900 to 1950, Women's Bureau, *Changes in Women's Occupations, 1940–1960*, bul. 253 (1954), p. 57; for 1967, Women's Bureau *Fact Sheet* (Nov. 1968).
*James J. White, "Women in the Law," *Michigan Law Review*, 65 (April 1967), p. 1051, gives the following percentages: 1963, 2.7; 1960, 2.6; 1957, 2.7; 1954, 2.3; 1951, 2.5; 1948, 1.8.

The goal of policy is not to reverse present forms of sex-typing nor even to equalize the proportion of workers of each sex in any occupation. Either of these objectives would be equally subversive of the two criteria—best job for the person and best person for the job. To further the general welfare, the objective rather should be to facilitate a division of labor that reflects the interests, values, and talents of individuals regardless of sex. Such a policy would, presumably work in the direction of putting the best person in the job.

"Best Job for the Person": The Under-utilization of the Talents of Women

A physician, we remember from introductory economics, may be a better cook than his cook, a better typist than his typist, and a better driver than his chauffeur. But in terms of the production of goods and services, the best job for him is the practice of medicine. From the point of view of the public interest, that is, the best job for any worker in the highest, most valuable one he is capable of performing.

Judged on the basis of this criterion, there is a considerable amount of underutilization or malutilization of the talents of women. Thus women with one to three years of college are not performing up to their capacities if they are service workers, including private-household workers, as 11 per cent of them were in 1968 (Table 6.3). Nor are at least some of the 48.5 per cent who were clerical workers.[1] And certainly women with four years of college are not optimally utilized as service workers and operatives, as 2.8 per cent of them were.[2] And surely at least some of the 6 percent of women with one year or more of graduate study

1. In 1960, about 4.6 per cent of men with one to three years of college were in service occupations; about 12.4 per cent of men with one to three years of college were in clerical occupations.
2. About the same proportion of men with four years of college were also service workers and operatives in 1960.

Table 6.3. Major Occupation Groups of Employed Women, by
Educational Attainment, March 1968
(*Women 18 years of age and over*)

| | | Elementary | High School | | College | | |
| | | | | Years of school completed | | | |
	Total	8 years	1 to 3 years	4 years	1 to 3 years	4 years	5 years or more
Professional, technical workers	15.0	.9	1.9	6.4	24.5	77.3	90.7
Managers, officials, proprietors (except farm)	4.6	3.8	4.4	4.9	5.5	4.5	3.2
Clerical, kindred workers	33.9	10.7	19.6	50.6	48.5	13.0	4.2
Salesworkers	6.5	5.8	8.4	8.0	6.1	1.4	.6
Craftsmen, foremen, kindred workers	1.1	1.8	1.8	1.0	.5	.4	.2
Operatives, kindred workers	15.6	31.9	27.8	11.8	3.0	1.0	.4
Laborers	.4	.8	.8	.3	.1	—	—
Private Household workers	5.8	14.7	7.7	2.6	1.6	.4	.2
Service workers (except private household)	15.4	25.5	25.7	13.2	9.4	1.4	.5
Farm workers	1.6	4.1	1.9	1.2	.8	.4	—
Number (in thousands)*	26,667	2,293	4,570	11,711	3,318	2,024	855
Percentage	100.0	100.0	100.0	100.0	100.0	100.0	100.0

SOURCE: Bureau of Labor Statistics, Special Labor Force Report.
*This total includes 478,000 women with no schooling or less than five years of schooling, about 90 per cent of whom were operatives and service workers, including household workers; and 1,418,000 women with five to seven years of schooling, about 84 per cent of whom were in the same occupations.

who were clerical workers, sales women, operatives, and service workers must have been capable of higher occupations.[3]

3. As also, of course, were the roughly 9 per cent of men with some graduate work who were in these occupations.

Table 6.4. Proportion of Degrees Awarded to Women, 1890–1968; Projections to 1978

	Degree		
Year	Bachelor's and First Professional	Master's	Doctorate
1978	45.9	31.7	11.2
1977	45.7	31.7	11.2
1976	45.5	31.8	11.1
1975	45.1	31.8	11.2
1974	44.5	32.0	11.3
1973	44.0	32.2	11.2
1972	43.6	32.3	11.3
1971	43.0	32.5	11.5
1970	42.3	32.8	11.7
1969	41.9	33.1	11.5
1968	41.3	33.2	11.7
1960	35.3	31.6	10.5
1950	23.9	29.7	9.6
1940	41.2	38.2	13.0
1930	39.9	40.4	15.4
1920	34.2	30.2	15.1
1910	22.7	26.4	10.0
1900	19.1	19.1	6.0
1890	17.3	19.1	1.2

SOURCE: Data to 1956 from U.S. Office of Education, *Statistics of Higher Education, 1955–56: Faculty, Students, and Degrees*, pp. 6–7. Data for 1947–1960: U.S. Office of Education, *Earned Degrees, 1959–1960*, p. 3. Projections to 1978: U.S. Office of Education, *Projections of Educational Statistics to 1977–78*, p. 31.

Although more young women have been entering college and achieving a first professional degree (Table 6.4), the proportion who have entered the higher level occupations still has not materially expanded since 1930 (Table 6.5, Figure 6.1). After a marked decline between 1930 and 1950—women contributed fewer entries to the 1967 edition of Who's Who (5 per cent) than to the 1930 edition (6 per cent)—there has, to be sure, been an upward trend. Even by 1969 the proportion of employed women who were in higher level occupations had recovered only to about the 1930 level. Because of the changing nature of the professions

Table 6.5. *Proportion of Employed Women in Professional* and Technical Occupations, 1870–1969*

1969	14.3	1910	9.9
1965	13.5	1900	8.2
1960	12.5	1890	7.8
1950	10.8	1880	6.7
1940	13.2	1870	4.9
1930	14.2		
1920	11.8		

*The data on proportion of employed women who are in professional occupations are equivocal.

SOURCE: The figures for 1940–1969 are from the Women's Bureau *1969 Handbook*, p. 92. The figure for 1960 is from the U.S. 1960 Census volume, *Occupational Characteristics*, Table 1. The most recent data are from monthly *Fact Sheets* of the Women's Bureau. The figures for 1870–1930 are from A. J. Jaffe and Charles D. Stewart, *Manpower Resources and Utilization* (Wiley, 1951), p. 503. The proportion of the total labor force in professional occupations rose from 2.6 in 1870 (*Ibid.*, p. 92) to 11.1 in 1960. The base for the figures to 1960 is the population 14 years of age and over; for 1969, 16 years of age and over. The base for the earlier years is not specified.

themselves, changing definitions, and changing computational bases, not too much emphasis can be placed on the details of the trends before 1940, but the general direction of the trends in Figure 6.1 is unmistakable.

A logical conclusion from the above trends is that although college-trained women are more likely than other women to become gainfully employed and although more women are college-trained now than in the past, they are taking positions lower than in the past and lower than their potential as measured in terms of education would indicate. The problem is not, therefore, that the talented women are not in the labor force but rather that they are not contributing at the level their talents would justify. We have no way to gauge how many women with talents other than those measurable by academic achievements are also in positions below their potential—how many, for example, are doing domestic work when they are capable of serving as health workers, or as saleswomen when they are capable of management. Their number is not inconsiderable.

The question may well be raised as to where the women who formerly went into the professions are now going. The answer seems to be that they are now going into clerical and kindred occupations (Table 6.6, Figure 6.1), the number of gainfully em-

Table 6.6. *Occupational Distribution of Women* in the Labor Force, 1940–1969*

	1969	1965	1969	1950	1940
Professional and technical workers	14.3	13.5	12.5	10.8	13.2
Managers, officials and proprietors	4.2	4.5	3.5	5.5	3.8
Clerical workers	34.0	31.5	29.1	26.4	21.2
Sales workers	6.9	7.6	7.8	8.8	7.0
Craftsmen and foremen	1.0	1.1	1.2	1.1	.9
Operatives	15.1	14.8	16.2	18.7	18.4
Nonfarm laborers	.5	.5	.5	.4	.8
Private household workers	5.5	8.2	7.8	10.3	17.6
Service workers (except private household)	16.2	15.1	13.6	12.6	11.3
Farmers, farm managers	.3	.6	.5	1.5	5.8
Farm laborers, foremen	2.1	2.2	1.2	3.9	
Total	100.0				

SOURCE: Data for 1940, 1950, 1965: Women's Bureau *1965 Handbook of Women Workers,* p. 89; data for 1960, U.S. Census of Population, *Occupational Characteristics,* Table 1; data for 1969, Women's Bureau *Fact Sheet,* July 1, 1969.

*16 years old and over.

ployed women in these positions increasing over 267 per cent between 1940 and 1968, from 2,530,000 to 9,289,000, and the proportion, almost 58 per cent, from 21.2 to 33.3 per cent (Women's Bureau, *Handbook on Women Workers,* 1969). Some, as noted above, are going into positions even farther away from their potential. "Nearly a fifth of our college-educated women are employed in these two relatively less demanding fields" (Keyserling, 1968).

Not all of the underutilization of the talents of women can be attributed to sex-typing of work or to the demotivation of women. We shall have more to say in Chapter 5 about the lack of control that women have over their working lives since so much depends on the men they marry and the unquestioned expectation that they adjust their careers to their husbands'. As a case in point, the career pattern of a woman with a graduate degree in health education may be cited: "Her marriage to a forest ranger-naturalist prevented her from continuing in health education. She found her subsequent jobs where there was a demand for female labor in isolated communities—telephone operator, typist, self-employed nursery school director . . ." (Ginzberg, 1966). Cases like this one no doubt account for a considerable proportion of the women in occupations below the level of their abilities. But a far larger proportion can be accounted for by the systematic demotivating of women that the socialization process produces.

There is, in addition, a form of underutilization of women that may be accounted for by a kind of demotivation labeled wastage. College-trained women, for example, constitute only a fraction of those capable of college work. "Young women probably account for about 3 out of 5 of those who have the ability to graduate from college but do not" (Harmon, 1965, p. 27). And the same kind of deficit exists as related to higher degrees. Only 37 per cent of the young women with the intellectual ability to earn a doctorate will even earn a bachelor's degree, and of these, only 1 per cent will actually receive the doctorate (Harmon, 1965, p. 28). And even all of this select grouping are not, as just noted, being used at the level of their abilities.

There is, then occupational wastage all along the line. Not all the women with the ability to achieve the doctorate will even get to college; nor all those who get to college earn the bachelor's degree; nor those who achieve the bachelor's degree win the doctorate. Among those who do achieve the bachelor's degree, many will not be in occupations that fully utilize their abilities. Lost somewhere in the pool of working women is a very considerable number with intellectual potential that has not been developed or, if developed even to the level of a college degree, is not being used. Thus, not only are the abilities of many talented women not being tapped at their highest potential level, but they may even be hidden and almost buried.

Subverting the Talents of Women

The data on the occupational distribution of women presented above reflect the fact that women in general are reared both at home and in school in a manner to suppress rather than to stimulate their highest talents. Child-rearing practices and school treatment deflect women from their highest potential achievement. Students of human development tell us that if, for example, we loosened girls' ties to their mothers' apron strings, if we encouraged them to fend for themselves, if we cultivated independence and self-reliance, if we rewarded their efforts to satisfy their curiosity, if we stimulated probing intelligence and vetoed easy answers, if we discouraged feminine submission, frowned on unthinking conformity to social rules, did not emphasize pleasing others, the achievement of women would be greater (Rossi, 1965). Women would, for example, enter science not only as teachers of science but as scientists, as creators and innovators rather than assistants. The work summarized by Maccoby does show that there is a relationship between child-rearing, educational, and socializing practices on one side and the intellectual style of girls on the other. The implication is that many girls might be salvaged for higher level professions if we made a deliberate attempt to do so.[4] At any rate, contrary to the assumptions underlying the education of girls, there is experimental evidence that a problem-solving approach can be cultivated in them (Maccoby, 1966, p. 51).

Alice Rossi zeroes in on the basic psychological incompatibility between the support and the productive functions of women. "A childhood model of the quiet, 'good' sweet girl will not produce any women scientists or scholars, doctors or engineers. It may produce the competent meticulous laboratory assistant . . . but not the creative scientists" (Rossi, 1965, p. 118). The supportive function for which the sweet girl is being processed does not make for a high level of creativity.

Girls fall behind boys in their intellectual achievement at precisely the time that the importance of pleasing boys is stressed to them. There is something rather poignant about Table 6.7. It

4. There are, no doubt, many frustrated administrators and managers trying to run offices without enough competent secretaries who would swear that there was no better use for women than performing secretarial services. The shortage of secretaries had reached almost crisis proportions in the late 1960's. See, for example, Herbert Kuperberg, "Secretaries: The Nation's Most-Wanted Women," *Parade*, Aug. 3, 1969, pp. 26–27.

Table 6.7. *Relative Superiority of Women Doctors in Six Variables* *

School Type	Language (1)	Social Studies (2)	Mathematics (3)	Science (4)	Normalized Rank (5)	Test Scores (6)
Public	5.5	3.2	2.5	1.9	4.6	1.9
Denominational	5.2	3.8	4.1	3.2	2.0	1.3
Independent	5.4	4.0	3.1	3.4	2.2	.9

*The figures in this table refer to the differences between the grade point averages of women and men in four high-school subjects (columns 1–4); differences between them in overall rank in high school class (column 5); and differences in intelligence-test scores (column 6). In public high schools, for example, the women who later achieved doctorates had averaged 5.5 points higher in language (70.0–64.5) than men who achieved doctorates.

hints at the lost or subverted talents of women. The data show that the high school girls who persisted in their career plans, who overcame the roadblocks to success, who did go on to achieve the doctorate, were superior to men who acquired this degree. They showed up so well, of course, because they were a selected population to begin with. But there were doubtless many other girls with equal potential who did not make the grade. Who stopped spelling the word that would put them above the boys. Who underplayed their own abilities. Who became afraid rather than proud of success. Who felt they would have to pay for success by giving up the attention of boys; or, conversely, felt they had to pay for the attention of boys by giving up success.

For, in effect, we put women in a situation where they must make impossible choices, where we punish them for success. We teach them how to fail:

Consciously or unconsciously the girl equates intellectual achievement with loss of femininity. A bright woman is caught in a double bind. In testing and other achievement-oriented situations she worries not only about failure but also about success. If she fails, she is not living up to her own standards of performance; if she succeeds she is not living up to societal expectations about the female role. Men in our society do not experience this kind of ambivalence, because they are not only permitted but actively encouraged to do well.

For women, then, the desire to achieve is often contaminated by what I call the *motive to avoid success*. I define it as the fear that success in competitive achievement situations will lead to negative consequences, such as unpopularity and loss of femininity. This motive, like the achievement motive itself, is a stable disposition within the person, acquired early in life along with other sex-role standards. When fear of success conflicts with a desire to be successful, the result is an inhibition of achievement motivation (Horner, 1968).

This is a psychological statement of the dilemma facing women having to perform incompatible functions, the stroking, supportive function assigned to women and the competitive demands of male sex-typed jobs. For it is in the male occupations that women are not permitted to achieve; in the female occupations, success is not denigrated. Women do not fear success as nurses, secretaries, or nursery-school teachers, only in the prestigious occupations sex-typed for men.

However conceived—in terms of psychological or sociological variables—the situation helps us understand why "a follow-up study of gifted children showed that while gifted boys tended to realize their potential in their occupations and creative output, gifted girls did not" (Maccoby, 1966, p. 28). It is not only those whose talents lie underutilized because they are deprived of cultivation that call for policies of retrieval but also those whose talents are misguided, repressed, discouraged, or deflected.

The Underutilization of Black Women

During the 1960's we became acutely aware of the non-, mal-, and underutilization of black people, men as well as women. We were reminded that the maintenance man in our building had gone to college, as had the woman who ran the elevator. In 1960, in fact, a fifth of all nonwhite men and women who had had at least a year of college were employed as operatives or as service workers, occupations undoubtedly below their qualifications. Some of the talent untapped by the economy found expression in leadership in voluntary, especially church-related, groups, much of it devoted to members of the black community itself.

In the 1960's we recognized that the neglect of the potential contribution of black men and women was as dysfunctional for our society as a whole as it was for the men and women themselves: "the waste of human talent, potential and actual, is nowhere more apparent than it is among American Negroes. The Negro need for a continually improving system of education and training is paralleled by the national need for a continually expanding source of trained manpower" (Fichter, n.d., p. 6). Neither black men nor black women are expendable.

The peculiar circumstances in which the black woman finds herself vis-à-vis black men give special poignancy to her situation. Like their white counterparts, some black women deliberately underplay and underdevelop their abilities in order to build up men's (Bernard, 1966). Such behavior is wasteful enough when engaged in by white women who hold their achievements below a ceiling of male achievement; it is even more so when engaged in by black women who hold their achievements below the even lower ceiling imposed on black men.

It is interesting to note, however, that young black women do not, like white women, exhibit fear of success. A study conducted at Howard University found that "for the black women, success in intellectually competitive situations with men does not elicit the fear of such negative consequences as anticipated by the white college woman. These data indicate that such mastery is not threatening; professional achievement does not lead to automatic rejection by the male; that a successful woman is an economic asset and attractive rather than threatening to a black man. Hence, success as here projected, is not to be feared" (Mednick, 1969). These findings are especially interesting because they illustrate the fact that there is nothing intrinsic in the white woman's fear of success in male sex-typed occupations; they also show a change in the younger as compared with the older generation of black women. In the past many superior black women did, as just noted, underplay their potential in order to build up black men.

A grimmer interpretation of the absence of fear of success in young black women would be in terms of their being inured to putting their men down. But, at least in the universe from which the present sample was drawn, the men did not view a woman's success as a reflection on them but rather as an asset they could profit by. The younger men, further, no longer needed the sacrifice of achievement by women to bolster their masculinity.

In recent decades teaching and social work have been the major professional contributions of black women. But there is evidence that some of them at least have interest in careers in science and do not feel they lack ability or that they have a personality unsuited for such a career. In a study of the 1964 graduates of predominantly Negro colleges, half of the women said they would find the work of research scientists very interesting, about half felt they did not lack ability for it, and only 17 per cent felt their personalities were unsuited for such a career (Fichter, n.d., pp. 91–93). Although these self-judgments prove nothing about the actual abilities and suitability of the women for scientific research, they do suggest a possible vein to explore. There is no compelling reason why black women, any more than white, should be contributing at anything less than their highest level.

Operation Retrieval

It is not only the underutilization of people who have already shown evidence of ability by academic achievement that calls for attention if we wish to implement the policy of "best job for the person," but also the loss of those, black or white, who have never had a chance to discover their abilities. Whatever may be the distribution of talents—by race, by class, or by sex—in our society we know there are many individuals who have greater potential than they will realize unless concerted efforts are made to retrieve them.

In the 1960's, programs calling for maximum feasible participation in community organization called forth a surprising amount of talent never before quarried. One study of a training program for women culled from welfare rolls found that about a third later went on to the local junior college, suggesting that there is available here a potential source of talent as yet untapped and, without a program for uncovering it, likely to be underutilized.[5] Another study looked at the data bank of Project Talent to learn what potential ability was available among the disadvantaged. It reported that among white high school girls whose parent(s) received public assistance during the students' life, 14 per cent scored above the national median for their sex and grade on the tests used; among black girls, the corresponding figure was 7 per cent.[6]

Medical services, according to President Johnson's estimate quoted in Chapter 3, are going to need an especially large increment of workers in the near future. Here, too, retrieval operations have found talents in hitherto unsuspected places. The Neighborhood Health Center of Montefiore Hospital in New York City, a prototype of such retrieval, trained women to be family health workers, nurse-midwives, laboratory technicians, and medical record clerks. Other potential jobs included obstetrical assistant and anesthesiology assistant. "Impressive" was the judgment of one of the physicians involved (Bowers, 1968). Women who, without such retrieval, would have spent their working lives either in jobs far below their potential or on welfare, were now upgrading maternity care in slum areas, filling "a crucial social need" and able to "fill uncounted vacancies at desperately shorthanded hospitals" (Sanders, 1968). The goal was "to help the qualified and ambitious move up the professional ladder—from family-health worker to nurse; from nurse to physician; from lab technician to scientist" (Sanders, 1968). The sky would be the limit for those with ability to scale the ladder.

In the past the school was spectacularly successful as an agency for locating talent; the abilities of generations of immigrant children were discovered in the schools. But the retrieval of talent now lost requires additional channels. Otis Dudley Duncan has raised the question of the school's adequacy:

5. Catherine Chilman, then of the Welfare Administration of the Department of Health, Education, and Welfare, was in charge of this project. The women were being trained to serve in child-care centers. Unfortunately the vagaries of funding left them without jobs when their training was completed. But the fact that so many continued their education suggests that a new world of possibilities had been opened up to them.

6. Perry Levinson, Welfare Administration, Department of Health, Education, and Welfare. Personal Communication.

One might wish to raise questions about the kind of society in which one institution, the school system, nearly monopolized the function of training and screening for occupational roles. On the basis of a general preference for pluralism, one could argue that there is a need for functional alternatives thereto. Indeed, military officials have recently been urging that the Armed Forces actually have fallen into the role of providing such an alternative; whether this is the particular alternative one would want to see perpetuated is another question. (Duncan, n.d.).

Certainly the schools have fallen down in the screening function, seining out, as they do, a large number of qualified girls from the more demanding occupations. Perhaps some service-oriented corps designed to accommodate young people eager to try themselves out in a variety of ways unhampered by traditional sex-typing of any kind of work could serve the screening function that schools have become too custom-bound to perform. At least some kind of ambience might be created in which all kinds of talents could be discovered without preconceptions about their propriety for either sex. Still, so long as sexism prevails it is doubtful if any single institution by itself can overcome its destructive effects completely.

"Feminine" and "Masculine" Uses of Women

It is hard to deny that the socialization and education of girls in ways that render them unsuited for such male-typed jobs as their talents equip them for must indeed be reexamined. We live in a world that sorely needs their special gifts. It is certainly contrary to the public interest to teach women to fail in male-typed professions, as it has been to teach black people to fail in white-typed occupations or as it would be to teach anyone to fail in any legitimate enterprise in which his best talents could find expression. If we could keep the socialization process open so far as it concerns preparing both boys and girls for adult functions, permitting individuated rather than sex-typed job choices, there would be considerably more flexibility and matching of talents and jobs. Better still, of course, would be a reduction, if not the total elimination, of sex-typing altogether.

For girls whose talents and interests lie in the more traditionally feminine areas, a question arises that is equally serious, if
not more so. It challenges a criterion for the utilization of the
talents of women in a context that allocates prestige to male
achievements and hence judges the best job for anyone to be a
job sex-typed as male: scientist rather than science teacher,
doctor rather than nurse, aggressor rather than nurturer. Are
women, or is anyone, more contributory, more valuable to the
general welfare in laboratories than in hospitals, libraries, offices,
or classrooms? Is it in the public interest to make success in male-
typed occupations the major measure of achievement? It seems
denigrating to make women feel they must achieve in male-
typed professions in order to be judged truly successful. This
standard is sexism in an especially virulent form, as noxious as
the argument, voiced by some men, that the costs to men of encouraging women to succeed might overbalance the benefits to
the total society.

In any event, if it is in the national interest to make optimum
use of the skills of all the people, the present situation does not meet
the criterion of "best job for the person." It implies a kind of
prodigality that those concerned with the public interest can
hardly view with equanimity.

REFERENCES

Alpenfels, Ethel J., "Women in the Professional World," in Beverly
   Benner Cassara (ed.), *American Women: The Changing Image*
   (Boston: Beacon Press, 1962).
Baker, Elizabeth Faulkner, *Technology and Woman's Work* (New
   York: Columbia University Press, 1964).
Bennis, Warren G. and Philip E. Slater, *The Temporary Society*
   (New York: Harper & Row, 1968).
Bennis, Warren G., "Organic Populism," *Psychology Today,* 3 (Feb.
   1970), 48.
Bernard, Jessie, *Academic Women* (University Park: Pennsylvania
   State University Press, 1964).
———, *Marriage and Family among Negroes* (Englewood Cliffs, N.J.:
   Prentice-Hall, 1966), pp. 90–91.
Bowers, John Z., letter to the editor of *Harper's* (March 1968), 6.

Caplow, Theodore, *The Sociology of Work* (New York: McGraw-Hill, 1964), Chapter 10.

Duncan, Otis Dudley, "Ability and Achievement," mimeographed, p. 18.

Epstein, Cynthia Fuchs, *Woman's Place, Options and Limits in Professional Careers* (Berkeley: University of California Press, 1970).

Fichter, Joseph H., *Graduates of Predominantly Negro Colleges, Class of 1964* (Washington, D.C.: Public Health Publication No. 1571, n.d.), p. 6.

Ginzberg, Eli et al., *Life Styles of Educated Women* (New York: Columbia University Press, 1966), pp. 91–92.

Grønseth, Erik, "The Dysfunctionality of the Husband Provider Role in Industrialized Societies," paper presented at the 7th World Congress of Sociology, Varna, 1970. The study cited by Grønseth is *Køn eller Kynne* (Stockholm, 1965), p. 20.

Groves Conference, April, 1970, summary of panel discussion.

Harmon, Lindsey R., *High School Ability Patterns: A Backward Look from the Doctorate* (Scientific Manpower Report no. 6, National Science Foundation, Aug. 1965).

Horner, Matina, "Fail: Bright Women," *Psychology Today,* 3 (Nov. 1969), 38. This article is based on Dr. Herner's doctoral dissertation, *Sex Differences in Achievement Motivation and Performance in Competitive and Non-Competitive Situations* (Ann Arbor: University of Michigan, 1968).

Jordan, Joan, "The Place of American Women, Economic Exploitation of Women," *Revolutionary Age,* vol. 1 (1968).

Kelly, E. Lowell, "Problems of Research: Design Difficulties," in Philip I. Mitterling (ed.), *Needed Research on Able Women in Honors Programs, College and Society* (Washington, D.C.: U.S. Office of Education, 1964), p. 65.

Kennedy, President John F., statement establishing a Commission on the Status of Women, 1961.

Keyserling, Mary Dublin, "Womanpower—An Underutilized Resource," reprint from *Unemployment Insurance Review* (Feb. 1968), p. 2.

Maccoby, Eleanor, "Sex Differences in Intellectual Functioning," in *The Development of Sex Differences* (Stanford: Stanford University Press, 1966), pp. 25–55.

G. P. Murdock, "Comparative Data on the Division of Labor by Sex," *Social Forces,* 15 (May 1937), 552.

Riesman, David, "Introduction" in Jessie Bernard, *Academic Women,* p. xxiv.

Rossi, Alice, "Who Wants Women in the Scientific Professions?" in Jacqueline A. Mattfeld and Carol G. Van Aken (eds.), *Women in the Scientific Professions* (Cambridge: M. I. T. Press, 1965), p. 7.

Sanders, Marion K., "The Doctors Meet the People," *Harper's* (Jan. 1968), 61.

Simon, Rita James and Associates, "The Woman Ph.D.: A Recent Profile," *Social Problems,* 15 (Fall 1967), 221-236.

Tuck, Ruth, *Not with the Fist* (New York: Harcourt, Brace, 1946), pp. 90–92.

Von Hoffman, Nicholas, "Gridiron 'Stud Party,'" *Washington Post,* March 13, 1970.

Weston, Peter, "The Motive to Avoid Success as a Function of Race and Social Class (unpublished Master's thesis, Howard University, 1969).

Women's Bureau, *1969 Handbook on Women Workers* (Washington, D.C.: U.S. Department of Labor, 1969), p. 92.

7

Cases in Point

Three Professions

Three professions—medicine, engineering, and management—all strongly sex-typed for men have been selected here to illustrate some of the extraneous factors involved in determining the sexual composition of the occupational structure of a society. The first, the case of the woman physician in the Soviet Union, illustrates how little skill and talent have to do with sex-typing of professions; the second, the case of women engineers, illustrates how sex-typing restricts and limits the horizons of a profession; and the third, the case of management, illustrates how specializing women to be nonaggressive and noncompetitive disqualifies them for top positions despite their abilities in the management aspects of these occupations.

The Woman Physician in the Soviet Union

The healing arts would seem to be especially congenial to persons with the values reported in the research literature as being particularly characteristic of women. Still, all over the world except in the Soviet Union (Table 7.1), women are only a minuscule proportion of the medical profession. If it were not for the experience of Soviet Russia we might have to conclude that although the profession of medicine is congenial to the values of women, they are not talented enough to pursue it successfully. The Soviet experience, however, demonstrates that this is not so (Field, 1957). Women physicians have maintained public health there at a high level.

Before the Revolution the percentage of Russian physicians who were women was less than 10 per cent; it is now between 75 and 80 per cent. The current proportion of women physicians is not a result of deliberate policy, except by inadvertence, on the part of the government or even a result of spontaneous flocking to the profession by women. It is related to the relatively low status accorded to the profession, "bright young men being still encouraged to become engineers." Like schoolteaching in the United States (Field, 1957, p. 72), medical practice "is often a means of marking time until marriage, and after marriage a way of supplementing the family budget. . . . Women physicians often are not able to devote themselves fully to a career" (Field, 1957, p. 93). The large proportion is related also to the greater willingness of women to submit to rigid bureaucratic control, for the physician is an employee at the mercy of sometimes unreasonable rules and regulations. Despite efforts to increase the supply of doctors, "the lure is still not strong enough," the shortages of both physicians and dentists persist.

Within the profession itself the prestigious positions go to men. Four out of five of those who hold high rank are men, just the reverse of the sex ratio in the profession as a whole. Eight out of 10 of the men physicians hold high status positions; only half that proportion of the women physicians do. The highest administrative and clinical posts are held by men.

In addition to bureaucratic regimentation and discrimination revealed by status differentials, the woman physician in the Soviet Union has had to cope with the prejudices of patients against women doctors, for the preferences of patients of both sexes still favor men, as they did before the Revolution. A study of a sample of emigrés interviewed just after World War II found about half giving equivocal replies to questions on preferred sex of physician; about a fifth had no opinion or preference. Among the rest, seven times as many preferred male doctors as pre-

Table 7.1. *Women as a Percentage of All Workers in Selected Professional Occupations in Eleven Countries*

				Occupation				
	Physicians[a]	Dentists	Lawyers[b]	(judges)	Engineers[c]	Scientists	Physicists	Chemists
U.S.A.	6.5	2.1	3.5	2.0	1.2	7.0	5.0	5.0
U.S.S.R.[d]	75.0	83.0	36.0	30–40	28.0	[e]	—*	—
U.K.[f]	16.0	6.9	3.8	[g]	.002	6.4[f]	—	—
Japan	8.3	3.0	3.0	—	—	—	—	—
Sweden[d]	15.4	24.4	6.1	6.7	1.3[h]	—	—	—
Germany (Fed. Rep.)[i]	20.0	—	5.5[j]	—	3.3[i]	—	—	—
Germany (G.D.R.)[k]	—	—	30.0	30.0	—	—	—	—
Italy[a]	4.9	—	2.8	0.5	1.1[h]	44.0[m]	8.1[n]	10.0
India[o]	9.54	3.89	0.74	—	—	—	—	—
Denmark[p]	16.4	70.0	—	—	—	—	—	—
Poland[q]	36.4	77.0	18.8	—	8.0	—	—	—

*Blanks indicate that figures are not available.

SOURCE: Cynthia F. Epstein, "Woman's Place: The Salience of Sex Status in the Professional Setting," paper presented at the 62nd Annual Meeting of the American Sociological Association, 1967.

a. In a rank ordering by percentage of women physicians participating in the NWIA Congress (Rochester, New York, July, 1966), the United States ranked fourth from the bottom in percentage of women physicians, just above Spain, Madagascar, and Vietnam. Countries (excluding Soviet bloc countries) with largest percentages of women doctors were: the Philippines (24.7); Finland (24.2); Israel (24.0); Brazil, Canada, Norway, Netherlands, France, and Australia had between 7 and 12 per cent. Source: American Medical Women's Association, *Report* of July 11, 1966.

b. The figure is only for barristers. From *Time*, Aug 27, 1965.

c. Additional (I.L.O.) figures cited in M Alexandrova, "Position of Working Women in Capitalist Countries," *Daily Review*, translations from the Soviet Press, Pushkin Square, vol. 9, no. 157 (2411), July 2, 1963; Canada has 24 engineers out of a total of 17,700; Australia has 6 out of 12,000; Italy, 220 among 28,200.

d. Soviet figures from L. Dubronina, *Soviet Women*, printed in U.S.S.R. (no date), and Professor V. Elyutin, D.Sc., "Higher Education in the U.S.S.R." (London, 1962), Soviet booklet #100. United States figures from Margaret Mead and Frances Kaplan (eds.), *American Women* (Scribners, 1965); Elizabeth Shelton, "Are the Scales Weighted against Women Judges?" *Washington Post*, Sept. 19, 1965, and U.S. 1960 census. Swedish figures from James Rossel, "Women in Sweden" (The Swedish Institute, Stockholm), p. 5. Figures on basis of 1960 census. Note too that these percentages are reflections of small absolute numbers; the 6.1 per cent for lawyers represents 80 out of a total of 1,530.

e. No percentage is given, only the absolute figure of 94,000 (Report of ferred female doctors. Even among women, though to a lesser extent, men were preferred (Field, 1957, p. 193). The situation had improved only slightly a decade later, in 1955; at that time it was estimated that still only 10 to 15 per cent of the women preferred women physicians as compared with the 7 per cent among the emigrés (Field, 1957, pp. 192–193).[1]

Sexist prejudices were especially slow to moderate in the villages:

> If in a village a woman doctor would be sent to take care of the inhabitants, they would say, "Ah, still another baba" (a slightly derogative term denoting an old, rather ignorant woman). Women doctors at the beginning were greatly distrusted by the peasant population. . . . These women doctors would come back to town in tears. But they finally managed to win the confidence of the population and to overcome these ideas among the people so that many of them managed to do good medical work (Field, 1957, p. 194).

---

the U.S.S.R. Central Statistical Administration, March 12, 1958, presented in *Facts on File,* March 13–19, 1958).

f. United Kingdom, 1961 Census, summary tables, General Register Office (Lawyers and judges, chemists, physical and biological scientists).

g. Only one woman Queen's Counsel has become a judge in 400 British courts, (*Time,* Aug. 27, 1965).

h. Includes architects.

i. Federal Republic of Germany, Helmut Steiner, "Social Origin and Structural Pattern of the Body of Judges in the G.D.R.; Comparative Approach to the Corresponding Body in West Germany," Sociological Study Group at the Institute of Economics, German Academy of Sciences, Berlin, mimeographed, May, 1966 (engineers, technicians, related trades).

j. Helmut Steiner, *op. cit.*

k. Figure from American Medical Women's Association, Inc. (1966).

l. Italy figures from 1961 Italian Census from Instituto Centrale di Statistica, Direzione Generale, dei servizi technici (May 19, 1967).

m. Biologists, zoologists, naturalists.

n. Includes mathematicians, astronomers, and geologists.

o. India figures from 1961 Indian census, vol. 1, part IIB (u), General Economic tables, Table B-V.

p. Denmark, 1960 census.

q. Poland, Magdelena Sokolowska, "Some Reflections on Different Attitudes of Men-Women Towards Work," *International Labour Review,* 92 (1965), pp. 35–50.

---

1. In general, each sex preferred its own sex about twice as often as the other; women preferring women over men in a ratio of 7 to 4 and men preferring men over women, 41 to 23.

Extraordinarily good medical work, one would have to conclude on the basis of the health record of the people.

> World War II provided the first comprehensive view of Soviet medicine at work against formidable odds. On the whole the view was impressive; so much so that it suggest a dramatic preview of what could very well become a new era in international medicine. . . . We are comparatively certain that the appallingly high sickness rates and death rates of the Russia of a generation ago are now greatly reduced. . . . There is good reason for believing that Russia's progress in health administration is by far the most rapid in the world today (Wilson, 1949).

What defects there were in Soviet medical services were attributed by the author of this report to bureaucratical administration and control—which were largely in the hands of men—rather than to any deficiencies or defects in the personnel.

That Russian women physicians were able to perform so well is all the more remarkable when we consider the handicaps they had to overcome, not the least of which was that of belonging to "the categories of Soviet population most deprived of free time—employed women . . . and housewives, whose duties include fixing meals and standing in queues while shopping" (Simirenko, 1969, p. 42).

The case of the Soviet physician illustrates the difference between the strictly technical-scientific or talent component and the sociological aspects of the sexual division of labor. It makes clear that the health of a population is quite safe in the hands of women physicians, that the small proportion which women contribute to the medical profession throughout the world in no sense reflects lack of talent or ability to perform the healing arts. It reflects, rather, the sexist sociological matrix in which medicine is practiced.

Women Engineers

The case of women engineers illustrates a different form of sex-typing, one that defines a profession in a restricted male way and thus limits the direction of its development.

A study of engineering aptitude as currently conceived reported that 7 per cent of those who had such aptitude were women (Marczech, 1966).[2] If all those who had this aptitude actually entered the profession, therefore, 7 per cent of all engineers would be expected to be women. Only Poland and the Soviet Union show this large a proportion of women engineers, and the proportion reported for the Soviet Union is so far out of line with those of other countries as to suggest differences of definition or classification. In most countries the paucity of women engineers cannot be due entirely to lack of women with engineering aptitudes.

In terms of sex-typing there is probably no profession more "masculine" than engineering. Understandably so, perhaps, because in the past it was largely applied to military installations, to massive building operations—mountain bridges, railway construction, tropical canals—often in out-of-the-way places not appealing or congenial to many women. Increasingly, however, it is being applied to industries where it can be practiced in pleasant offices under congenial circumstances in no way prejudicial to women. And, in fact, the number of women enrolled in engineering schools more than doubled between 1949 and 1963 (Table 7.2).

There is nothing intrinsically masculine in engineering techniques; they can be applied equally well for achieving all kinds of goals, small as well as large, "feminine" as well as "masculine." It is primarily the image of engineering in the massive, primarily military, uses of the past that has given it a characteristically masculine aura. The sex-typing therefore persists.

Some insight into the mechanisms by which sexism operates in engineering can be inferred from a study of a national sample of junior and senior women engineering students (Robin, 1963). They came to engineering school with exceptionally high grades; in engineering school, however, their grades averaged lower than those of the men, suggesting the possibility of a faculty bias in grading similar to the bias documented in school teachers when

2. A Department of Labor study some five years later reported that 40 per cent of all students with engineering aptitude were women. See *New York Times*, Aug. 19, 1969.

Table 7.2. Number of Women Enrolled in Schools of Engineering;
Number of Degrees Awarded to Women, 1948–1963

1963	1,800	173
1962	1,559	169
1961	1,486	168
1960	1,539	174
1959	1,662	146
1958	1,718	133
1957	1,783	97
1956	1,434	95
1955	1,167	75
1954	1,161	76
1953	926	52
1952	696	71
1951	625	95
1950	683	224
1949	763	167

SOURCE: Ralph E. Dunham and Harold A. Foecke, *Engineering Degrees,*
1962–1963 and Enrollments, Fall, 1963 (Office of Education, 1965), p. 8.

they are led to expect superior performance in certain students
and not in others.[3] As compared with men students, these young
women were interested in a more feminine way of being an
engineer, a way that emphasized design rather than control or
domination of the environment.[4]

That this feminine way of being an engineer did not fit the
faculty's sexist concept of the engineer's role was shown not only
by the lower grades awarded to the women, but also by the fact
that, judged in terms of an instrument designed to describe the

3. An almost amusing example of the impact of gender-related treatment
by the environment is offered by the clinical case of a chromosomally male
child who was erroneously attributed female gender at birth and reared for
14 years as a girl. When he was being treated as a girl, he was a mediocre
student. But when allowed to become a male, he became an excellent student. "For example, he came to be among the first in his class in mathe-
matics, a subject in which he had done very poorly when he thought he
was a girl" (Stoller, 1968, p. 70).

4. Both the men and the women recognized the importance of good relations with fellow workers for the quality of one's own work, but the men
ranked "social skills" higher than the women did, and technical skill and
training lower, suggesting that the women felt they had to rely more on
competitive superiority than on "the club factor."

ideal engineer as the faculty saw him, the women fared less well than the men. This fact suggests that men have appropriated engineering, see only its masculine control-and-domination aspects, and therefore have blind spots for any other kinds, or at least a denigrating attitude toward them. Certainly this is their attitude toward any feminine way of being an engineer: that is not engineering as they conceive it.

Soviet sociologists, it may be pointed out parenthetically here, seem to recognize that there is something contrary to the public interest in such sex-typing of the professions. They express a certain apprehension: "whatever the causes of such phenomena, society is hardly to be served with a perspective when all the engineers are males, while doctors and teachers are females" (Simirenko, 1969, p. 41). They imply concurrence with a conclusion expressed by Bruno Bettelheim: "Most work that men can do, women can also do, but they will do it differently. . . . There are no essentially male or essentially female professions, . . . all are human professions and . . . they can become more human as we allow men and women to make their essentially human, but specifically male or female contribution" (Bettelheim, 1965). There may be a great deal more to engineering than control and domination. The public interest may sometimes require a job to be done for which a control-and-domination kind of engineer is not the best person. There may be many kinds of "designing women," including engineers with a penchant for design.

Management

If we disengage the entrepreneurial from the strictly management functions, it can be seen that most women are engaged in performing management functions. Women in the past were accustomed to managing great estates when their husbands went to war; the chatelaine of a great manor house in the middle ages was managing a not-insignificant enterprise. Until workshops and homes were separated, women managed domestic industries. In a rural setting, men managed the fields, women the household, and one was as vital and productive as the other. Women have managed abbeys, convents, hospitals, schools, colleges. Today more women are engaged in household management, shrunken as it has become, than in any other single occupation. Planning, budgeting, procurement, administration are not exclusively male talents; women are quite capable of performing all of them.

In the management of business and industry, however, women are conspicuously absent. A Harvard dean is frequently quoted to the effect that there are so few women in management positions that there are not enough to warrant study. Not the technical but the sociological aspects of industrial and business management militate against success for women in this occupation. It is the bureaucratic, hierarchical organization seemingly, until now, demanded by large-scale enterprise that, by layering management and thus introducing status and power differentials, places them at a disadvantage. For whenever there is a status-power differential in a two-sex organization, women will be assigned to the lower levels.

The traits called for in the entrepreneurial, as distinguished from the management, aspects of business and industrial enterprises—aggression and competitiveness—are socialized out of most women by their specialization in the supportive function. If they retain strong achievement motivation, they are socialized to satisfy it by way of their husbands. If they seek to achieve in their own right, they still operate through men. It is one of the most publicized secrets of successful business women that they often have to manage through men, from behind the scenes, implementing their ideas through men who are allowed to take the credit for them (Bernard, 1968).

Antidiscrimination Policy Becomes Antinatalist Policy

The rationale for policies to encourage women to enter the labor force has been that they would supply a wide range of services demanded by the general welfare. Only recently has it been argued that such policies served the general welfare also as methods of controlling population. Since a very considerable research literature documents the fact that in industrialized societies there is an inverse relationship between fertility and labor-force participation by women, it is now being argued that "normative barriers against the employment of women in professional and other white-collar employment should be undermined by governmental policy whenever possible" (Weller, 1968, p. 521). Antidiscrimination policies became antinatalist policies. Nonofficial policies in industry have always tended to be antinatalist. Women workers often were fired if they became pregnant, and even if they were not, few if any provisions were made to help them accommodate a pregnancy. But now official policy was becoming antinatalist also. There were better uses for women than childbearing.

Women, President Kennedy said in 1961 as he established a Commission on the Status of Women, "should be assured the opportunity to develop their capacities and fulfill their aspirations," and services should be provided "which will enable women to continue their role as wives and mothers while making a maximum contribution to the world around them." In 1961 there was as yet only incipient concern about the imminent population crisis, and that chiefly among the ecologists, demographers, and social scientists. Within a decade it became a major public issue. A full-time devotion to motherhood was no longer a taken-for-granted way for women to pursue happiness. The public interest did not call for women to produce many children; in fact, it called for quite the reverse. The time might conceivably come—after a nuclear holocaust, for example—when policy makers might wish to stimulate births, but not now. In this new context, helping women to pursue happiness outside of the nursery was as important as utilizing them effectively in the labor force. A job or career had to be made an attractive alternative to excessive maternity. It was therefore in the public interest to make participation by women in the labor force appealing whether or not it supplied essential services or contributed to the gross national product.

REFERENCES

Bernard, Jessie, *The Sex Game* (Englewood Cliffs, N.J.: Prentice-Hall, 1968), Chapter 11.

Bettelheim, Bruno, "The Commitment of a Woman Entering a Scientific Profession in Present-Day American Society," in Jacqueline A. Mattfeld and Carol G. Van Aken (eds.), *Women and the Scientific Professions* (Cambridge: M. I. T. Press, 1965), p. 7.

Field, Mark G., *Doctor and Patient in Soviet Russia* (Cambridge: Harvard University Press, 1957).

S. Marczech, "Why Don't Women Go into Engineering?" *American Engineer,* 34 (Aug. 1966), 28.

Robin, Stanley Shane, *A Comparison of Male-Female Roles in Engineering* (Doctoral dissertation, Lafayette, Ind.: Purdue University, 1963).

Simirenko, Alex, "Post-Stalinist Social Science," *Transaction* (June, 1969).

Stoller, Robert J., *Sex and Gender, On the Development of Masculinity and Femininity* (New York: Science House, 1968).

Weller, Robert H, "The Employment of Wives, Role Incompatibility and Fertility," *Milbank Memorial Fund Quarterly,* 46 (Oct. 1968), p. 507.

Wilson, Charles Morrow, *One Half the People* (New York: Sloane, 1949), pp. 228–229.

IV

The Pursuit of Happiness: Adjusting the Lives of Women to the Establishment

President Kennedy's nicely orchestrated preamble to the act establishing the Commission on the Status of Women had touched all bases. The pursuit of happiness by women was hampered by prejudices and outmoded customs that conflicted with our commitment to human dignity, freedom, and democracy. The right of women to develop their capacities and fulfill their aspirations should be assured. But women's pursuit of happiness involved more than policy statements sanctioning it. Somehow it involved reconciling the conflicts among their functions, especially the conflict between their productive and other, primarily procreative, functions.

The traditional statement of the problem of reconciling these functions accepted the status quo and looked for ways to ease the problems of the working wife or mother. An enormous literature has examined the pros and cons of the "working wife," the "employed mother," and the "marriage versus career" dilemma. On a hit-or-miss basis, thousands of individual women have had to work out one kind of accommodation or another. So far all these

147

discussions have taken for granted the current sexual specialization of functions. Child rearing and homemaking have been accepted as intrinsically women's work; the objective has been to show how carrying those loads can be eased. All the adjustments are viewed as being made by the women themselves within a taken-for-granted Establishment.

Chapter 8 examines the general situation of women workers, Chapter 9 focuses on professional or "career women."

8

Reconciling the Incompatible Functions of Women

One Role, Two Roles, Shared Roles

Until very recently a one-role ideology for women prevailed everywhere. The implicit ideology behind policy was that women's place was in the home, that she should work outside the home only if she had no male provider to take care of her. As recently as 1936, 72 per cent of a Gallup poll sampling disapproved of married women working if their husbands could support them. In 1938, 90 per cent of a sample of men said married women should not work, and 88 per cent of a sample of women agreed that married women should give up their jobs if their husbands wanted them to. These findings are understandable in a depression decade. But even as late as 1969 a substantial proportion of the population—a whopping 40 per cent—still held to that one-role ideology. "Women should stay home and take care of their families. Even if the kids are in school, a woman's obligation is still to make a home for her husband" (*Washington Post*, 1969).

As so often happens, ideology was not even within hailing distance of actual practice for, regardless of ideology, married women living with their husbands were flocking into the labor force at a rapid rate (Figure 8.1), and in 1967 almost half (48.4

149

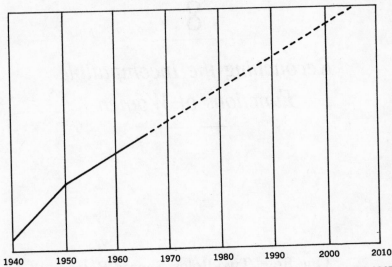

Figure 8.1. Proportion of Married Women, Husband Present, in Labor Force, 1940-1967.
Source: Women's Bureau, **1969 Handbook on Women Workers** (1969), p. 26.
Projection (Dotted Line) by Present Author.

per cent) were mothers, some (24.8 per cent) with small children (Women's Bureau, 1969). And many men who might reply to a poll in terms of the nineteenth-century one-role ideology would not hesitate to accept support from young working wives for their own professional preparation. They might also welcome the work of middle-aged wives which relieved them of the onerous responsibility of supplying to these bored, frustrated, depressed women their only interest in life.

It was, therefore, truly a giant step forward when official policy finally caught up with the twentieth century and began to recognize other than sheer necessity as a reason for married women, even mothers, working. Such shifts do not come suddenly. At first the contribution that working women were making to the "cultural and economic life of the nation" was recognized as legitimizing their labor-force participation. It was recognized in Great Britain in the Report of a Royal Commission on Population in 1949:

It would be harmful all round, to the women, the family and the community, to attempt any restriction of the contribution that women can make to the cultural and economic life of the nation. It is true that there is often a real conflict between motherhood and a whole-time "career." Part of this conflict is inherent in the biological function of women, but part of it is artificial. . . . We, therefore, welcome the removal of the marriage bar in such employments as teaching and the civil service, and we think that a deliberate effort should be made to devise adjustments that would render it easier for women to combine motherhood and the care of a home with outside activities.

Thus the first rationale for accepting the two-role ideology was based on a general-welfare criterion. The pursuit-of-happiness idea did not enter into it, except in the very negative form of "helping the poor dears carry the double load." The publication in 1956 of *Women's Two Roles* by Alva Myrdal and Viola Klein may be taken, simply for the sake of convenience, as a turning point. There were other reasons than sheer necessity that justified labor-force participation by women. In that book the authors not only documented with cold, hard demographic and economic data the need for women's contribution to the labor force, but they also recognized as a justification for work outside the home that "women no less than men need for their happiness both emotional fulfillment in their personal relations and a sense of social purpose" (Myrdal and Klein, 1966). And President John Kennedy agreed. He agreed not only with the Royal Commission—that services should be available "which will enable women to continue their role as wives and mothers while making a maximum contribution to the world around them,"—but also with the Myrdal-Klein thesis that "women should be assured the opportunity to develop their capacities and fulfill their aspirations."

When Alva Myrdal and Viola Klein reissued their volume in 1966 they felt they had been too defensive in the earlier edition. For by that time "the practice of going out to work, at least part-time had become so widespread among women in their thirties and forties, irrespective of social class, that those who failed to do so now almost have to give an explanation for staying home." Now it was the one-role, nonworking woman rather than the two-role, working wife who was on the defensive. And policy no longer rested exclusively on the general-welfare rationale.

But the crux of even this new Establishmentarian two-role policy was the acceptance of the traditional sexual specialization of functions that, as the Royal Commission saw it, created a conflict "inherent in the biological function of women." Women, it was taken for granted, were still exclusively responsible for child rearing. All that policy could do was help overcome the artifical difficulties entailed in carrying out this function. Until Movement Women began to challenge this stance, it was taken for granted by everyone. All the research assumed it, and all the programs and plans. The problem was viewed as one of devising the best way to reconcile women's domestic and work roles.

Movement Women did not see why women alone should be saddled with the conflicting functional imperatives. Reproduction, to be sure, could not be shifted. But in and of itself, bearing a baby did not interfere all that much with labor-force participation and, as we shall presently see, it was interfering less and less. It was the child-rearing function that did. They therefore argued that not only for the sake of women but for the sake of children too—and even for men—this function be shared by men.

Varying Pursuits of Happiness

When President Kennedy said that women "should be assured the opportunity to develop their capacities and fulfill their aspirations" and that services should be provided to "enable women to continue their role as wives and mothers," while at the same time "making a maximum contribution to the world around them," thus officially sanctioning the two-role pattern, it sounded to some women like a charter for liberation. But for others, adding a maximum contribution to the world around them while they continued their roles as wives and mothers was not an auspicious prospect. For them the pursuit of happiness involved only minor or casual interest in labor-force participation, or none at all— "one-and-a-half" roles at most. The pursuit of happiness led them to the hearth and nursery. Not having to work at all continued to be a great desideratum for them.

Myrdal and Klein had described the nineteenth-century model of the lady of leisure that still lingered on into the middle of the twentieth century. To those who hold hard, underpaid, disagreeable, menial jobs, work is not a form of self-fulfillment; it is demeaning. Understandably, therefore, just not having to get up in the morning to go to work would be a big step toward happiness for them. Still, even four-fifths of a sample of women on assistance rolls and women of the "working-poor" class—who would be most likely to have the dull, uninteresting, and menial jobs—would prefer full-time jobs to staying home (Center for Research on the Acts of Man, n.d.). So would their counterparts in Russia: "The married woman who works bears a double burden, but her position in society is superior to that of the woman who does not work. I once asked several women in a factory why they worked. I deliberately chose women whose earnings were low and whose work was more monotonous than housework. They replied that no matter how hard they worked in the home, they never got credit for it. Here they received respect and appreciation" (Current Digest of the Soviet Press, 1968).

The deteriorating effect of housework as an occupation on the mentality of women has been commented on for almost a century. There is increasing evidence that it can also have a deteriorating effect on mental health as well, as measured in terms of symptoms of psychological distress. Thus, working women, three-fifths of whom are married, show less than expected frequencies of such symptoms whereas housewives show greater than expected frequencies (Bernard, 1971; 1972). Understandably, therefore, just the right to take a job, to be released from the boredom of housework, from its isolation, from its unstimulating round of menial tasks, and to have the companionship of other adults, to be in the swing of things would contribute to happiness by way of self-fulfillment for many women. About 15 per cent of the wives in one study gave "getting out of the house" as a reason for working (Orden and Bradburn, 1969, pp. 253–268). In another study of employed women, both married and unmarried, "three of every five indicated that they would work even if they (and their husbands) had enough money to live comfortably without working." Among black women, two out of three did (Shea, et al., 1970, p. 213).

For others, just a job by itself would not be enough; pleasant work and surroundings would have to be added. But, as would most men (Veroff and Feld, 1970, p. 207), they would still want to work even if the net monetary rewards were not much greater than the added cost involved in taking a job, as is often the case. Women in this category might not worry too much about discrimination or other rights; a secondary place in the world of work would satisfy their modest pursuit of happiness.

At the top, however, are women who want a career. They want a job at the highest level of their talents, a job they know they are the best person for; they want careers in the fullest sense of the term. Work is not for them just something extra thrown in; it is a major focus of their lives. They need it for self-fulfillment. They mind anything thrown into their path as an obstacle to equal opportunity.

Actually, all these varying forms of pursuing happiness were available to women, at least theoretically, as the work histories of women have shown.

Work Histories

On the basis of two research streams, one dealing with the life cycle and one on labor-force analysis, several classifications of the work histories of women have been made. They show that the choices of women are not necessarily between one-role and two-role patterns but among many ways of combining them, for they may overlap, run sequentially, or run concurrently in the so-called "double-track" manner.

Donald E. Super, noting a lack of data on the careers of women, attempted to apply a modified form of a male schema to women and came up with: (1) the stable homemaking one-role pattern, in which women have no labor-force experience; (2) the conventional one-role pattern in which the work and the domestic roles are sequential, the young woman working in a stop-gap job until she marries and then retires from the labor force; (3) the stable working, two-role pattern in which the woman remains in the labor force, whether or not she marries; (4) the double-track two-role pattern in which the woman continues in her work after marriage and even after motherhood; (5) the interrupted pattern in which a one-role and a two-role pattern may alternate or run sequentially; (6) an unstable in-and-out-of-the-labor-force pattern according to whim, which might be labeled a one-and-a-fraction-role pattern; and, finally (7) a multiple-trial pattern consisting of a sequence of unrelated jobs, unstable, with no genuine life work (Super, 1957, p. 76).

Sophia Cooper arrived at a slightly different formulation. She described the seven Super patterns as follows: (1) lifetime continuous employment; (2) a double-track pattern combining employment and homemaking throughout adult life; (3) an interrupted pattern in which the woman takes time off to rear children and then returns to uninterrupted employment; (4) a truncated pattern in which women work until marriage or the birth of a first child and then leave gainful employment forever; (5) intermittent reentry and exits from the labor force, resulting from lack of identification with a career; (6) a multiple-trial career pattern in which the need or desire to work remains but the kind of work varies; and (7) a pattern in which a girl goes directly into homemaking with no interval of gainful employment at all (Cooper, 1963).

It seems clear that the women following the several Cooper work-history patterns are not all motivated in the same way, and the same policy criteria would not apply with equal cogency to all. Those in the first three kinds of pattern appear to be much more work-oriented, even career-oriented, than those in the other four, especially the last. They are probably also among the most talented and least in need of special incentive to reduce the number of children they bear or of lures to attract them into the labor force to provide essential services. But they may also be among the most needy, working whether they want to or not. The fifth pattern tends to characterize the work history of women who take jobs to earn enough for specific consumer goods—a new refrigerator, a new automobile, a boat, a family trip. The sixth reflects the work history, hardly a pattern, of a woman who enjoys working if the job is interesting but who rarely finds any that can really engage her full commitment for long periods of time. She is an amateur; whether or not she is in the labor force depends on the availability of work she enjoys. It is hard in this day and age to figure out who the girl is who follows the seventh pattern, never entering the labor force at all. She is probably the high-school dropout who marries immediately. It is for her that "operation retrieval" would be most fruitful, so far as both increasing labor-force participation and reducing the number of children borne are concerned.

Unfortunately, we do not know what proportion of women can be classified according to the several patterns either at any given moment or over a life span. We do know that fewer than one in ten fall into Cooper's pattern 7 (Garfinkle, 1969, p. 5). More detailed information about the career histories of professional women is obtainable from a questionnaire study by Eli Ginzberg and his associates of 311 women of unusual distinction (Table 8.1, Table 8.2). One would not expect a schema based on the life histories of this set of extraordinary women to conform to that based on the population as a whole. It is all the more remarkable, therefore, that the data coincide as well as they do.

Ginzberg and his associates (1966) distinguished six patterns: "continuous," "minor breaks," "intermittent," "periodic," "terminated," and minor or no-work-at-all histories. Ginzberg's "continuous" pattern corresponded to Cooper histories 1 and 2; his "minor breaks," "intermittent," and "periodic" to Cooper histories 3, 5, and 6; and "terminated," "truncated," and "minor or none,"

Table 8.1. Work Histories of 311 Educated Women

Work History	Per Cent
Continuous	36
Minor breaks	14
Intermittent	12
Periodic	14
Terminated, temporarily or permanently	13
Minor or none	11
Total	100

SOURCE: Eli Ginzberg and Associates, *Life Styles of Educated Women* (New York: Columbia University Press, 1966), p. 78.

to Cooper histories 4 and 7. The similarity between the two schema suggests that the problems are generic, characteristic of both talented and average women, though with varying degrees of urgency. For more detailed analysis, Ginzberg telescoped his categories into three: continuous, broken, and terminated. Among his subjects, half fell into the first, slightly more than a quarter into the second, and slightly fewer than a quarter into the last. Marriage and motherhood were decisive influences in determining which of the patterns would prevail, the single and the childless married women being, understandably, much more likely than women with children to be in the continuous category. Alice Rossi reported that only a third of the women in her "housewife" category were in the labor force, 70 per cent of those in the "pioneer" category (Rossi, 1965, pp. 79–80). Overall, in 1967, almost two-fifths (37 per cent) of married women living with their husbands were in the labor force and 61 per cent of them had children under 18. Over a lifetime, the cumulative proportion would be larger.

Table 8.2. Work History of 311 Educated Women by Family Situation (in per cent)

Work History	Single	Married, No Children	One Child	Two Children	Three or More Children
Continuous	91	83	48	29	7
Broken	7	15	29	39	40
Terminated, temporary or permanent	2	2	23	32	53

SOURCE: Eli Ginzberg, et al. *Life Styles of Educated Women* (New York: Columbia University Press, 1966), p. 92.

One Role, Two Roles, and the Achievement of Happiness

Current research shows that "two roles are better than one" even, or perhaps especially, if the one role is the domestic role. Thus, among women who choose some form of the two-role pattern, who opt to combine marriage and work, the result tends to be felicitious. E. W. Burgess and Leonard Cottrell (1939) reported a generation ago that happiness in marriage was associated with the wife's working if she wanted to or not working if she did not want to. Arnold Rose (1959) some years later found among middle-aged mothers of college students that more of those who were in the labor force expressed life satisfaction than did those who were not. Among educated employed women, Ivan Nye (1963) found that general satisfaction tended to be high. In fact, for women with high achievement motivation, work outside the home made motherhood itself more satisfying (Veroff and Feld, 1970).

That the one-role pattern—full-time motherhood as a life career—is not an optimum choice in the pursuit of happiness today was suggested by a study of middle-age depression among 490 women hospitalized for mental-health impairments. Among these women, it was found that those who had devoted themselves exclusively to rearing children accounted for 82.0 per cent of all depressed cases. Women who had not invested so exclusively in the maternal role contributed smaller proportions (Bart, 1970).

Perhaps even more to the point was the conclusion of another study showing that the by-now anachronistic, highly differentiated role-specialization of family functions—father the provider, mother the domestic specialist—was bad for marriage. It led to marriages that were merely "empty shells." This study was unique in that it was based on a panel of 400 marriages studied over many years. E. W. Burgess and Paul Wallin in 1939 had interviewed a thousand engaged couples; three years later, a second wave of interviews was undertaken with 666 of the original couples, then in the early-marriage phase. And in 1955–1960, a third wave of interviews reached 400 of the couples. The original hypothesis assumed that qualities and traits in the couples themselves could be predictive of the future course of the marriage. This hypothesis was not borne out, for it did not make adequate provision for "the dynamic element resulting both from changes in the social circumstances in which the couple finds itself and changes in the relationship between individual husbands and wives (Dizard, 1968, p. 1).

Because of the nature of the process by which the original sample was selected, these couples tended to be educated, middle class, homogeneous. Everything seemed to be going for them. The deadening of the marriage, its reduction to an "empty shell," could not be explained by anything present at the time of marriage. It resulted from the rigid differentiation of functions between husbands and wives:

Decreasing husband-wife happiness and permanence is disproportionately common in those marriages which move toward a greater degree of role differentiation. Most of our couples began their marriages with relatively low levels of separation between husband and wife roles. Most wives worked to help augment the family's income and we surmise that, given these other features, husbands could be found frequently helping their wives with traditionally feminine household tasks. By the middle years, however, this reasonable undifferentiated role arrangement had undergone alterations. As role differentiation increases, husbands and wives in our sample are increasingly likely to argue over family decisions; they are increasingly likely to suffer losses in happiness; and, finally, they are much more likely to give increasingly serious consideration to separation and/or divorce. Increasing role differentiation does anything but enhance the husband-wife relationship. The husband-wife relationship becomes more segmental, the emotional content of the relationship begins to lose force. Love declines, less affection is demonstrated less often, and husbands and wives are less likely to be happy with their marriages. The implication is that the wife should diversify her marital roles and thereby make her life and her marriage more satisfying—to herself and her husband (Dizard, 1968, p. 1).

And, by implication, to her children also (See Chapter 12). The one-role style of life, it appears, for many if not for most women clearly is not the best way to pursue happiness.

It would seem, therefore, that in terms of self-actualization in the pursuit of happiness a policy making it easier for women to follow the two-roles option would be indicated. Actually, despite Kennedy's brave promises, policy has been notoriously lagging in its efforts to help women reconcile the two roles.

Before pursuing this topic, however, a brief parenthetical note on the "cost" of the one-role pattern to the general welfare as well as to women themselves.

A Parenthetical Aside: The "Costs" to the General Welfare of the One-Role Pattern

Although our concern in Part IV is not primarily with the general-welfare goal of policy, at least a nod in the direction of the "costs" to the economy of the one-role domestic pattern is warranted here.

If a young woman enters the labor force at age 20, marriage will "cost" the economy about ten years of lifetime labor-force participation; the woman who never marries will spend about 45 years in the labor force; the woman who marries but remains childless, about 35. One child "costs" the economy ten more years, for the expected work life of women with one child is 25 years. A second child "costs" an additional three years of labor-force contribution since women with two children will contribute 22 years to the labor force. The third child "costs" only two additional years, and fourth-or-higher parities cost three additional years.

Table 8.3. Average Number of Years of Labor-Force Activity Remaining for 20-Year-Old Women in the Labor Force, 1960, 1950

Year	Single	Married, No Children	One Child	Two Children	Three Children	Four or More Children
1960	45.3	34.9	25	22	20	17
1950	40.5	34.0		23		

SOURCE: S. Garfinkle, "Work in the Lives of Women," paper presented at the meetings of International Union for the Scientific Study of Population, London, 1969.

The "cost" of marriage to society in terms of professional achievement rather than in terms of years of labor-force participation among career women is negligible. Among single career women, 63 per cent achieve good or high levels; among married women without children, 60 per cent do. But the advent of children precipitates a marked decline in the professional contribution. Only 41 per cent of mothers with one child, and 39 per cent of those with two, reach a good or high level of achievement. If there are more than two children, only 17 per cent achieve at the good or high level.

Table 8.4. Achievement Level of 226 Career Women by Family Situation

Achievement Level	Single	Married, No Children	One Child	Two Children	Three or More Children
High	24	23	12	8	11
Good	39	37	29	31	6
Medium	30	37	38	40	40
Low	7	3	21	21	43

SOURCE: Eli Ginzberg and Associates, *Life Styles of Educated Women* (New York: Columbia University Press, 1966), p. 102.

There is, of course, no way to evaluate the production of children against the production of goods and services in terms either of the general welfare or the pursuit of happiness. There is reason to believe that the "costs" of children in terms of labor-force participation are declining, as we shall note presently in our comments on fertility in the 1960's.

In any event, the days of the one-role pattern when a woman could restrict her entire life to her domestic functions are past for an increasing proportion of women. More and more of them will be opting for a double-track form of the two-role pattern, and facing enormous problems trying to reconcile their demands. In general, two ways to deal with them have arisen. One approach accepts the present sexual differentiation of functions and tinkers with the institutional patterns of "existing social arrangements" to help women reconcile the incompatible demands made on them as mothers, homemakers, and workers. This is the approach dealt with in the remainder of the present chapter; it deals with ways to adjust the lives of women to the Establishment. The other approach rejects this position and zeroes in on the sexual differentiation of functions itself; it argues for shared rather than rigidly differentiated roles. Not tinkering with the machinery but a complete overhaul is called for, to adjust the Establishment to the needs of women rather than the other way round. This shared-roles approach is dealt with in Chapter 13.

Opportunity to Develop . . . and Fulfill?

If we were, in fact, to limit the discussion in Part IV to the goal of assuring women "the opportunity to develop their capacities and fulfill their aspirations on a continuing basis irrespective of national exigencies," as President Kennedy specified, we would stop right here. For all plans and programs for helping women reconcile their two roles have always given self-fulfillment (let alone improvement of marriage!) a very low priority, and even then, usually only in response to a national exigency.

Through special protective legislation of one kind or another, women had been helped in their worker role for many decades because they were among the most exploitable of all workers. And, trivial as some of it may have looked—clean washrooms may not seem all that important to people who have always taken them for granted and hardly know what any other kind is like—it did make some contribution to the well-being and comfort, if not the self-fulfillment, of working women. Only since such protection has been used as a technique for discriminating against women—by barring them from certain kinds of work or from overtime, for example, or restricting some kinds of night work—has there been a movement to get rid of it. Such labor legislation did nothing to help women reconcile the two roles; it just tried to control the exploitation of women in the second role.

But the crux of the problem of the two roles lies in child care, for so long as this function is assigned exclusively to women, some kind of help in carrying it out has to be provided. For the most part early attempts to deal with the two-role dilemma were dominated by the lingering one-role ideology. Married women were discouraged from taking jobs; they were fired if they married while employed. Certainly when they became mothers they should not work if they could help it. In the early years of the century the movement known as Mothers' Pensions developed, designed to supply income to poor women without husbands so that they could stay home and look after their children rather than enter the labor market. Their time was worth more in the home than in the work force, an ideology that was later embodied in the Aid to Dependent Children provisions of the Social Security Act of 1935.

Then came the exigencies of World War II. The one-role ideology became a luxury the economy could no longer afford. Women were needed in the factories and munitions plants, so under the Lanham Act day-care facilities and nursery schools sprang up in housing projects all over the country—no problem at all. But after the war they lapsed. A recrudescence of the one-role ideology, reflected in the so-called feminine mystique, took place.

Benefits to women are rarely emphasized in any proposals for legislation on child care. Children, yes. Society, yes. But legislation in behalf of women themselves? Legislation designed to afford "the opportunity to develop their capacities and fulfill their aspirations?" These are the lowest of all priorities. If they sneak in at all, it has to be under some other guise. Thus in 1968, at one of the conferences of the Commission on the Status of Women, community representatives were instructed to make clear to their communities "that child care benefits are for the whole community, nor just for low-income mothers. . . . [There are] economic gains to all sections" (Commission on the Status of Women, 1968, p. 48). In 1970 the Report of the Presidential Task Force on Women's Rights and Responsibilities, urging liberalization of support for child-care centers, noted that "lack of adequate child care facilities has been found to be a major deterrent to solution or even significant progress in providing greater educational opportunities for children, reducing the welfare burden, giving greater dignity and self-respect to mothers on welfare, filling critical manpower needs in shortage occupations and [finally, at the end of the list] providing real freedom of choice in life style for women" (Item 3H). A grudging step was taken in the 91st

Congress (1970) when a proposed bill in the Senate, though directed primarily to children in poor families, permitted attendance of other children at cost or part of cost of tuition and a proposed bill in the House provided for children in families of all classes. The prognosis for early implementation was by no means bright.

For even though the passage of the Social Security Act of 1967 requiring women on assistance rolls to accept training or employment has made provision for care of their children a necessity, still, even for such hardship cases, the supply of facilities for child care has remained abysmally low. In 1965, only 2 per cent of the children of working mothers were benefitting from group care. In 1968 there were only 13 federally administered day-care centers in Washington, D.C.; 99 in New York City (Commission on the Status of Women, 1968, pp. 37, 39).

In order to eke out the meager facilities available from government support, unions, private industry, housing developers, and school systems were experimenting with ways to provide child-care services. By 1969 the situation will still unimproved. Most women were still having to find their own ways, one by one, to deal with the "incompatibility between employment away from home and their domestic duties." We did not even know in detail what solutions they were arriving at. "Exactly what ways these are has not yet been ascertained," but there was evidence that substantial proportions were being taken care of by the mothers themselves. It was brutally clear that hardly anyone was taking seriously the relief women might need for their own self-actualization. Quite aside from the pursuit-of-happiness point of view, and just in terms of the general welfare (for the entire economy would grind to a screeching halt if all married women, who were 58 per cent of the female labor force in 1967, left their jobs), it seems outrageous to thoughtful people that women themselves should be saddled with the entire cost of reconciling the two roles and that so little real help has been forthcoming from any source—government, community, or industry.

Although the provision of child-care services has been one issue on which there has been widespread consensus among those who attempt to adjust their lives to the Establishment, questions have

Table 8.5. *Child-Care Arrangements of Working Mothers*
(February, 1965) *

Type of Arrangement	Children under 14	
Care in child's own home	45.5	
Father		14.9
Other Relative		21.2
Nonrelative		9.4
Care in someone else's home	15.7	
Other arrangements	38.8	
Care in group-care center		2.2
Child looked after self		8.1
Mother, while working		13.0
Mother worked only during child's school hours		15.0
Other		.5

SOURCE: Based on Table 22, *1969 Handbook on Women Workers* (Women's Bureau, 1969), p. 49.

*One study of employed women found that the daily costs of child care ranged from a median of $1.83 for women earning less than $1.00 per hour to $4.00 for those earning $3.00 or more an hour (John R. Shea et al., *Dual Careers: A Longitudinal Study of Labor Market Experience of Women*, vol. 1. Center for Human Resource Research, Ohio State University, 1970, p. 137.

recently been raised from the points of view both of helping women pursue happiness and of the general welfare.

Movement Women, for example, have been having second thoughts about surrendering the socialization of their children to child-care centers controlled by members of the Establishment who would, they fear, socialize their children along lines they disapprove of. They were "concerned with what happens inside the day-care center," for already in conventional centers "by the age of four, children are assimilating the idea that a woman's place is in the home. They are learning to follow directions and rules without asking why." Therefore, "in order to develop a radically structured day-care program we must not allow any control to be in the hands of the universities and corporations. . . . Control must rest with those who struggle for and use the day-care center" (Gross and MacEwan, 1970, p. 28). Men, of course, as well as women.

The other second thought had a different slant. It raised the question of the effect of making motherhood too easy, thus encouraging women to have children. "If the major goal is to lower fertility, the wholesale establishment of on-the-job facilities for the care of children seems self-defeating, as does the establishment of neighborhood child-care facilities by the state" (Weller, 1968, p. 521).

So far as President Kennedy's twin recommendation—home services for women—is concerned, forget it. Such services were hardly being considered at all. One can scarcely help marveling at the callous, cynical, almost punitive attitudes widely held toward the problems for women intrinsic in the two-role ideology.

Antinatalism and the Two-Role Ideology

The two-role ideology received an unexpected boost when population growth became a matter of great popular concern. In the past, even if one did not believe that marriage, motherhood, and domesticity were always the preferred life pattern for women or the best way for them to pursue happiness, it was not necessarily contrary to the general welfare to grant women the right to seek self-fulfillment exclusively through motherhood. Let them, if that was what they thought (even if mistakenly in many cases) they wanted. The public interest was not threatened.

But in the 1950's, half of a sample of Cornell University women said they wanted four or more children—18 per cent said five or more (Goldsen, 1960, p. 218)—and 84 per cent of Vassar women said they wanted three or more (Freedman, 1967, p. 137), and a tenth of the married housewives in Alice Rossi's (1965, p. 82) sample said they wanted five or more children. In 1960 almost a fifth of the women 25 to 29 years of age not in the labor force actually had four or more children (U.S. Census, 1960) and in 1969 the average number of children ever borne by women 35 to 44 years of age not in the labor force was 3.56 (Bureau of the Census, 1970, Table 1)—17 per cent higher than in 1960. When these figures were known, and when the fertility of women 35 to 39 years of age in 1969 (the most fertile cohort born in the twentieth century) was 50 per cent above replacement needs (Bureau of the Census, 1970, Table 1, p. 1), we began to wonder whether the public interest might not well call for channeling the pursuit of happiness by women in other directions, especially when there was reason to question whether exuberant maternity was really producing all that much happiness anyway.

In the era of the one-role pattern, women had been praised for staying home and having babies; employment outside the home had been deprecated in fact precisely because it lowered the birth rate. In the new context, it began to seem that we would have to ask them to not stay home in order to not have so many babies. Employment was now being advocated because it would have precisely that effect. "The employment of . . . married women should be encouraged," not necessarily because it contributed to the production of needed goods and services or even to the self-actualization of the women themselves, but rather because it lowered the birth rate. And because white-collar employment was a deterrent to early marriage, it should also be provided to young unmarried women upon graduation (Weller, 1968, p. 521). Higher education, because it retarded population "by increasing the span of time between generations," should similarly be encouraged. What women had once demanded as a right was in process of being almost imposed as a duty. Antidiscrimination policy was blended into an antinatalist policy.

Strangely enough, however, women in the 1960's proved to be truly confounding. Improbable as it may seem, with all the difficulties they had to contend with, women were learning, somehow or other, how to cope with the problems of reconciling their childbearing and their work functions. Bearing children was having less and less effect on labor-force participation. Or, conversely, labor-force participation was having less effect on childbearing.

In 1960, for example, white women in the labor force had borne only 57.5 per cent as many children as white women not in the labor force. But in 1969, they were having more than two-thirds as many (68.7 per cent). The effect of employment status, as distinguished from labor-force participation, did not change that much in the same time period: in 1960, employed white women were having about three-fourths as many children as unemployed white women (76.3 per cent); in 1969, about the same (78.5 per cent). Women employed full time in 1960 had had only two-thirds as many babies as those employed part time (68.1 per cent); but almost three-fourths (73.2 per cent) as many in 1969. Labor-force participation was still antinatalist, but decreasingly so.

Table 8.6. Effect of Labor-Force Participation and Employment Status on Number of Children Ever Borne, White Women (Standardized for Age) 1960, 1969

	1969	1960
	per cent	per cent
In labor force as per cent of those not in labor force	68.7	57.5
Employed as per cent of unemployed	78.5	76.3
Employed full time as per cent of employed part time	73.2	68.1

SOURCE: Bureau of the Census, *Fertility of the Population: January 1969*, series P-20, no. 203 (July 6, 1970), table 4, p. 12.

We have discussed one-role and two-role patterns as though there really were choices for women all along the line, as though they deliberated and selected a role pattern that suited them, fully aware of all the alternatives. Not at all, say avant-garde women. Actually women have little real choice. They are coerced by social pressures. They are at the mercy of chance events. They have little control over their life styles.

Coercion? Chance? Choice?

One does not have to deny Mervin Freedman's conclusion that "the satisfactions that accrue to most women in bearing and nurturing children provide a tremendous store of contentment . . . and that despite boredom and housework, diapers, and the like, marriage and children are satisfying experiences for most women" (Freedman, 1967, p. 150)—as indeed they are for most men—in order to question the implied corollary that these satisfactions are enough to fill a lifetime. Even the remarkable agreement on a preference for domesticity among about a fifth of superior women reported in Chapter 1, or Ralph Turner's finding among high-school girls that almost half looked forward to a life of domesticity (Turner, 1966, pp. 13–18) did not imply that domesticity by itself was enough. Avant-garde women were challenging even the authenticity of these preferences. Judith Blake Davis, for example, noted that "traditional feminine roles and activities are well designed to circumvent . . . the subjective awareness of the opportunity costs involved in childbearing" (Davis, 1965, p. 1195).

Bruno Bettelheim rebuked critics who raised questions of this nature:

> I am always suspicious if the protagonists of a cause accuse those not interested in it [in this case, greater participation in the labor force] of deluding themselves. The truth of the matter is usually that those others, far from deluding themselves, meet the problem of their lives in ways which seem more appropriate to them or, probably more correct, the problems of their lives are different from those of the leaders of the cause. Maybe in regard to their participation in intellectual leadership contemporary [domestically inclined] American college women don't delude themselves at all, but simply know what they want. Maybe the present [pioneer-type] leaders of the feminist movement are behind their times and try to fight old battles all over again, while our [domestically inclined] college girls know that women have won the war for equality and are ready to settle down to a peaceful coexistence on this new basis. Maybe those are in error who think that, given the existing social arrangements, it is preferable for most intelligent women to pursue a profession when compared with settling down, for example, to a suburban existence (Bettelheim, 1964).

The operant words here are "given the existing social arrangements," a "given" that Movement Women were not willing to concede.

It must be noted that both Freedman and Bettelheim were referring to women of the 1950's, the era of the feminine mystique. That was a time when psychiatrists were telling women to indulge their biological functions without subversion by feminist doctrines and thus derive fulfillment so that "we shall attain the goal of a good life and a secure world in which to live it" (Rheingold, 1964). Women should settle for one role, the domestic, but if that was not feasible, for a merely secondary position in the world of work in exchange for a primary position in the home. The whole apologia of the feminine mystique was based on this "forget it" ideology: go home, have babies, be satisfied.

Even many pioneer-type women succumbed to this "cooling the mark out," which is a way "of reconciling failures to their lot, of 'adjusting' people to their fate. This process protects the social system from the aggressions of the unsuccessful, of the aggrieved, of its victims" (Bernard, 1969, p. 351). It "applies to any situation in which a person with a genuine grievance is led to accept the situation rather than making something of it. . . . Cooling occurs whenever a person with a genuine grievance is reconciled or adjusted or in any other way pacified so that he decides to accept a bad situation rather than rebel against it" (p. 370).

But even under "the existing social arrangements," the psychiatric tenets about what made women happy were suspect. Judith Blake Davis was among those who argued that many domestically oriented women were, if not deluding themselves, then being deluded by others about their own best path to happiness. How much genuine choice is involved, she asked, in the desire expressed by young women for motherhood? How many found fulfillment in bearing children because that was the only way to pursue happiness they had been taught or even permitted to consider seriously? Are they truly presented with genuine alternatives? Do they know what they are missing? She tells us that "family life as we know it has been a forced march for more people than we usually care to admit, and . . . many people might be happier if they did not fill such roles." Women are "propelled into reproductive unions . . . as a career, as the principal focus of their lives" (Davis, 1970, p. 68). Motherhood as a value is inculcated into girls from such an early age that alternatives are hardly given serious attention. Without such alternatives, most young women find motherhood at least a socially acceptable way to invest their talents. But they really do not have a choice. The socialization process, by way of "peer group pressures, cultural norms, parental training, teachers, role expectations, and negative self-concept" (Freeman, n.d), which deprives them of self-confidence discourages them from taking career plans seriously. The "better dead than unwed" ideology propels young women into marriage, and because all feel the same way, they hesitate to delay marriage too long for fear that all the desirable mates will be taken by the time they get around to selecting one.

There is a modicum of evidence to support Judith Blake Davis' contention. When there are attractive alternatives to marriage, women do delay it. Among women 14 to 44 years of age in 1960, the marriage rate in all age-at-marriage categories was higher among those who were not employed than it was among those who were employed. Marriage among those not employed had no competition from alternatives in the form of jobs. And the higher the level of the job among those who were employed, the lower the marriage rate. Income was also related to marriage rates. The higher the incomes of women at almost any age, the lower the marriage rates. Marriage, in brief, had more competition when incomes were higher and attractive work was available.

There is also evidence to support Judith Blake Davis' statement in studies of marriage. Although married women report their marriages as happy to about the same extent as married men, when studied in a different context, more married than unmarried women are reported to be depressed, phobic, passive, and troubled by psychosomatic symptoms. One possible explanation of this paradox is that they have been so thoroughly socialized into believing that marriage and motherhood are the major components of happiness that they judge themselves happy by definition: they must be happy because they are married and have children. Another possible explanation is that they have been socialized into a state of poor mental health in order to fit the requirements of marriage as now structured. Poor mental health is now the "cause" of their marital happiness (Bernard, 1971).

Chance is a large component in the life style of women. Of

special relevance is the "moratorium in the development of a self-concept" which students of career motivation and occupational choices among young women have noted in the late teens and early twenties. This is the period in which both young women and young men have the developmental task of finding themselves in their working lives and finding mates. For young men the two tasks may go on concurrently; their careers are not dependent on the girls they marry.

For young women, however, the two tasks cannot go on concurrently. Young women cannot make any firm decisions about their futures until their marital status is settled, until they know the man they are going to marry, for their entire future hinges on that one contingency; everything has to wait until that pre-eminent decision has been made. It is difficult to make a dedicated attack on professional training in the emotional limbo that precedes that crucial decision; it is almost impossible for most young women to take their future careers seriously during those years. "John may want to be a lawyer, physician, engineer, farmer, statistician, radio announcer, but Mary, nine times out of ten, can see no further than her marriage." Understandably so, since any plans she makes may be invalidated by her marriage. She prepares for a career as laboratory technician only to marry a rancher in the wilds of Montana. So all she wants is "a little job that will put her immediately into the company of men." It is this "perceived lack of control over the central adult role anticipated by women" that produces the moratorium referred to above. Chance in the form of the man she happens to marry may decide what pattern—one role, two roles, or shared roles—her life will follow. Without any genuine "confrontation of choice" a young woman "emerges a pawn in the game of fate" (Mulvey, 1963, p. 384). Whatever young women may think in their late teens, for most, as the research cited above suggests, some combination of work and domestic roles will optimize the happiness they are pursuing by way of self-actualization.

It was precisely to provide such a "confrontation of choice" that counseling services were among those the Commission on the Status of Women was to recommend.

Preparation for Choice: Counseling

Among the next steps Myrdal and Klein had recommended in 1956 were individual adjustments by women themselves, including definite planning for the two roles, thoughtful choice of vocation, a serious attitude toward work, and care to keep vocational skills up to date (Myrdal and Klein, 1966, pp. 154–162). Help in making these adjustments is usually viewed as one of the functions of counseling. "In a democracy offering broad and ever-changing choices, where ultimate decisions are made by individuals, skilled counseling is an essential part of education. Public and private agencies should join in strengthening counseling resources," said the Commission on the Status of Women. A series of regional conferences sponsored by the Women's Bureau and the Office of Education were therefore held in 1964 and 1966 to implement the recommendation, one of the functions specified being that of "helping girls to understand and accept their dual role as homemakers and workers." The expression "helping girls to . . . accept their dual role as homemakers and workers" is the kind that makes Movement Women grind their teeth. Still, the idea was more valid than appears on the surface, for it was not so much encouraging women to accept the homemaking role that was envisaged as encouraging them to accept the worker role. As it turned out, however, it was not preparing them to accept two roles but, let us say, one role and a half.

The profession of counseling was not equal to the challenge. The whole profession, not only the counseling of girls, has been caught up in the paradox of policy discussed in Chapter 3 above. The President's Commission on National Goals had articulated it like this:

> The status of the individual must remain our primary concern. All our institutions—political, social, and economic—must further enhance the dignity of the citizen, promote the maximum development of his capabilities, stimulate their responsible exercise, and widen the range and the effectiveness of opportunities for individual choice. . . .

But still:

> . . . the productive skills and the creativity of the American people have been major factors in the great economic achievements of the United States. The ability to produce has been closely allied with the system of education. Preparation of the individual for occupational competency through vocational education can be of unique assistance to the national economy during this period of technological, economic, and social change. . . . (Corwin and Clarke, 1969, p. 316).

The first of these directives would require counselors to lead girls to stop thinking of themselves as weak, unintelligent, incompetent, incapable; it would try to undo the damage that fifteen to twenty years of malsocialization had done to their self-concept. "The image a woman has of herself and the other members of her sex is not that of an autonomous, whole human being who is expected to contribute to the many and varied activities that constitute the life of a changing society in a changing world. She views herself as limited to very few roles in life. . . . She neither feels capable of, nor interested in, serving in other capacities—economic, political, academic, etc." (Bunch-Weeks, p. 7). A primary concern with maximum development of girls would direct counselors to enlarge girls' horizons, show them all the options open to them, supply them with accurate information, help them think boldly in terms of their highest potential and of ways to overcome hurdles (Eyde, 1970, p. 24–28). It would seek to release them from what Jo Freeman calls "the gilded cage" into which the socialization process consigns them.

But the second directive would lead counselors to steer them into the safe, especially clerical, jobs, no matter how much beyond that level their talents qualified them to reach. In this sense, counseling becomes merely "an institutionalized means of defending the existing social order" (Corwin, and Clarke, 1969, p. 316). Social adjustment becomes "the guiding principle, and the progressivism which had promised to redirect the spirit of education in the interests of the socially deprived [is] turned into an adaptive philosophy in defense of the status quo" (Corwin and Clarke, 1969, p. 316).

Critics leveled other serious charges against counseling also as it impinged specifically on girls. It was charged with being anti-intellectual (Eells, 1964, p. 37). It was charged with contributing to the perpetuation of sex-typing of jobs by steering girls into jobs sex-typed for women: "The guidance counselor at school is a great help! For instance, this year, when I went to check about next year's courses, she said to take a whole year of typing, instead of only one semester, so that I could get a better job in the future" (Elston, 1970). Counseling was charged with discouraging nonconformity and merely perpetuating old patterns. Thus one pamphlet issued by Movement Women cited this item from a Canadian Department of Labour release: "If you are a girl, marriage is the career you may have in mind. You will probably work in paid employment for a while before marriage. You may want to return to work after your family is grown up. You may even combine marriage with a career. Women are most numerous in such fields as teaching, office work, personal and domestic service, health service and welfare work. But they are making careers for themselves in practically all fields of work, and girls can find many interesting and rewarding opportunities if they care to look." In the meanwhile, though, learn to type. Instead of attempting to counteract all the forces that have robbed girls of self-confidence and a positive self-image, counseling has been charged with reinforcing them. Counseling has even been used, allegedly as a way of "cooling the mark out," of discouraging girls and women from doing anything about their grievances.

Some argue that it is unfair to expect counseling to overcome all the forces at work to determine the course of girls' lives. Some are defeatist: the investment of time and energy in career preparation before girls have settled the major issue, marriage, is almost wasted. The emphasis on marriage presents a roadblock that even the most dedicated counselor would be hard put to overcome. As Judith Blake Davis says, motherhood as a value is inculcated into girls from such an early age that alternatives are hardly given serious attention. Still, if girls and young women could be shown that there are some choices available to them, it might be possible for them to make more judicious decisions. For, as we shall see in Chapter 9, there are some variables that are, or can be, subject to at least a modicum of control.

REFERENCES

Bart, Pauline, "Depression in Middle-Aged Women: Some Sociocultural Factors," paper presented at meetings of Society for Study of Social Problems, 1968; "Mother Portnoy's Complaint," *Transaction,* 8 (Nov.–Dec. 1970), 69–74.

Bernard, Jessie, "Functions and Limitations in Counseling and Psychotherapy," in Donald A. Hansen (ed.), *Explorations in Sociology and Counseling* (Boston: Houghton Mifflin, 1969).

———, "The Paradox of the Happy Housewife," in Vivian Gornick and Barbara K. Moran (eds.), *51 Per Cent* (New York: Basic Books, 1971); *The Future of Marriage* (New York: World Book 1972).

Bettelheim, Bruno, "The Talented Woman in American Society," in Philip I. Mitterling (ed.), *Proceedings of the Conference on Talented Women and the American College* (1964, mimeographed).

Bunch-Weeks, Charlotte, *A Broom of One's Own* (n.d., mimeographed), p. 7.

Bureau of the Census, *Fertility of the Population: January 1969* Series P-20, (203), July 6, 1970, Table 1.

Burgess, E. W., and L. S. Cottrell, Jr., *Predicting Success or Failure in Marriage* (Englewood Cliffs, N.J.: Prentice-Hall, 1939).

Center for Research on the Acts of Man, University of Pennsylvania, Unpublished study.

Commission on the Status of Women, *1968: Time for Action,* Fourth National Conference, Washington, 1968.

Cooper, Sophia, "Career Patterns of Women," *Vocational Rehabilitation and Education Quarterly,* (13–14) (1963), 6 ff., 21–28.

Corwin, Ronald G., and Alfred C. Clarke, "Social Change and Social Values," in Donald Hansen (ed.), *Explorations in Sociology and Counseling* (Boston: Houghton Mifflin, 1969), p. 316.

Current Digest of the Soviet Press (Dec. 1968), 11.

Davis, Judith Blake, "Demographic Science and the Redirection of Population Policy," *Jour. Chronic Diseases,* 18 (Nov. 1965), 1195.

———, statement at hearings before subcommittee of the Committee on Government Operations, House of Representatives, 91st Congress, 1970, p. 68.

Dizard, Jan, *Social Change in the Family* (Chicago: Community and Family Study Center, University of Chicago, 1968), p. 1.

Economics and Research Branch, Department of Labour, Canada, *Looking Ahead to the World of Work.*

Eells, John S., Jr., "Women in Honors Programs: Winthrop College," in Philip L. Mitterling (ed.), *Proceedings of the Conference on Talented Women and the American College* (1964, mimeographed), p. 37.

Elston, Cindy, "At High School," *Quicksilver Times Supplement* (Oct. 18–28, 1970), p. 12.

Eyde, Lorraine D., "Eliminating Barriers to Career Development of Women," *Personnel and Guidance Journal,* 49 (Sept. 1970), 24–28.

Freeman, Jo Ann, *The Building of the Gilded Cage* (n.d. mimeographed).

Freedman, Mervin, *The College Experience* (San Francisco: Jossey-Bass, 1967).

Garfinkel, Stuart, "Work in the Lives of Women," paper prepared for International Union for the Scientific Study of Population (London, 1969), p. 5.

Ginzberg, Eli, et al., *Life Styles of Educated Women* (New York: Columbia University Press, 1966), p. 78.

Goldsen, Rose K., et al., *What College Students Think* (Princeton, N.J.: Van Nostrand, 1960), p. 218.

Gross, Louise and Phyllis MacEwan, "On Day Care," *Women, A Journal of Liberation* (Winter 1970), p. 28.

Mulvey, Mary Crowley, "Psychological and Social Factors in Prediction of Career Patterns of Women," *Genetic Psychology Monographs,* 68 (1963), 384.

Myrdal, Alva, and Viola Klein, *Women's Two Roles* (London: Routledge and Kegan Paul, 1966).

Nye, F. Ivan, "Personal Satisfactions," in F. Ivan Nye and Lois Wladis Hoffman (eds.), *The Employed Mother in America* (Chicago: Rand McNally, 1963), p. 321.

Orden, Susan and Norman M. Bradburn, "Working Wives and Marriage Happiness," *Amer. Jour. Sociol.,* 74 (Jan. 1969), 253–268.

Rheingold, J., *The Fear of Being a Woman* (New York: Grune and Stratton, 1964).

Rose, Arnold, "Factors Associated with the Life Satisfaction of Middle-Class, Middle-Aged Persons," *Marriage and Family Living,* 17 (Feb. 1955), 15–19.

Rossi, Alice, "Barriers to the Career Choice of Engineering, Medicine, or Science among American Women," in Jacquelyn A. Mattfeld and Carol G. Van Aken (eds.), *Women and the Scientific Professions* (Cambridge: M.I.T. Press, 1965).

Shea, John R., et al., *Dual Careers: A Longitudinal Study of Labor*

Market Experience of Women, vol. 1 (Columbus: Center for Human Resource Research, Ohio State University, 1970), p. 213.

Super, Donald E., *The Psychology of Careers* (New York: Harper, 1957), p. 76.

Turner, Ralph, "Is It Vive la Difference?" in report of a Women's Bureau conference, *Exploding the Myths* (Dec. 3, 1966), pp. 13–18.

United States Census of Population, 1960, *Employment Status and Work Experience,* Table 8, p. 61.

Veroff, Joseph, and Sheila Feld, *Marriage and Work in America* (Princeton, N.J.: Van Nostrand, 1970).

Washington Post, September 21, 1969.

Weller, Robert H., "The Employment of Wives, Role Incompatibility and Fertility," *Milbank Memorial Fund Quarterly,* 46 (Oct. 1968), 521.

Women's Bureau, *1969 Handbook on Women Workers* (Washington, D.C.: Department of Labor, 1969), pp. 32, 43.

9

Women at the Professional Level

Career Patterning

The discussions of role patterns so far has been fairly general. That is, it applies to women of all occupational levels. All have to struggle to find ways to reconcile their several functions. But for women at the highest levels, in the technical, scientific, and professional occupations, there are unique and peculiar additional problems. Not only do they, like other working mothers, have to find ways to provide for child care, but also, like their male confreres, they have the by-no-means ignorable problem of acquiring difficult professional skills and competencies before they enter their work roles and of maintaining them during interruptions, if any, in their work—or career—histories.

Thinking and policy have therefore taken quite different tacks in dealing with women in the several work-history patterns. For those in the lowest levels, on assistance rolls, policy has been designed to encourage—*coerce* would not be too strong a term—a two-role pattern. For women in the middle occupation and income brackets, who worked, when they did, because they enjoyed working or wanted to increase family income, there has been, despite recommendations by one commission after another, little positive encouragement in the form of help, either by government

179

or by industry, especially in the form of child-care assistance, but neither has there been, as in the era of the one-role ideology, positive and active discouragement. But for women in the highest levels to whom the term *career women* is sometimes pejoratively applied there has been, if anything, active discouragement, even in some cases hostility. The career woman is required to order her life in complete conformity to the demands of her profession and to pay whatever price is exacted for deviation from them. Some of the possible ways of doing this are summarized here.

There are four variables whose timing, at least theoretically, allows them to be partially controlled by professional women in planning how to accommodate their child-bearing and child-rearing functions to the demands of their careers: (1) age at marriage, (2) age at childbearing, (3) age at professional preparation, and (4) age of assumption or resumption of professional practice. These are certainly not independent variables; each depends on the others. The first will, of course, usually precede the second; and the third, the fourth.

It might well be argued that women actually do not have partial control over these variables. The pressure on them to marry, as just noted, is so great that they feel they must marry fairly young, for if they wait all the desirable men will be committed. They have a valid point there, too, for the optimum age at marriage, as judged in terms of stability under present circumstances, is 22 for women and 24 for men. With so much pressure put on them to marry ("Better dead than unwed") it is doubtful if there really is much choice involved. But at least theoretically some control is possible. The age at which they bear children is also only partially under control despite the increasing dependability of contraception. And the age at which professional preparation is undertaken may depend on a variety of factors, including availability of support and access to facilities.

Granting that there are practical forces limiting any young woman's choices, we can still examine some of the possibilities for different patternings. In general, eight kinds of patterns, subsumed under three general categories—early interrupted, late interrupted, and uninterrupted—are possible as shown. The numbers refer to the four major contingencies in the careers of women, namely (1) marriage, (2) childbearing, (3) professional preparation, and (4) assumption or resumption of professional practice.

Eight Career Patterns

A.	3	1	2	4		Early-interrupted pattern
B.	3	4	1	2	4	Late-interrupted pattern
C.	3	1	4	2	4	" " "
D.	1	3	4	2	4	" " "
E.	1	3	2	4		" " "
F.	1	2	3	4		Uninterrupted pattern
G.	1	–	3	4		" " "
H.	–	–	3	4		" " "

The length of the interruptions is, of course, itself a variable. It might be as brief as a short maternity leave or as long as the time it takes for a last child to reach college, the future seeming to tend more toward the first option than the second. Garfinkle (1969) reports "the rather astonishing change which is taking place in the work lives of women, namely that the effects of the birth of a child on work life continuity is rapidly diminishing" (p. 5). He reports many cases in which women work almost to the time of delivery "and then returning to work after a time lapse hardly longer than a somewhat lengthy vacation or the time their husband might require to recover from a fairly minor illness" (p. 5.). The crucial component is the timing of the break between *3* and *4* and its length.

The Early-Interrupted Pattern

It has become customary to derive an overall picture of "the average woman" in terms of an early-interrupted work history: labor-force participation until the birth of the first child, return when the last child is in school or soon thereafter.

Among talented women, Ginzberg's study showed about one-fourth in some form of interrupted pattern. Freedman reported an early-interrupted pattern as preferred among Vassar seniors (Freedman, 1967). And a study of undergraduates in a predominantly black college and also in a surburban community college also found this pattern the most preferred by both men and women.

Actually the early-interrupted pattern is probably the worst possible in terms of professional development. Havelock Ellis in his *Study of British Genius* noted that either very early marriage or fairly late marriage, or no marriage at all, was characteristic of achieving women. They thus "escaped from, or found a *modus vivendi* with, domestic and procreative claims." The early-interrupted pattern is contrary to all of these escapes. It interrupts the woman's career at a time when it is least stable, so that temporary defection is most serious; and when she herself still lacks the competence, aplomb, experience, and self-identity to cope with its costs.

Those who advocate or accept the early-interrupted pattern grant that some retooling or rust-removal may be required upon re-entrance into the professional field, and a variety of programs have been instituted to supply it. For certain occupations this may be a suitable solution. But for those in the learned, scientific, or technical professions, it is not auspicious; this holds true regardless of sex. Speaking of the interruption of careers of men by military service, J. Douglas Brown noted that the losses were probably irreparable:

> It will never be possible to estimate accurately the number of creative scientists and engineers who were lost from the flow of trainees because of the interruptions and diversions of careers arising from World War II. Experience in organized military activity may contribute greatly to maturing a man's capacity in dealing with his fellows [just as, of course, marriage and motherhood may contribute to the maturing of a woman's]. It does not, however, offer an effective substitute for the exact, integrated, and continuous training afforded by a scientific or engineering program in a university or by intensive specialization in creative effort in industry. Interruption in the development of a scientist or research engineer, as with a medical

doctor, appears to be costly in terms of quality and quantity of the end product. Too many men fail to return to their previous training programs or lose the momentum which carried them to the higher levels of attainment (Brown, 1954).

Women may lose their momentum also. Studies of the achievement motivation of women after graduation from college give equivocal results. One reported "a dramatic decrease in achievement motive [among 137 Radcliffe alumnae] between 5 and 10 years out of college" and attributed this "moratorium of achievement striving" to the assumption of family responsibilities during those years (Baruch, 1966, p. 102). But another study, of Jackson College graduates of the classes of 1953 and 1958, questioned five years after graduation and then again ten years after, found no such decline. In fact, this study found higher scores on achievement-striving among the older than among the younger subjects, suggesting an increase rather than a decline in the first decade after graduation (Eyde, 1968). Until we know more about the way motivations operate to lead women to re-enter active professional careers, little more can be said about how much reliance can be placed on its persistence.

Even if they do return, Alice Rossi, who very much disapproves of the early interrupted pattern, points out, the years of greatest achievement potential have been lost. The early-interrupted pattern should not, she argues, be "widely or uncritically accepted until we have better answers to the question concerning the effect this withdrawal has upon the contributions we may expect from her. If we judge from the dozens of researches Harvey Lehman has conducted on the relationship between age and achievement, the answer to this basic question must be a qualified 'not very much' " (Rossi, 1965, p. 102). This objection to the early-interrupted pattern on the basis of achievement has good research support. Lindsey P. Harmon, for example, studying the careers of science doctors, found "when the married women return to professional work they have returned to professional jobs that tend to be either teaching or research, but less frequently the balanced combination . . . characteristic of the men and of those women whose professional careers have been uninterrupted." This means, in effect, that they return "as an important reservoir for assistants and technicians and the less demanding professions, but only rarely for creative and original contributors to the more demanding professional fields" (Rossi, 1965, p. 107).

Ginzberg and his associates substantiated this criticism. They found that the achievement level of women with interrupted work histories was far below that of women with uninterrupted work histories, fewer than a third as many showing a high achievement level and five times as many showing a low achievement level (Table 9.1). It is quite possible that a selective bias

*Table 9.1. Achievement Level of Educated Women
by Career Patterns*

Achievement Level	Work History (in per cent)	
	Continuous	Broken
High	23	7
Good	41	10
Medium	29	47
Low	7	36
Total	100	100

SOURCE: Eli Ginzberg et al., *Life Styles of Educated Women* (New York: Columbia University Press, 1966) p. 100.

was at work here: the most highly motivated women may have been the ones who continued their work despite the distractions of family obligations, while for the unmotivated, marriage and children may have been an acceptable excuse for low achievement. Equally likely as an explanation, however, is the fact that the women with uninterrupted work histories were single or childless. Since work history and family situation were themselves closely related, it is expectable that family situation was also related to achievement.

The downward mobility characteristic of the early-interrupted pattern was demonstrated in a study of a less gifted population base on a representative national sample of 34,662 households.

In this sample it was found that women originally in professional and technical occupations tended to return to clerical and sales positions, and women originally in clerical and sales positions to (nondomestic) service jobs. "This pattern of downward mobility . . . appears to be related to extensive periods of absence from the labor force. . ." (Shea, 1970, p. 171).

Criticisms of the early-interrupted career pattern in terms of achievement and downward mobility are basically from the point of view of the optimum utilization of human resources; they evaluate the pattern in terms of the loss it implies in creativity or achievement. They apply to men as well as to women. For many women, loss in achievement is more than compensated for by the satisfactions they derive from their domestic role; but such women are likely to be in the terminated career category rather than in an interrupted pattern.

Subtler and more relevant from the self-actualization point of view is Alice Rossi's argument against the early-interrupted pattern: that if a woman is enticed to withdraw from her career for a number of years, her husband and children will evolve a style of living dependent on her contribution as wife and mother. When she seeks to return to her work, far more reorientation and readjustment on everyone's part is called for than would have been if all had become accustomed to her role as an independent and active professional from the beginning.

The Late-Interrupted Patterns (B, C, D, E)

The late-interrupted patterns appeal to young women who are not in any hurry to undertake motherhood at an early age although, like the young women opting for the early-interrupted pattern, they might want the companionship of marriage at a fairly early age (D, E). In any event, after graduation or marriage they go right into professional or graduate training and practice, remaining with it for a long enough time to acquire self-confidence and to prove their mettle. Some might feel secure enough in their professional identities after five or six years; others might want to postpone motherhood ten or even fifteen years. In either case, by the time they do choose to have children they will be in a better position psychologically, socially, professionally, and even financially, to clear the hurdles.

There was a time when higher education and marriage for men as well as women (D, E) were held to be incompatible. Students were expelled if or when they married; but reversal of this policy took place, first for men and then also for women, especially at the graduate level. The merit of marriage under these auspices is that it is initiated in an atmosphere in which both partners are assumed to have the privilege of intellectual pursuits. Such a pattern, established early in a marriage, should have a good chance to continue later on in the nonacademic world outside.

Among women not even ready to make the commitment required in institutionalized marriage, let alone motherhood, the delayed marriage conducive to career facilitation is sometimes made possible by relationships that supply intimacy and companionship without demanding a permanent commitment. On the campuses of many universities, young men and women are finding suitable ways of relating to one another in which it is taken for granted by both that women have legitimate intellectual interests. Marriage may or may not result. Either way it makes possible a period of development toward autonomy on the part of young women, obviates premature marriage which might have a stunting effect, and makes for greater psychological independence. In such unions there is no need for the young woman to put the young man's career ahead of her own.

Uninterrupted Patterns (F, G, H)

Since marriage itself need offer no obstacle to either professional training or practice, and if neither marriage nor children intervenes, as in pattern H, the career pattern is also uninterrupted. Although statistical data on labor-force participation of women do not tell us the proportion of women who fall into these several patterns, it can be assumed that practically all of the small number of women who never marry follow uninterrupted patterns, and most of the married but childless women probably do also.[1] In the Ginzberg sample, 91 per cent of the single women followed the H pattern; and 83 per cent of the married but childless women, pattern G.

Pattern F contemplates the possibility of marriage and children at a fairly early age, followed by professional training and uninterrupted practice thereafter. It is not a pattern that has received favorable consideration in the literature on career patterns for women for a number of reasons. Most thinking about careers has assumed a male model as standard; and there is a substantial research literature discouraging to a policy of early marriage.

In view of the assumptions against pattern F, it is difficult to make a persuasive case in its favor. But at least the data, however fragmentary, on which it rests deserve consideration. Two studies, one of women in social work, a profession sex-typed for women, and one of women with doctorates, showed that those who married and had their children before they received graduate or professional training were more likely to participate in the labor force on an uninterrupted basis than those who married after they had taken professional training (Astin, 1967; Tropman, 1968). It can be argued that only highly motivated women would have undertaken professional training after motherhood, so that a highly select population is involved. Still, even limiting the pattern to highly motivated women, it makes sense.

Another line of argument is more circuitous. It casts aside all assumptions based on male career patterns and tries to think

1. The marriage rates of professional women have been notoriously low. Among physicians who graduated from medical school between 1925 and 1940, 31 per cent had not married as reported in a study published in 1957; among social workers 30 years of age or over in 1950, 40 per cent had not; professional and managerial women in 1950 showed 38 per cent unmarried (professional administrators were less likely to be married than executives); among editors and reporters in 1950, 46 per cent were married; of women executives and those in high-level administrative positions, 53 and 55 per cent respectively were married (Bernard, 1964, pp. 313–314). In a study of women doctorates, the marriage rate was 52.7 per cent, or 59.4 per cent if religious were excluded. In the Ginzberg (1966) sample, 28 per cent had not married, a proportion lower than in most of the other studies, but still 4.5 times the proportion in the general population. The proportion of younger women who are married among professional women is higher than the proportion among the older, suggesting that the proportion of married is on the increase.

solely in terms of the way young women develop. We noted above that young women find it impossible to make serious career plans until they know who their husbands are going to be, for everything depends on that crucial choice. Further, many also find it impossible to think seriously beyond having children. They may give a kind of vague nod in the direction of some kind of work later on in their lives, but they lack genuine conviction. Since they really cannot think seriously in terms of a career until the urgent marriage-and-motherhood imperatives have been met, it would seem to be the part of wisdom to go with rather than against this tide. We might think of the period of, say, 18 to 22 years as the "motherhood" stage in a young woman's life, a stage she would pass through and "outgrow" or "get over." Following this line of thinking, we would take it for granted that she had to get motherhood "out of her system" before she could plan beyond it. By the time she was about 25 she would be ready to resume her training wherever she had left off and continue uninterruptedly into her profession with fresh rather than dated preparation, with no need for re-tooling.

Certainly a caveat with respect to too-early marriage is in order. Too-youthful marriages tend to be less stable than later ones, but not less stable than those delayed too long.[2] Alice Rossi (1965) emphasizes the loss of autonomy that young women experience when they marry young. Martinson (1955) concludes that young women tend to marry out of weakness rather than strength; and Hurley and Palonen (1967) advise against having children too early. Young marriages might require subsidies, perhaps in the form of long-term loans. Still, for many young women this timing of the two roles might prove optimal.

One of the pluses of this pattern has to do with the perspective in which it puts the lives of women. It accustoms us to see how small a part motherhood takes in the total life of a woman, how much in this day and age, it is a young woman's enterprise. It frees us to think of women in a wider context.

2. The optimum age at marriage in terms of stability is 24 for men and 22 for women. Marriages entered either before or after these ages are less stable. See United States Census of Population, 1960: *Age at First Marriage,* Table 10.

Quasi Interruptions: Part-Time Work

When we spoke of the "one-and-a-half-role" pattern above, we referred to women who assigned a merely casual importance to their jobs. But there are some women to whom work would be a serious investment even if undertaken only on a part-time basis. Alice Rossi (1965) believes that under certain conditions, part-time employment may be a good solution for mitigating interruptions; Myrdal and Klein (1965) do not.

Part-time work may take several forms: part-time the year round or either part-time or full-time work during less than a full year. The second, except in the case of school teachers, is only a euphemism for seasonal unemployment, having the disadvantages of both part-time and full-time work. Usually what is meant by part-time work is anything less than the customary 40-hour week the year round.

The practical obstacles to the part-time solution for the problems involved in the uninterrupted pattern are considerable. The proportion of all women who have been part-time workers in one form or another has remained fairly constant for the last two decades. What the possibilities are for increasing the supply of such employment under existing conditions we do not know; that would depend on the willingness not only of women but also of employers. In 1969, the proportion of the female labor force employed in voluntary part-time work—as distinguished from those working part-time involuntarily and from those who wanted part-time work but were unemployed—varied by age, being lowest in the very years when children were youngest. In 1971, Committee W of the AAUP was recommending that part-time academic appointments for both women and men be institutionalized with all the privileges and prerogatives of full-time appointments, an ideal prototype solution for many.

The situation for professional women may not be as stringent as that for other women. They can arrange their schedules to take care of their maternal responsibilities; those who have special gifts may find it possible to paint, write, or practice at home.

The Two-Career Family

In the form of so-called "antinepotism" rules, there has been a strong opposition to two-career families in the United States. The teaming-up of husbands and wives has been discouraged. In France, however, legal provision is made to ensure that in the civil service, the teaching profession, and other careers, the husband or wife of a person already employed in a given district should have a certain priority for posts in the same area. In the assignment of personnel in the Soviet Union, the general rule, despite numerous exceptions, is that husbands and wives should not be separated. Not just a system of joint fellowships, but one, where practicable, of joint appointments (a system just the opposite to that represented by the antinepotism rules currently on the books), if not always enforceable, would help women in the pursuit of happiness. The idea is to think not in terms of separate, isolated individuals but in terms of an organic unit consisting of husband and wife, allowing for individualism or individuating as desired.

In the case of at least some women, finally, the integration of family and career is achieved in a relationship that is called the colleagueship. Where both husband and wife are in the same profession,[3] they may operate as a team, or at least in tandem as they did under the domestic system of production. Such unions seem to be remarkably successful. In a study of women who competed for the 1942–43 Westinghouse Science Scholarship awards, it was found that "three out of five had husbands in the same or allied fields and were unanimous in stressing the support their husbands gave in their attempt to complete their advance training and remain in their fields after marriage. Two cases of col-

---

3. In 1967, 40.0 per cent of all husbands who were professional, technical, and kindred workers were married to wives who were also professional, technical, and kindred workers. See Women's Bureau, *1969 Handbook on Women Workers*, p. 38. This does not, of course, mean that they were in identical professions or technical work. Among married women with professional and engineering degrees, it is reported that 55 per cent had married men with the same degrees (Women Engineering Graduate Society of Women Engineers, 1964).

leagueship, one at Harvard University in the behavioral and social sciences, and one at California in biology, are presented in autobiographical detail in *Academic Women*. The going may still be rough even with a husband to offer support, but at least the split in the woman's life is reduced and the entire burden of her career is not placed on her shoulders alone. She does not have to pursue her happiness in a path 180 degrees apart from his.

Although the so-called "androgynous life" of wives and husbands in the two-career family has been greeted as the wave of the future (Bird, 1968), it should be noted that in such marriages, the wife's career is almost always subordinate to that of the husband. In one study of 53 such two-career families, the wife's career was viewed as merely a kind of hobby, an avocation rather than a vocation, in a substantial proportion with a traditional orientation. The woman's primary role was defined as that of a wife rather than of a professional, and the husband was the status-giver and source of income. In some, the neotraditional, the wife's income was used and her profession was taken more seriously, but she still had sole responsibility for the children. Among those with an egalitarian orientation, some women deliberately kept their incomes down. Marriages in which the wife's income was greater than the husband's—labeled "matriarchal" by the researcher—were characterized by more problems than were the other three types (Paloma, 1970). The two-role ideology has a great deal to recommend it for helping women pursue happiness, but it is far from a guarantee of success.

The one clear and unequivocal conclusion that emerges from all the studies on the career patterns of women is that career pattern is not a simple or unidimensional variable; certainly the research so far has not located all the relevant variables or measured their impact convincingly. "Given the existing social arrangements," there does not seen to be any ideal way to reconcile the domestic functions assigned to women with the demands of their work roles as currently defined.

It is argued by some radical women that in view of the fact that we are going to need the services of professional women and are going to have to offer women attractive alternatives to motherhood, it is in the public interest as well as the interest of women themselves to take the career problems of women seriously, to make the careers of women as respectable and worthy as those of men, to see their career problems as amenable to rational solutions, to institutionalize them and hence render them predictable and assimilable. And so long as women seek careers, they should be permitted to run the course with a minimum of handicaps.

But while some women are insisting that career patterns of women be made as nearly like those of men as possible, there are others who are asking if this is not actually just one more illustration of sexism? Is this not accepting the male pattern as the standard against which to judge all patterns? Is this not taking for granted that the careers of men are *the* correct, proper, appropriate patterns for everyone? That the careers of all must follow the male pattern or be unacceptable? That the values implicit in achievement are the best values for everyone? Along with many others, including young male radicals, they ask if the game is worth the candle.

Is the Game Worth the Candle?

The concept of career leads to the heart of one of the major upheavals we are undergoing today. It is tied up with the whole value-complex associated with achievement. Freud pointed out that we paid for civilization and its achievements with a sacrifice of personal gratifications; what men gave to their work was what they took from their families (Freud, 1958). And Talcott Parsons (1949) reminded us that in no sector of our society did "the dominant patterns stand in sharper contrast to those of the occupational world than in the family." Career success demands qualities that are precisely opposite to those demanded for family life. The work and family roles of men must therefore be kept strictly segregated lest one interfere with the other, and usually if there is a conflict it must be resolved in favor of the career. The payoff for this enormous investment in achievement by men in their occupational roles has been the enormous productivity of the economy. In this context, the powerful achievement drive implied in a career was functional. It might extort enormous costs from the individually driven men and their families, but it created affluence.

Young radicals in the 1960's were beginning to challenge the validity of this view. They looked around at their parents' generation and decided that the game of success—the rat race—was not worth the candle of human deprivation that it cost. Erik Grønseth, a Norwegian sociologist, concluded from a careful analysis of the ramifications of the occupational roles of men that although as now structured they might be functional for the status quo, they were nevertheless dysfunctional for society as a whole: "What is 'functional' for the short-term upkeep of a competitively, compensatory 'achievement'-oriented, 'open'-class social order, and for an integration based on this kind of 'achievement'-principle, may in the long run prove totally disintegrative" (Grønseth, 1970).

Disintegrative for marriage as well as for a whole society. We have quoted research evidence on the destructive effects on marriage of too-great role specialization. The emphasis there was on the wife's role, and the implication was that the wife should diversify her marital roles to make her life and her marriage more satisfying both to herself and to her husband.

But the implications for the husband's role are also pertinent. For a husband-father to be successful in the provider role he must invest enormous amounts of time in his work, time that could otherwise be devoted to his family. He must cultivate competitiveness, aggressiveness, rationality, calculation—traits, as Parsons has pointed out, not compatible with those required for happy family relationships. Thus (this study reported) the more successful the father was in his career, the less likely his marriage was to be successful. To avoid this result:

The husband can simply hold back and not get overinvolved in his occupational pursuits. Recent work in occupational sociology indicates that this may in fact be occurring within certain middle class occupations, especially those in the large corporations. Frequently noted, in this regard, are the problems of middle management. At this level, the number of higher positions drops off precipitously and one of the adaptations to the strain inherent in the quest for promotion is simply to stop trying and transfer energies from the corporation to the family (Dizard, 1968, p. 79).

Philip Slater also raises questions about using the male concept of career, as it is now institutionalized, as the standard for either women or men. Perhaps, after all, it isn't that worthy of emulation. Perhaps male careers could also bear a bit of looking into. What would be wrong with a career pattern in which success does not demand the complete absorption the present male pattern does? For both men and women who preferred it?

In *Academic Women* it was pointed out that not all women were willing to invest this much of their lives in their careers; they did not want to put all their eggs in one basket. In a male context, such an attitude seems frivolous, lacking in seriousness. Now Philip Slater suggests that maybe these women were making more humane choices than the career-stricken men:

> "Career" is in itself a masculine concept (i.e., designed for males in our society). When we say "career" it connotes a demanding, rigorous, preordained life pattern, to whose goals everything else is ruthlessly subordinated—everything pleasurable, human, emotional, bodily, frivolous. It is a stern Calvinistic word. When a man asks a woman if she wants a career, it is intimidating. He is saying, are you willing to suppress half of your being as I am, neglect your family as I do, exploit personal relationships as I do, renounce all personal spontaneity as I do? Naturally she shudders a bit and shuffles back to the broom closet. She even feels a little sorry for him and bewails the unkind fate that has forced him against his will to become such a despicable person. The perennial success of this hoax perhaps contributes to the low opinion that men so often have of feminine intelligence (an opinion which, as any teacher knows, is otherwise utterly unfounded).
>
> A more effective (revolutionary, confronting) response would be to admit that a "career" thus defined, is indeed undesirable—that (now that you mention it) it seems like a pernicious activity for any human being to engage in, and should be eschewed by both men and women. Of course, she doesn't want a "career," nor do most humans, with the exceptions of a few males crazed, by childhood deprivation or Oedipal titillation, with insatiable desires for fame, power, or wealth. What she wants is a meaningful and stimulating activity, excitement, challenge, social satisfactions—all the things

that middle-class males get from their jobs whether they are defined as "careers" or not. Rarely is she willing, however, to pay the price that masculine narcissism seduces men into paying in our society. She therefore accepts the definition of herself as the inferior sex, instead of adopting the revolutionary stance of the black militant ("black is beautiful"), and saying: "My unwillingness to sacrifice a host of human values to my personal narcissism and self-aggrandizement makes me the superior sex."

Such a stance would in fact liberate both sexes: Women would be freed from the suffocating stagnation of the artificial domestic role in which they have been imprisoned; men would be liberated from their enslavement to the empty promise (ever receding, always redefined as just out of reach, and unsatisfying even when grasped), of "success." Both could then live in a gratifying present, instead of an illusory future and an ill-remembered past (Slater, 1970).

Philip Slater is here shamelessly plagiarizing the ideas of Movement Women who propose to do precisely what he proposes: liberate both women and men from the crippling effects of artificial role constrictions. Adjusting the Establishment to the lives of women rather than the lives of women to the Establishment.

References

Astin, Helen S., "Personal and Environmental Factors Associated with the Participation of Women Doctorates in the Labor Force," (mimeographed, 1967).

Baruch, Rhoda, *The Achievement Motive in Women: A Study of the Implications for Career Development* (Unpublished doctoral dissertation, Harvard, 1966), p. 102.

―――, *The Interruption and Resumption of Women's Careers* (Harvard Studies in Career Development, No. 60, 1966).

Bernard, Jessie, unpublished study of students at the Federal City College, Washington, D. C., and Montgomery Junior College, Bethesda, Md.

―――, *Academic Women* (University Park: Pennsylvania State University Press, 1964).

Bird, Caroline, *Born Female, The High Cost of Keeping Women Down* (New York: McKay, 1968), Chapter 8.

Brown, J. Douglas, "Meeting Requirements for Scientific, Engineering, and Managerial Manpower," in William Haber et al. (eds.), *Man-*

power in the United States: Problems and Policies (New York: Harper, 1954), p. 194.

Dizard, Jan, *Social Change in the Family* (Chicago: Community and Family Study Center, University of Chicago, 1968), p. 79.

Eyde, Lorraine D., "Work Motivation of College Alumnae: Five-Year Followup," *Jour. Counseling Psych.,* 15 (March 1968), 199–202.

Freedman, Mervin, *The College Experience* (San Francisco: Jossey-Bass, 1967), Chapter 10.

Freud, Sigmund, *Civilization and Its Discontents* (Garden City, N.Y.: Doubleday-Anchor, 1958), pp. 50–51.

Garfinkle, Stuart, "Work in the Lives of Women," paper prepared for International Union for the Scientific Study of Population, London, 1969, p. 5.

Ginzberg, Eli, et al., *Life Styles of Educated Women* (New York: Columbia University Press, 1966).

Grønseth, Erik, "The Dysfunctionality of the Husband Provider Role in Industrialized Societies," paper prepared for the 7th World Congress of Sociology, Varna, 1970.

Harmon, Lindsey P., *Profiles of the Ph.D.'s in the Sciences,* NAS-NRC pub. no. 1292 (1965), p. 61.

Hurley, John R., and Donna P. Palonen, "Marital Satisfaction and Child Density among University Student Parents," *Jour. Mar. and Fam.,* 29 (Aug. 1967), 483–484.

Martinson, Floyd M., "Ego Deficiency as a Factor in Marriage," *Amer. Sociol. Rev.,* 20 (April 1955), 161–164.

Myrdal, Alva, and Viola Klein, *Women's Two Roles* (London: Routledge and Kegan Paul, 1956), p. 162.

Paloma, Margaret M., "The Myth of the Egalitarian Family: Familial Roles and the Professionally Employed Wife," paper prepared for meetings of American Sociological Association (Aug. 1970).

Parsons, Talcott, "The Social Structure of the Family," in Ruth Nanda Anshen (ed.), *The Family; Its Function and Destiny* (New York: Harper, 1949), p. 262.

Rossi, Alice, "Barriers to the Career Choice of Engineering, Medicine, or Science among American Women," in Jacqueline A. Mattfeld and Carol G. Van Aken (eds.), *Women and the Scientific Professions* (Cambridge: M.I.T. Press, 1965).

Shea, John R., et al., *Dual Careers: A Longitudinal Study of Labor Market Experience of Women,* vol. 1 (Columbus: Center for Human Resources Research, Ohio State University, 1970), p. 171.

Slater, Philip E., "What Hath Spock Wrought?—Freed Children, Chained Mothers," in *The Pursuit of Loneliness, American Culture at the Breaking Point* (Boston: Beacon Press, 1970), reproduced in *Washington Post,* March 1, 1970.

Tropman, John E., "The Married Professional Social Worker," *Jour. Mar. and Fam.,* 30 (Nov. 1968), 661–665.

V

Protest

The assumptions on which rest the policies, programs, and plans for helping women reconcile their work and domestic roles when they conflict are now being challenged by a vocal and articulate and analytically sophisticated group of women. President Kennedy's statement was a brave try. But as the radical women are now teaching us to see, it assumed as a matter of course an unchanged status quo. Policy makers might challenge, as indeed they did, the sexual division of labor. But the sexual differentiation of functions entered their thinking only marginally. The pursuit of happiness for women, radical women insist, also demands modification of the Establishment. They were not to permit policy makers to escape the implications of the demographic revolution. No more than conventional women were these radical women unified in their goals or programs. But they did see that approaching the problem only by way of the job or career side of the dilemma was wholly inadequate. The sexual allocation of functions must also be re-examined and revised. Why, they asked, should all the costs of reconciling the contradictory pressures on women have to be borne by women alone?

A Personal Note

Although, as indicated in Chapter 1, I am indebted to Movement Women for many insights, it goes without saying that I do not speak for them. No one does. They are quite capable of speaking for themselves, and they reject the very idea that anyone should speak for them. Nor do all members endorse all the positions cited here, but all concur in the necessity for a radical—in the literal "root-and-branch" sense—restructuring of society, especially the sexual specialization of functions. For this goal, standard forms of protest are not adequate.

I have selected for discussion what I know best about Movement Women from my own contacts with them and from the burgeoning available literature. Some of them will fault my selection of emphases as giving too bland a picture of their feelings, too academic a statement of the issues, too sociological an interpretation of the Movement's functions. They would have preferred more blood-and-guts: "Our anger is our message! Remove that and you miss the whole point, you defang us! The specific things we say or do aren't half so important as the rage we express." I recognize that another selection of emphases could give such a daimonic or Dionysian picture. If the impression I leave is too Apollonian, it is my view, not theirs. Believe them, not me.

10

The Protesters

Functional Sharing, Not Concessions

All the thinking so far reported, and the facts upon which it is based, follow deeply rutted grooves, some more than others, but all to some extent. All the research, all the policies, all the ideas take as given the permanence, even the inevitability, of "existing social arrangements," that is, of current ways of institutionalizing both work and family relations. The present sexual specialization of functions and division of labor are taken for granted. Of proposed changes, some may ask, "Why?" But rarely do any ask, "Why not?"

But now there is a generation of radical women to whom much of this discussion sounds flat, stale, and unprofitable. They do ask, "Why not?" about changes. Perhaps equally subversive is their question, "Why?" about "existing social arrangements." For just as young campus radicals have asked us to re-examine the university, and black militants have questioned all our work and educational institutions, so these young women ask us to re-examine the functional specialization in the family.

The only sexual specialization of function they accept is the actual bearing of children, and even regarding this function there are some who look forward to the surrogate or "artificial womb . . . as a humane and liberating development for women" that will free them from the nine-month gestation period. They do not take it for granted that child rearing is the exclusive function of women; they propose that men share with them the responsibility for it. Child rearing is the most important function in any society; it should be everyone's responsibility—our's, men's as well as women's.

They do not allow men to escape merely by assuming a liberal stance, agreeing to open all jobs to women or helping them so that they can perform the "two roles." More is required: not only permitting women to share the jobs men have appropriated but also themselves taking on functions women have hitherto been specialized to perform; it is not only a negative matter of removing job barriers but also a positive one of sharing all responsibilities.

Parenthetical Note

Before describing who these young women are, a parenthetical note. There is not likely soon, or ever, to be a definitive study of the Women's Liberation Movement. The members would not cooperate with such a study; Movement Women do not want to be defined by outsiders. (I hope this description is not taken as an attempt to impose a definition on them; it is intended only as a statement of the way the Movement looks to me.) They recognize no spokeswomen. No one speaks for them. They recognize no leaders. No elite. No representative. They reject the media attempts to personalize them, to exploit colorful personalities among them:

> . . .the mass media work to serve interests directly opposed to our own. For example, we are attempting to build, within our movement, nonexploitative ways of relating to one another based on trust and concern rather than political expediency. We have serious personal/political intentions in breaking down hierarchical and elitist structures, and for experimenting with leaderless groups and collective decision making. In dealing with the media these revolutionary principles and practices are destroyed. The media work to create leaders, they know no way of relating to us on our own terms. Being interviewed and presented as a leader is a real ego trip—the media bring out the most counter-revolutionary traits in people. Elitism, dissension, and division are the ultimate results.

Creating leaders also increases the power of the mass media to define our movement for us. What the media-created leader says becomes a standard, usually very restrictive, for the whole movement. Then the press discredits the entire movement by discrediting the leader through attacking her personal life rather than dealing with her politics. . . . The media-created liberated woman is not merely unusual and exceptional, but a total weirdo—a bra-burner, man-hater, lesbian, sickie!

Each time we respond to the mass media we legitimize them and the reality they are defending, and we risk sacrificing all that we are working for. It is time to call a halt to all dealings with the mass media—no more interviews, no more documentaries, no more special coverage. We don't need them and we don't want them.

To respect their position as expressed here, which I honor, I am violating the canons of scholarly work and withholding citations to the work of specific women when I quote it except when it is a report or analysis of scientific research.[1] My own integrity is the only guarantee I can offer that I am using bona fide materials in context. Nor do I single out individual women for special attention.

Who They Are

Without stopping to try to explain why the Women's Liberation Movement arose precisely when it did, a brief historical overview of it will help to put it in perspective.

It may sound amusing to speak in terms of stages of development of a movement that emerged as an entity only in the late

1. The main sources have been *Female Liberation Newsletter; New Left Review; Motive* (March-April 1969 issue); *No More Fun and Games, A Journal of Female Liberation (The Female State); Revolutionary Age; Up from Under; Voice of the Women's Liberation Movement; Women, A Journal of Liberation; Notes from the Second Year: Women's Liberation.* In addition, the numerous other mimeographed papers circulated by individual groups, especially the papers published by the New England Free Press. The names of the women quoted or cited include Fran Ansley, Ti-Grace Atkinson, Judi Bernstein, Judith Brown, Charlotte Bunch-Weeks, Ellen Cantrow, Joanne Cooke, Dana Densmore, Roxanne Dunbar, Beverly Jones, Diane Kadish, Joan Jordan, Stella Kingsbury, Ann Koedt, Laurel Limpus, Susan Lydon, Nancy Mann, Kate Millett, Juliet Mitchell, Peggy Morton, Ellen O'Donnell, Cynthia Ozick, Kathie Sarachild, Linda Seese, Meredith Tax, Betsy Warrior, Marilyn Salzman Webb, and Myrna Wood.

1960's. Still, in our fast-paced society stages follow one another at a dizzying rate. In general, several distinct stages, perhaps five, can be delineated in the history of the Women's Liberation Movement. During the first stage it was still within the womb of the New Left, sharing its civil rights and peace convictions. The second stage was one of increasing disillusion with the New Left and growing rage at its male chauvinism, culminating in a third, or transitional, stage or secession or liberation. There followed a stage of astounding expansion as more and more women were attracted to the movement, women not at all of the original New Left orientation. This stage was also characterized by widespread media publicity, no respectable journal feeling it could afford not to have at least one issue devoted to it. The reaction against this media definition of the movement referred to above inaugurated a fifth stage, preparation for the long haul, working out solutions to problems of definition, strategy, tactics, communication, means, ends, formulating issues, analyzing trends, reaching out, learning, teaching.

Because so much of the character of the movement was determined by the women who initiated it, an introductory glance at who they were is in order here. Despite an almost virulent anti-elitism, they were without doubt an elite group themselves, belonging to that 7 or 8 per cent who were found by Elizabeth Drews in her study of talented high school girls to be both talented and motivated, and to the 7 or 8 per cent who were pioneers among the women in the class of 1961 as reported by Alice Rossi. But they are far from homogeneous.

Diversity

No more than their campus and black counterparts were the original Movement Women a homogeneous, compact, formally structured organization. They were ideologically diverse—Marxist, Maoist, Fidelist, Marcusean, Quaker, Christian, anarchist, passionately environmentalist and conspicuously non- even anti-Freudian. Some were nonideological.

They were also occupationally diverse. One group included a nurse's aid, a poet-mother, a student, a welfare mother, a biochemist, a teacher, a computer programmer, and a former prostitute.[2] Other groups included academic women and novelists.

They were far from standardized as personalities. Some enjoyed "the colorful dress of a turned-on generation of women who are asserting themselves as females as well as intellectual-politicos," but others could hardly wait for uniforms, hopefully culottes with pockets. (This suggestion would win my vote). Still others objected to the very thought of a uniform. Adopting a uniform "would simply be substituting one restriction for another. The problem is not current fashion per se; it's the rigidity with which it is prescribed by the fashion industry. We are not liberated unless we can choose freely between a hair shirt and a sequined dress. We must fight conformity, not develop our own." Some enjoyed "being women who love men" while others were so outraged by the aggressive, the predatory, the competitive, and destructive male that they would gladly have seen him and all his kind gathered in preserves where they could no longer disrupt human communities. Some accepted the existence of sociologically relevant sex differences but deplored them as evidence of brainwashing; others were agnostic on the subject. Some were married and some were not, although marital status per se was not important in a culture that accepted unofficial unions.

They differed, finally, also in style. The wit and humor of a Pat Mainardi stood out, for wit and humor are not usual qualities of revolutionaries, but the scholarly analyses of a Kate Millett, the heavy academicism of a Naomi Weisstein, the Faustian passion of a Roxanne Dunbar, the exquisite tenderness of an Ellen O'Donnell were also all part of the movement's literature. Their journals differed also, each with its own stamp. There was not, in any of them, the superficiality that goes under the name of sophistication in the slick journals; but there were passion and commitment and intellectual sophistication in most of them.

Young, White, Middle-class

A member of one group tells us that they "all fit the young, white, middle-class, activist description." And the first national

---

2. Compare with occupational distribution of women in the labor force, Table 6.6.

Women's Liberation Conference in November 1968 with representatives from 30 states all over the country, was also described
as "lily-white and . . . middle class."

Young women who were in their twenties in the 1960's are
members of a cohort raised in that strange, as yet incompletely
accounted for, postwar period characterized by what Betty
Friedan has labeled the feminine mystique. All of a sudden it
seemed (though of course it was not all that sudden) middle-
class women reverted to nineteenth-century "one-role" models of
femininity. They left college, married early, had lots of babies,
baked bread (!), wove fabrics, and in general sought self-fulfillment in togetherness in the cave (Cassara, 1962). It passed. By
the 1960's young women were returning to school and to the professions. But almost certainly many of the young women reared in
the heyday of the feminine mystique were scarred by it and were
beginning to react against it by the 1960's.

One young woman, for example, describes her anger with her
mother's acceptance of a subordinate and secondary position in
the family:

> . . .our lives were shaped by two predominating facts: first, that my
> mother's work was understood to be a sort of high-quality diver-
> sion, and that my father's was really the work that counted; second,
> that my father and I were the real centers of my mother's life. . . .
> My mother was terribly unsure of herself, distrusted her perfectly
> good mind and imagination and—albeit with frequent humor—was
> continually self-deprecating.

The "lily-whiteness" of Movement Women was by no means
an expression of racism. Quite and completely the contrary: it
troubled them. In fact, one Movement Woman noted that it was
from black women they had learned what women were capable
of. In their Movement apprenticeship days with SNCC,

> White women saw the black matriarchal society and began to dis-
> cover an alternative to the lives of their white, middle-class
> mothers [presumably of the feminine mystique generation]. We
> realized the biological-inferiority-of-women argument to be a lie
> and a myth. We saw [black] women rule their own roosts, not
> merely deciding what color car to buy. We noted that the leader-

ship of the Southern grassroots organization—MFLU and Mississippi Freedom Democratic Party (MFDP)—was female. . . . At
the same time, we saw the dangers of the matriarchal society—the
oppression of black men. We do not advocate such a society.

Despite the leadership contributed by black women in SNCC—
Ruby Doris Smith Robinson was the most powerful woman in the
organization—their intellectual contributions, Movement Women
noted, were ignored.

Like their white male counterparts, Movement Women cov-
eted the unchallengeable issues that black militants had. The
black cause was so just, so fair, so irrefutable in principle that
any revolutionary movement would want to have it on its side.
The Movement Women had more right to its support in terms of
history than others, for there had been a long tradition associ-
ating the issues in the abolition movement and the woman's rights
movement in the nineteenth century. In fact, the legal status of
black people had been designed on the pattern of the legal status
of women, as Gunnar Myrdal (1944) told us a generation ago:

> In every society there are at least two groups of people, besides the
> Negroes, who are characterized by high social visibility expressed
> in physical appearance, dress, and patterns of behavior, and who
> have been "suppressed." We refer to women and children. Their
> present status, as well as their history and their problems in so-
> ciety, reveal striking similarities to those of the Negroes. . . . In
> the historical development of these problem groups in America
> there have been much closer relations than is now ordinarily re-
> corded. In the earlier common law, women and children were
> placed under the jurisdiction of the paternal power. When a legal
> status had to be found for the imported Negro servants in the
> 17th century, the nearest and most natural analogy was the status
> of women and children. The ninth commandment—linking to-
> gether women, servants, mules, and other property—could be in-
> voked, as well as a great number of other passages of Holy Scrip-
> ture. . . . The paternalistic idea . . . held the slave to be a sort of
> family member and in some way—in spite of all differences—placed
> him beside women and children under the power of the pater-
> familias."

It was tempting to show how closely parallel women and
blacks were in high social visibility, ascribed attributes, rational-

ization of status, accommodation attitudes, and discrimination;
and throughout the writings of Movement Women there were re-
curring references to some women as "Aunt Toms," as "field niggers" (in contrast to men who were "house niggers"), and other
black analogies. But others rejected this borrowing of issues as
devaluing them for use by black people:

> We should not . . . imitate the rhetoric of the Black movement. It
> must be frustrating for Black people to see their language taken
> out of context and destroyed not only by the society's media, but
> also by young white radicals, and now by women. Phrases like
> "Aunt Tom," "Jane Crow Law," and "shuffling" have no place in our
> movement. These terms have specific meaning for Black people,
> male and female. Language which is historically and socially at
> odds with the subject of analysis not only cheapens one's analysis,
> but is an insult to the absolutely necessary struggle of the Black
> people in this country, a struggle necessarily related to our own.

Some of the Movement Women dreamed hopefully of uniting
black and white women in a joint attack on racism. "There is now
the possibility of the split between black and white workers being breached by women, black and white—cutting across the
color line through organization on the basis of sex—raising specific demands to meet the needs of women and children and re-
unifying the working class." But it was hard for most black
women to take the grievances of white women seriously. Though
they recognized themselves as victims of both racism and sexism,
racism seemed to them far more urgent than sexism. Thus, quite
aside from any antiracial theoretical position of their own, Movement Women were overwhelmingly—and guiltily—white. A situation not of their own choosing.

The Movement Women were also middle class, but not entirely. One woman described the wretched rural poverty she grew
up in, as the daughter of a sharecropper, grandchild of an Indian
woman and a drunken Irishman, moving from one farm to another. Another was a member of one of the richest dynasties—
banking and oil—in the United States. One was the daughter of
a coal-miner. As though forestalling the expectable charge of
deviance, one young woman described her own archetypically
middle-class background, in part, like this:

My family is a perfectly normal American family—the kind that might produce an astronaut. My mother is an excellent cook and seamstress who has an R.N. and a beautiful laugh. . . . My father is a Methodist minister. . . . My sister is a high-school senior who's going to major in Home Ec. My brothers are a pre-ministerial college senior, a sports-and-art-loving high-school junior and a nine-year old Cub Scout. I was a Girl Scout, myself, and I took piano, ballet, drama and swimming lessons, went to scout and church camps, sang in choirs and choruses and folk groups. . . . Last June I graduated from Randolph-Macon Woman's College.

It was Christian idealism that motivated her to find shelter under the hospitable ideological umbrella of the Women's Liberation Movement. It had become clear to her that dealing with the problems raised by women demanded "basic changes in our assumptions about the organization of society—from the family to the school to the church to the economy to the state. . . . All this is clearly Christian. . . . It assumes working for justice and equality and dignity 'on earth.' "

Intellectually Sophisticated

However diverse they were in occupation, ideology, background, and personality, most Movement Women were intellectually as well as emotionally committed. They were activist, to be sure, but they were not necessarily anti-intellectual. Their convictions may not always have grown out of intellectual analysis; but most felt they had to have an intellectual defense for them. They were admittedly not objective; they were selective. But they insisted that what they selected be intellectually respectable.

Some Movement Women dipped their pens into their veins to write on the basis of their own experience what men had sometimes written with pale ink on the basis of highly derivative research findings. Most were familiar with the relevant literature. They were, in fact, essentially translators into the language of activism of the findings of objective research. What the researchers may have said in dull, inert statistics and tables, they said in the stirring rhetoric of revolution. Where, for example, the social psychologists might speak of socialization, they found programming or brainwashing, or, as one of their forebears did 60 years ago; "domestication" (Coolidge, 1912). Whereas researchers studied "attitudes toward feminism" (Kirkpatrick, 1955), Movement Women spoke of *male chauvinism* or *sexism*. Discrimination was translated as *oppression*. A functionalist might say precisely the same things as these women said. They might, for example, make the same role analyses (Lopata, 1966). But when Jessie Bernard (1942) or Helen Lopata (1966) analyzed the social role of the housewife, it sounded like a matter-of-fact description; when Movement Women did, it sounded like a call to arms. When the functionalist made an analysis, it sounded, whatever his avowed intention might be, like a justification or rationalization, not merely like an explanation. When Movement Women made analyses they sounded like indictments. At a time, it might be added parenthetically, when radical men were rejecting the whole theoretical basis for functionalism—at a meeting organized by the radical caucus of the Eastern Sociological Society in 1969, the very use of the term *functionalism* produced jeers and guffaws of contempt—Movement Women were thoroughgoing structure-functionalists. Their analyses were in terms of a system or establishment or culture that programmed its members from early infancy to perform certain functions for its—not their own—benefit and brainwashed them to like it.

Why They Are

Unlike the young women attracted to the hippie subculture or the "groupies" attracted to the acid-rock subculture, many of whom allegedly accept and even seek subservient, even masochistic, roles vis-à-vis men (Davidson, 1969), Movement Women will settle for nothing less than equality. The original organizational impetus for the Women's Liberation Movement came from the shock of having such equality denied to them by radical men, and they have not recovered. Radical to begin with, they were further radicalized by their treatment, first in the civil rights movement and then in the student protest movement.

A pattern of rejection of leadership for women in the radical movement had originally been set in SNCC (Student Non-violent Coordinating Committee) in a situation where it might have had some rationale, for Northern white women in the South were not permitted to move about freely, especially after dark, nor, as a corollary, permitted to use project funds or cars. Where all white workers were in constant jeopardy, the white women were especially vulnerable. It was understandable, however much resented, that they were not permitted to undertake the more dangerous exposed tasks. That policy seemed to women far less justifiable, however, when it was taken over by SDS (Students for a Democratic Society). Women who had never felt oppressed before came to feel so now.

They were not even listened to. "How many times," asks one indignant woman, "have you seen a woman enter the discussion only to have it resume at the exact point from which she made her departure, as though she had never said anything at all? How many times have you seen men get up and actually walk out of a room while a woman speaks, or begin to whisper to each other as she starts?" It is hard for women to speak out in public at best, and "in that kind of hostile, unresponsive atmosphere, it is difficult for anyone to speak in an organized, stringent manner." Insulted, angered, ignored, "she wonders why she is bothering at all."

One young male informant, when asked if it was true that at meetings the men might sometimes stop just long enough to let a woman talk but as soon as she stopped, pick up where they had left off, replied, after turning the question over in his mind thoughtfully, "Yes, that's about the way it is." Why? Another thoughtful pause. Then: Strategy was a mind-reading act. You had to know how the opposition would act and react to what you did. The opposition was male. The men understood better than the women did what to expect from them. Women read men one way; men, another. Strategy based on the way women read the male opposition just didn't seem to fit the facts. It was as simple as that. The men do listen to the chicks. Even patiently. "But what they say just doesn't sound relevant. So we just go on, as they say, as though they hadn't said anything. So far as we can tell, they haven't. Men on opposite sides of the barricades understand one another better than women understand either side." What could women actually contribute? (As he and a male companion who had been sitting quietly next to him got up to leave, the companion looked back over his shoulder and said, "They don't listen to me, either.")

Another informant had a similar apologia:

> When a man vents his hatred of capitalism you know he knows what he's talking about; it has forced him to play its rotten game— fight, win, claw your way to the top, devil take the hindmost—or be co-opted and accept defeat in a 9-to-5 meaningless mental cubbyhole. It's in his guts and the other men know what he's talking about. The chicks throw the same words around and it sounds— like confetti. I suppose when they talk about male oppression it's the same in reverse. They all seem to know what they're talking about. It's hard for us to. We have some common ground in opposition to the draft because if we lose, they lose us.

Accustomed, as university or college students, not only to being heard in classroom and seminar, but even to having their opinions solicited by their professors, radical women found this rejection by radical men traumatic. The situation seemed all the more anomalous in an organization ostensibly dedicated to equality.

Equally traumatic was the sexism or male chauvinism that accepted without question the sexual division of labor. We are no longer surprised when we hear of unions that exploit their own employees; or black liberators who oppress their followers. It should not be surprising, therefore, that in an age that has a law forbidding discrimination in employment on the basis of sex, such discrimination persisted among radical men. Even the beloved Che Guevara had betrayed a lack of appreciation of the place of women in revolution, assigning them such age-old feminine jobs as cooking, teaching, social work, nursing, sewing. This showed that "even the best of men . . . are not above cynically taking advantage of the servile mentality created in women by the inferior role they're forced to play. In this respect they're defeating their own ends . . . to establish a completely rational humane society where every individual is allowed to live up to his or her full potential."

Many of these women belonged to a generation who had never in their own homes been asked to serve the coffee or perform personal-service chores around the house for their fathers and brothers. Mother, especially if she was under the thrall of the feminine mystique, did all that. And they were not about to do these things for men—also accustomed to mothers who brought in the coffee—however radical. It is hard to tell which sex found the confrontation more shocking. "Men talk about restructuring society, but ask them to make a cup of coffee and all hell breaks loose. Men laugh at changes that would affect half of the world's population. A new society must not perpetuate the inequality of women."

Even in the nondomestic chores, the women found to their dismay that they were still expected to perform the same sex-typed jobs—typing, mimeographing, general clerical work. "Only certain roles are open to women within the Movement," they complained. "Women do office work and even run offices, but are covertly discouraged from articulating political positions and from taking organizational leadership." The articulation of grievances became increasingly vituperative.

Some "were turned off by the hypocrisy that permitted women to remain in service positions, that refused to listen to women in meetings, and . . . even dared to deny that women were oppressed." Others felt they could no longer tolerate the male chauvinism and even corruption they found in SDS. One bitter woman denounced the whole male radical movement as "a diseased product of a diseased society." It was as chauvinist as the outside world, as competitive. On some campuses it had simply "replaced the sorority and fraternity." It was elitist and not equalitarian. Some segments of the radical movement resembled Mafia-like operations. They were as competitive and as full of internecine fighting. They considered any dishonest and corrupt act as justified because it was a rebellion or a protest against a corrupt society. These were the same excuses as those used by policemen, lawyers, and politicians. Even punks and hoods and gangsters used the same line of reasoning to justify their behavior.

And, finally, the women found to their dismay that they were still only sex objects. Stokely Carmichael's tenet of October 1965 was repeated with indignant and horrified shock by women for a long time thereafter. He had said that "the only position for women in SNCC is prone." (One Movement Woman commented, "I never knew whether he meant prone like a slave or prone like a very active screw. Did it ever occur to him that some women might prefer to do it like, say supine?")

Recognition of the issues women were raising was finally accorded by SDS in 1968. In December of that year it passed a National Resolution on Women recognizing women as "the oldest and largest continually oppressed group in the family of mankind," and proposing a four-point program: (1) launch a campaign to bring the wages of women employees in universities up to the level of men's; (2) begin the struggle for women's equality in high schools, state schools, teachers' colleges, junior colleges, and trade schools, especially beauty schools, secretarial schools, and nursing and other job-training schools for women; (3) relate the women's rights struggle to other repressive institutions such as juvenile courts, girls' homes, women's detention centers and prisons, family courts, welfare, labor battles; and (4) challenge the counseling practices that steer women into auxiliary occupations, demand the teaching of women's struggles, and challenge course content and direction. If was no doubt good as far as it went, and most of the programs were taken over by women. But it was too little and too late. It was regarded as mere tokenism. It did not emphasize the major concerns of women, which were coming increasingly to be seen as those related to sexism.

> The resolution covers several important areas of Female Liberation, particularly "male supremacy." Yet there is nothing in the resolution which would suggest what many of us mean by Female Liberation. The resolution calls for "free speech" within SDS. The masculine structure of SDS is built-in, and not much will change if a few specially selected women are allowed to speak pedantically enough to share some power with the big guys, and exert power in a new territory of their own—women.
>
> Marriage or living arrangements, an overwhelmingly important and absorbing matter in the day-to-day lives of the majority of people, including SDS organizers, was simply not discussed. But the programmed subservience of women in the domestic situation assures continued masculine domination in public. Most SDS people come from privileged families, and though they question many of the

values of their heritage, they do not seem to question the economic and psychological basis of the middle class—the nuclear family and the private possession of children. In fact, by jazzing it up a bit with drugs, colors, music, approved affairs, even a few orgies (group "love"), intimate meetings, they have managed to make the coupling and breeding tradition of the bourgeoisie appear more attractive than ever before. But the frills do not diminish the oppressive nature of the institution for the female, and especially the children (male and female).

Clearly the SDS did not really understand what female liberation meant nor was it a congenial ambience for women to seek for liberation in.

Separatism and Secession

The idea of separatism was not easy for the radical women in SDS to arrive at, nor to implement. There was a long period of discussion of the pro's and con's. Segregated groups, caucuses, "co-ed" groups were experimented with. They satisfied some of the women, but not all. Some rejected the mere tokenism that they felt was all they could ever expect from co-ed groups.

Others were defensive. They concluded that a process which is the reverse of co-optation—it might be labeled de-optation—was called for. Not a splinter group—a term that all wise in the ways of the organization quail at—but an independent power source that could parley on a more nearly equal basis and make its own independent contribution to the Movement. Attacking such a movement would not weaken the Movement. The idea "that female liberation would be divisive, because women would be fighting the agent of their oppression—men. . .reveals the prejudice against women. That is, men make revolutions; women [merely] help. And if men have pressures on them from women, their power as fighters is diminished. I fail to see how women fighting the authoritarian power-hunger in men can but greatly aid the revolution." Let men fight their own battles and stop "trying to tell us what to do."

Still others felt that the revolution itself, in fact, had to be protected against men: "Fascism is a man's game, not very appealing to women. . . . I do not think men can be trusted as long as they hold the kind of personal and social power they do, and they will hold it until it is taken from them, when women refuse to continue the game." Thus, not only "for their own salvation" but also "for the good of the movement, women must form their own group and work primarily for female liberation." Boring from within or trying to influence policy from the inside could not succeed so long as male chauvinism existed. The efforts of women had to be harnessed, exploited, used, and this could be done only from the outside. Organized autonomously as women outside they would have more influence than as separate individuals inside, or even as caucuses.

For some of the women, experiences in jail had given them a foretaste of liberation, paradoxical as it might seem.

> In the jailhouse, they experience perhaps the only taste of independent radical female expression given them. There they are segregated by sex, and the someone who always assumes leadership is this time a woman. They find out about each other, probably for the first time. They learn that the others, like themselves, are generally brave, resourceful, and militant. If they stay in jail long enough, they begin to organize themselves and others in the cellblock for prison reform, etc. They get up petitions, smuggle out protest letters and leaflets, mount hunger strikes and other forms of resistance. They manage very adequately to sustain the abuses, self-imposed disciplines, the loss of status, and the fear, which their brothers face. Outside, of course, jailhouse reminiscence is dominated by the men. And the women desegregate themselves, recalling only rarely a faint affection for their former cell-mates. It is little wonder then that for some women, jail may be the first time that they know their sisters and work with them in radical organizing where they're at.

They felt they needed to withdraw, finally, because they needed the refuge from male domination to work through their own identities. Like black people, they felt the need of experience in achieving consciousness of themselves. In order to satisfy this need, "women should undergo . . . self-examination with each other, but away from men. American Negro organizers have decided that the development of 'black consciousness,' liberation from white society's definition of the Negro, can only be inhibited by the assistance of even the best white organizers. Only after the Negro has confirmed his own identity will he have the assurance to form equal alliances with those whites who share his struggle for political democracy and social justice." Similarly, women must fortify themselves against the punishment of the male chauvinist and the paternalism of the male liberal. Once women have shared the process of self-discovery and the experience of independent decision making, they are ready for the real struggle.

Difficult as it was to break with the men, a substantial number did. Their humiliation had to be intense before they could actually do it, and their ideological and strategic differences profound. Finally, however, at least some of them—the "feminists" among them—did. The separatist policy proved right for them. In 1969 they were reaching and radicalizing thousands of women with their message. Complaints against sex discrimination received by the Equal Employment Opportunities Commission increased in 1970, "mostly as a result of women's liberation" (*Washington Post,* July 21, 1970). Many women with wounds quite different from those of the original Movement were spontaneously attracted to it, including women who were simply horrified at the consequences of male aggression; college students, high school students; working women; formerly nonpolitical housewives, even wives of "Movement men" who had previously had no politics of their own. The nucleus of the Women's Liberation Movement around whom the new members gathered carried with them the original idealism of the New Left. They, rather than their former male counterparts, were the true heirs of the ideals professed in the Port Huron Manifesto.

SDS still wished to recover the assistance of the "feminist" Movement Women. But when in the fall of 1969 it invited them to participate in the National Action in Chicago, the so-called Days of Rage, one Movement Woman who rejected the invitation waxed indignant at the effrontery of SDS men in trying to determine the nature of women's struggle.

The women who remained within the SDS—the so-called "politicos"—followed a different pattern. To highlight the contrast between the approach of the "feminists" and the "politicos" of the SDS, including Weatherwomen, one Movement Woman cited the story of the so-called Motor City Nine.

[The Motor City Nine] went into a classroom in Macomb Community College, barricaded the doors, and talked about imperialism, racism, and female oppression. When two men wanted to leave the room, they experienced SDS's idea of democracy: the women responded to such an exhibition of male chauvinism and general pig behavior by attacking the men with karate. Above the article there is a picture of the women. They are wearing jeans and leather jackets and generally look like the equivalents of the Young Lords, a Chicago youth gang.

The author of this paragraph bemoans such SDS tactics—aggression, loud talk, putting down and beating down the opposition, manipulation, elitism—and reminds the women that "the way we struggle now determines the nature of the society we will create."

Even these women were finding it impossible to work with the men; they were meeting "separately to discuss how to combat male chauvinism among their fellow revolutionaires."

The smug, leering, "vive la différence," male Playboy types, the coy "but-I-love-men" female types, the "I-agree-with-their-goals-but-not-their-tactics" liberal types, all of whom put Movement Women down, probably have no idea of the mettle of the women they are talking about. These are not frustrated beauty contestants nor sexpots *manquées*. The correct groups to contrast them with are certainly not beauty contestants nor sexpots, nor even PTA members or bridge-club members. It is, rather, the Weatherwomen who were being blown to bits in basement bomb factories or fleeing the country to escape indictments or actually being indicted for their part in the Four Days of Rage in the fall of 1969. Not how much angrier Movement Women were than conventional women, but how much more temperate they were than their erstwhile fellow-revolutionaries was the crux of the matter. The revolution they were seeking could not be achieved by violence.

On Their Own

When, in effect, the Movement Women "went public," a change came over the membership. The Movement now attracted many women who would never have been attracted to a woman's caucus within SDS, and certainly not to the Weathermen. Older women who found it answered a need for them. "Happy housewives" who found to their own surprise that they really weren't so happy after all. Brilliant women who could straddle both the conventional organizations like the National Organization for Women and the Movement. When asked how she could belong to both, one talented woman replied, "NOW appeals to my mind; Women's Liberation is my soul."

The growth was phenomenal. In little over a year "the women's movement has mushroomed from a sprinkling of groups in major cities to a movement of perhaps 100,000 women in over 400 cities. . . . Regional and local conferences have taken place all over the nation, reflecting an excitement [generated by] a movement whose time has come." But size had its perils. Some might ask, "Will success spoil Women's Liberation?" but others looked upon it as a challenge. They blossomed. Fearful and alienated women gained self-confidence:

Perhaps more important than its growth in size, the women's movement* has grown rapidly in its self-confidence, its analysis, and its program over the past three years. My first women's liberation group, which like many consisted of women active in the New Left, spent much of its first months struggling with our own fears and resistances. We were uneasy about whether we should be spending so much time on ourselves, whether our problems were really a common oppression, and whether other women would respond to us. In contrast, today many of us work full-time with women's liberation; we have not resolved all the issues facing us, but we are confident about our priorities. Where once we felt alone, now we do not have enough time, energy, or resources to respond to the growing interest in this movement. Similarly, women everywhere are speaking out boldly—in the church, in senior and junior high schools, in traditional women's organizations, in black liberation groups, in professional associations, in labor unions, and many other places.

*Even its name has been subject to careful scrutiny and change. Some groups now speak of the Female Liberation Movement, to show that all women of all ages are included, not just adults. We have assumed that the term "women" includes all females. [Footnote in the original].

Once on their own, Movement Women had to learn, often the hard way, their own style of operating. Without false pride, without having to save face, without arrogance, they had to set about to learn about themselves, to diagnose their weaknesses and their handicaps and how to overcome them, to learn how to admit failure when they recognized it and how to pick themselves up and continue on their way. The ways they dealt with all these "developmental tasks" are amply documented in their writings.

The challenges they faced were two-fold, defensive and offensive. For their defenses they had to learn the womanly arts of self-defense, both physical and psychological; for the second they had to work out the most congenial modus vivendi—it could hardly be called organization—and sort out and assign priorities to issues and work out strategies. Their success was substantial, if uneven.

The Defensive Aspects of Liberation

> Women . . . have to be hyper-aware of their surroundings. . . . Walk down a city street without being tuned in and you're in real danger; our society is one in which men rape, mug, and murder women whom they don't even know every day. You'd better keep track of what car is slowing down, and of who is walking up behind you.

Well-mannered, politely reared, middle-class men outside the Movement found it incredible that there were women who feared sheer physical male brute strength. They found it hilarious that Movement Women were turning to judo and karate. Despite the fact that an untold number of women actually were assaulted and raped each year, it was hard to evoke from middle-class men anything more than an amused "no woman is ever raped unless she asks for it." They could not even imagine the antenna that women carried, signaling possible threats and dangers. They themselves would never dream of accosting a woman. It did not occur to them that the man behind them might.

Movement Women took physical self-defense seriously, not only as a genuinely needed protective technique but also as a symbolic form of liberation. They learned, incidentally, also how to manage and maintain the hundred-and-one mechanical gadgets modern life is filled with in order to free themselves from dependency on men for these chores.

Even more important were the psychological defenses they evolved. They learned early their own vulnerabilities and how to protect the jugular. They created shields against the most barbed male spears. When they could, they disarmed men. If being pretty (many Movement Women are, in the modern collegiate manner) is not the be-all and end-all of your life, then being told you aren't doesn't bother you. If you aren't trying to appeal sexually to men (most Movement Women are not), it doesn't dismay you to be told you have no sex appeal. If you have no fear of Lesbianism (as few Movement Women have), you don't panic at the epithet. If you have learned to understand the roots of "bitchiness" (most Movement Women have), you can face that charge with equanimity. If you're not trying to be feminine in the old-fashioned way (most Movement Women are doing their best not to be), you don't mind being told that you're not feminine. (A persuasive case could be made for the position that Movement Women are more feminine in their orientation than most women, far more sexually aware, far more sensitive to the nuances of the relations between the sexes, far more knowledgeable about men; they can be as provocative in their reverse coquetry as young women who pursue allure almost as a career). Given all these *if's,* all the barbs are blunted or they glance off without leaving a dent. Thus disarmed, men are nonplussed. They are left slack-jawed. These are not women as they define women. Certainly not in the sexist tradition.

Such defenses serve an offensive function also. Any man who has ever been confronted by an attractive young woman who faces him coldly and noncoquettishly, who does not yield when he attempts to beat her down, who does not cop out when he hurls epithets at her, has had a chilling experience. To the credit of a great many of them, it should be said that they do begin to get the point. It had just never been brought home to them before. They may not know how to deal with the problem, but they recognize that there is one.

Defense against the weapons of men was only one part of the
defensive aspect of the Movement. Defense against the manifold
forms of "resisting consciousness" among women was also essential, including "anti-womanism, glorification of the oppressor,
excusing the oppressor (and feeling sorry for him), false identification with the oppressor . . . , romantic fantasies, utopian thinking, and other forms of confusing present reality with what one
wishes reality to be, thinking one has power in the traditional
role—can 'get what one wants,' has power behind the throne,
etc., belief that one has found an adequate personal solution or
will be able to find one without large social changes, self-cultiva-
tion, rugged individualism, seclusion, and other forms of go-it-
alone, self-blame, ultra-militancy." These would never do. They
reflected a false consciousness. Women could not solve their
problems one by one, by themselves. Liberation had to be a joint
project and it had to extend far beyond the immediately personal
niche of each separate individual woman.

Mounting such a joint effort was by no means easy.

REFERENCES

Bernard, Jessie, *American Family Behavior* (Harper, 1942), pp.
525–537.
———, "The Status of Women in Modern Patterns of Culture,"
Annals Amer. Acad. Pol. & Soc. Sci., 375 (Jan. 1968), 4–14.
Cassara, Beverly Benner (ed.), *American Women: Their Changing
Image* (Boston: Beacon Press, 1962).
Coolidge, Mary Roberts, *Why Women Are So* (New York: Holt,
1912), Chapter 9.
Davidson, Sara, "Rock Style, Defying the American Dream," *Harper's*
(July, 1969), 53–65.
Kirkpatrick, Clifford, *Family as Process and Institution* (New York:
Ronald, 1955).
Lopata, Helen, "The Life Cycle of the Social Role of Housewife,"
Sociology and Social Research, 51 (1966), 5–22.
Myrdal, Gunnar, Richard Sterner, and Arnold Rose, *An American
Dilemma* (New York: Harper, 1944), vol. 2, p. 1073.
Washington Post, July 21, 1970.

11

Strategies and Tactics

Modus Vivendi

The specific offensives mounted by Movement Women are discussed in Chapter 12. Our concern here is not with the contents of the issues involved—sexism, marriage, the nuclear family —but with the organizational strategic problems involved.

In contrast to the conventional form of organization used by NOW and other women's groups, Movement Women evolved— or are evolving, for it is still in process—an extremely amorphous but organic form of operating, hardly a form of organization at all in the usual sense. There are small groups everywhere; there are annual meetings, but no official leaders. Everyone talks. Everyone listens. Everyone is heard. There are no rigidities. Flux and movement rather than formal structure are what characterize them. Groups form as needed and then dissolve; they join to work together for certain ends, then separate and go their own way. There are localities in which there are groups that are stable and sure of themselves; but even they have their share of uncertain, vulnerable, groping groups to which young women attach themselves hoping to find an external solution for their problems. They will not find it, for it is a tenet of Movement Women that such psychological dependency in women is not to be fostered. Women are, rather, to be encouraged to work out their own destinies; no one can do it for them. No one will impose leadership on them, or even supply it to them. Some come looking for a sorority; they are not catered to. Some come looking for therapy; if they get it, it comes as a by-product. Some come looking for an escape from the alienation that plagues so many upper middle-class young women when they leave the congenial world of academia where they have been dealt with as intellectual beings and find themselves now in a world that sees them simply as young women of no particular significance otherwise.

Such an escape from alienation they do find. For a major function of these groups is precisely that of releasing the young and the by now not-so-young women from their isolation from one another. They find articulated all the grievances they have felt but never been able to express. They experience community, fellowship, identification, sisterhood. Chivalry had put women on a lonely pedestal that had cut them off from other women; equality with men had frequently been interpreted by men as justifying bad manners or ill treatment. As individuals, women could be bullied, mowed down, one by one. But with a community back of them, women could stand up to their oppressors. They had an identity. They received the kind of emotional support men's organizations had never offered. In their own groups they found an audience that listened to them, that even heard them, that never put them down, that was on their side. As single individuals they could easily be psychologically undone by sexism; united with other women, they felt stronger when confronted by it. They felt stronger even when they were alone.

At a time when so many new things are happening for the first time in history, it is hard to see them one by one. But surely one of the most interesting is the sudden burst of solidarity among these women. Not yet by the million perhaps, but in increasing numbers, they turned from their domestic loneliness and ran toward one another, discovering one another, losing their sense of aloneness, of isolation. One theme that runs through all the writing and thinking of Movement Women is this joyous release: We are not alone! We know one another! We understand one another! We are not lone individuals, unique in our oppression. We are part of a great company! We are worthy! We are not inferior! It would be dramatic, even melodramatic, to use the Marxist figure of speech, but it is psychologically true. These women feel psychologically unchained.

Amorphous and leader-shy groups of such women might be, but communication remained essential. For communication among themselves, many groups began to publish "rags" at irregular intervals; some published newsletters; some put out periodicals, varying in content, emphasis, and quality. One group, finding that there was need also for a newspaper written from the angle of Movement Women, established such a bi-weekly newspaper, *Off Our Backs, A Women's News-Journal,* "written by women to be shared with other women who are also struggling for liberation." Its prospectus explained the need it was to serve:

> Male supremacy pervades this society, preventing direct and honest communication between women. Nowhere, in either the underground or Establishment press, are our issues adequately analyzed or discussed. . . . We have become convinced that we can no longer work where we see repeated failure to print articles of importance to our sisters and ourselves, and where degrading sex ads and nudie photos are the accepted norm of "political" coverage. Our political and economic analysis, necessary for building the revolution, is regarded as inconsequential by even the most "radical" of publications. We have been denied print space to develop our analytic and poetic abilities. We feel the needs of the growing women's movement can no longer be served by an occasional article or special supplement. We need to create and support our own media.

All these publications radiated a passion that compensated for unpolished format. If they were more polished and conventional, they would lose their clout, for the acceptance of conventional literary style, like the acceptance of conventional dress, is itself a kind of acceptance of the status quo. They have a style of their own, that is powerful precisely because it forces readers to hear what the writers are saying. A less rugged style would lull rather than communicate.

Communicating with the outside world poses problems of its own. Sheer polemics run the risk of losing impact by repetition. They tend to become shrill and hence to turn readers off rather than on. It is hard to say the same things over and over again in a fresh way. It sounds so déjà vu that finally no one pays attention any more, and the really new message does not get across. To meet such situations, more dramatic forms of communication have to be devised.

On issues Movement Women shared with other groups, they could share in strikes, picketing, sit-ins, and men's other disruptive tactics. But they felt the lack of a means of communication as dramatic as, for example, burning draft cards. Men could refuse induction and burn their draft cards, but all that women could do in opposing the draft was to help the men. It was more difficult in one-sex activities to provoke, let us say, the radicalizing brutality of the billy club. There were fewer current news events to exploit. There were no "places where women could say 'No' and cause the same disruption as men did in saying 'No' to the draft." The grievances they wanted to air did not lend themselves to public assault. They occurred in private or, if anything did happen in public, disruption might victimize rather than radicalize other women and the blow would simply glance off them. How to demonstrate against the use of sex to sell just about anything and everything? How to demonstrate against the coquetry of women or the subservience of secretaries or the intimidation of wives? Even black militants had given up attacks on Uncle Tom; they did not reach the enemy. Disruption of abortion trials and hearings, demonstrations at a Miss America contest in Atlantic City, at bridal fairs, at Playboy Clubs, on Wall Street, and at exclusively male bars, and guerilla theater were among the ways—always designed for maximum symbolic value —for communicating to the Establishment. The aim was not only shock value, but also raising questions whose answers would be educational. (Sometimes they overestimated the intellectual level of their audience, as when one group used guerrilla theater on Wall Street to convey the message that "the nuclear family was synonymous with the patriarchy of the American business corporations" or that the witch was symbolic of the persecution of nonconforming women.)

Since they were dealing with nonrational structures, whether or not they were any longer functional, rational debate was not useful. Pitting one nonrational but highly symbolic pattern against another forced an examination of the challenged pattern. Exclusion from a bar unless one had a male partner could hardly be that important, and ordinary, sensible women would not consider it worth attacking. But as representing a pattern of social life that demanded couples, that discriminated against individual women, it was important. A couple-organized social life gave cogency to the witty "better dead than unwed" conclusion of Movement Women. After several months, there was some let-up in this form of communication. There remained recognition of the usefulness of occasional dramatic, even theatrical, not to say shocking, disruptions to attract the public's eye; but the Movement Women also recognized the long, hard "organizational" task ahead of them.

Strategic Issues

Like others who seek to change the world, Movement Women had to ask, do you change structures first and through them "the hearts and minds of men" or do you change "hearts and minds of men" first and through this process change institutions? Though their almost Pavlovian psychology would have lead one to predict the first option, actually they seemed to follow the second. To change structures you have to amass power; this means coalitions and alliances. But the restrictive emphasis on the cleavage between the sexes as the major one in history and in contemporary life limited access to coalitions and alliances. It all but blotted out recognition of class; it blurred ethnic (except racial) factors.

Black men, Kenneth Clark reminded Movement Women in a confrontation at the 1970 convention of the American Psychological Association, could not forget white women's complicity in the degradation of black men in the era of lynchings; and most black women found racism more onerous than sexism.

Unaccepted, then, if not actually rejected by blacks, by workers, and by the poor—who had all the really powerful issues—Movement Women were aware of their essential isolation from the major battlefields of the day, of the contrast between their cosmopolitan perspective and the narrow middle-class parochialism enforced on them by their restricted tether. Other groups invited their cooperation, and often got it from individual members, but few such groups were willing to support Movement Women. (Some conventional women's organizations refused even to use the adjective "feminist" to describe their own orientation, fearful lest they be identified with Movement Women). Movement Women were quite correct in their assessment of their battle as potentially "even more earth-shattering than the awakening of blacks." But it was an even harder one to fight.

In the absence of allies and coalitions, solidarity among women's groups became increasingly important. During the time when the Movement Women were still within the womb of the New Left, there had been a wide generation gap between them and older reform-minded women. The differences were both ideological and procedural, the young women favoring direct action, the older women more traditional parliamentary approaches.

After liberation from SDS, the generation gap was bridged. The young women came to see that it was strategically erroneous to do anything to widen cleavages among women, that with so few allies, they could not afford to reject any women's organization. A change came over its rhetoric and its general tone. There was less emphasis on the ideological and strategic and tactical differences between Movement Women and the more conservative NOW organizational approach. Solidarity or sisterhood became the emphasis: no more criticism. Even one of the most radical of the Movement Women rebuked critics of NOW:

> Even the present liberal demands of NOW are not contradictory to our communist thesis, since those women are advancing the legal equality of women so that we have a clear field for the battles we are fighting, and such rights give women breathing space. It is disheartening to hear radicals condemning such reform activity as counterrevolutionary. Not everyone has to involve herself in such activities, but we should be glad that someone is doing it, and not condemn them for their labors which are ultimately necessary for our own fight, into which we hope to bring the women of NOW, when they see the reality of the system.

Not then, so much by way of a strategy of coalitions and alliances to change structures directly as by a strategy of changing the way people saw their world, especially the way women did. The technique was one of "consciousness raising."

> Consciousness-raising includes all those ways in which women are brought to see their oppression as a group and are confronted with the question of what they will do about it. Susan B. Anthony stated it clearly in 1872: "I do pray, and that most earnestly and constantly, for some terrific shock to startle the women of the nation into a self-respect which will compel them to break their yoke of bondage and give them faith in themselves; which will make them proclaim their allegiance to women first. . . . The fact is, women are in chains and their servitude is all the more debasing because they do not realize it. Oh, to compel them to see and feel and to give them the courage and the conscience to speak and act for their own freedom, though they face the scorn and contempt of all the world for doing it!" . . . But consciousness-raising is not simply awakening to one's condition. It must also be the process of finding the courage and confidence to move. Central to this process, then, is the development of a positive self-image for ourselves as women. . . . Because we have been taught that men are superior and not so limited, most women, especially those who strive to "get ahead" look up to and identify with men, resulting in a dislike of other women and a hatred of ourselves as women. In order to change this self image, groups can encourage each woman to develop a fuller sense of herself, helping her to take the time and energy to pursue her own identity and interests, and pushing her to develop previously thwarted talents and abilities necessary for the common struggle. Through sharing and working together on projects and in discussion groups, women have begun to see each other not as competitors or inferior companions but as sisters in a common struggle who can and must be loved and trusted.

The kind of change Movement Women were hoping to bring about in the self-conceptions of women had been labeled "radicalizing" when used by the New Left on students. Like "radicalizing," the raising of women's consciousness of their oppressed status was a process sociologists had called *mass conversion:*

By the term mass conversion we designate a wholesale shift in self-attitudes, not necessarily religious ones, in a direction that is discontinuous with earlier commitments. . . . From a psychological point of view, whether there can be a *complete* about-face in fundamental values is debatable. Some psychological antecedents to the "new" beliefs seem to be present in every convert. In the view of William James, a conversion meant that the submerged side of a divided self was brought to the fore. . . . The convert . . . is given a new identity and a sense of selfhood anchored in new group affiliations from which he can return only with the greatest difficulty. . . . Mass conversion, then, can be viewed as a collective movement in status or as a shift in the norms of some group which fundamentally reorients the relationships of participants to the rest of society, even while the participants strive to maintain consistency. The mass of potential converts is found among those partly excluded from what they consider effective participation in society (Lang, 1962, pp. 353–354).

The "psychological antecedents" required for this form of conversion were present in thousands of women who had never shared the New Left experience. What Movement Women were saying struck a responsive chord in even the seemingly most conventional women.

Why *Now?*

To explain why the time for the Women's Liberation Movement had come at this particular moment would require an explanation of why the civil rights movement or the New Left, or the peace movement had come when it came; and explaining these movements would require an explanation of the whole withdrawal of consent by the governed to time-honored authority which characterized the 1960's. It was a time of secularization of all kinds of ancient norms, a desacralization or removal of their sacred aura. All kinds of status relationships were being challenged, status relationships between the sexes no less than others.

The challenge to the inferior status of women was far from new. It had begun almost two centuries earlier. But for effective impact it had to wait until there were enough women to whom the issue was relevant. In the past such women had been rare. Toward the end of the eighteenth century it became possible for some women other than rich heiresses or those to the manor born to achieve relatively independent status. They could become teachers or writers or actresses. The Enlightenment and the French Revolution contributed a suitable intellectual ambience; they encouraged the challenge to authority that had to accompany independence, however minuscule the proportion for whom it was possible still was. They adumbrated a future when independence would be possible for all women. Mary Wollstonecraft, Fanny Kemble, and Georges Sand in England, the United States, and France exemplified the emerging trend. They could leave a bad marriage and make a go of it on their own.

Once it became possible for any women to achieve the status of independence, all the problems of such status began to emerge for them. At first such problems appeared in such a small avant garde that they seemed too unreal to warrant any attention from most women, far removed from the status of independence. But the history of the nineteenth century was to be one in which independence was to become possible for an increasing number of women. As more and more women recognized that independence was indeed possible, the intellectual and ideological discussions and controversies that had begun with, let us say, Mary Wollstonecraft, found an increasingly extensive and attentive audience. It is interesting to watch not only the ideological controversies as they expressed themselves in the avant garde, but also the ripples from the dropped pebbles spreading to wider and wider audiences as more and more women found independence possible, if not always truly feasible. The controversies today sound remarkably like those of the nineteenth century, and understandably so, since they are dealing with the same issues. What has changed is the size of the audience for whom they are relevant. By the last third of the twentieth century, they had become relevant to practically all women. The "psychological antecedents" were there.

So also were the demographic factors to which we have so frequently called attention, that required totally new values in relation to the functions of women. The procreative function that had all but determined the position of women in the past was no longer to be the major preoccupation of their lives. Coming to terms with all the implications of this revolution demanded a total restructuring of the relations between the sexes. Movement Women were among the most prescient in sensing this. The processes of change were writ large in their own lives.

Coda

At the end of Chapter 3 we presented a brief resume of Soviet legislation vis-à-vis women, noting how it followed the demands of the state as seen by policy makers, now encouraging labor force participation, now childbearing. How independent the new women's movements in industrial societies are of regime, status quo, or policy makers' conception of the public interest can be seen in the similarity between the concerns expressed in the U.S.S.R. and those expressed here at home. There is the same concern with "unisex" or "monosex," and with the denigration of the relative status of men. Here, for example, is an excerpt from the Soviet press:

> Women work on a par with men today and even wear trousers. Where is this emancipation leading? Are women becoming masculine? Is a third type developing, something between a man and a woman? Many readers ask these questions in letters to this newspaper. . . . This newspaper's Public Opinion Institute questioned 4,020 young parents about their hopes for their children's futures. Naturally, the parents dreamed up the Ideal Woman and the Ideal Man. What is interesting is that they were one and the same person. . . . Let us consider the problem.
>
> There are several factors in the psychological "offensive" of women against men. The first is education. The weaker sex is already a bit stronger in education, 58 per cent of the specialists with higher or technical secondary education are women.
>
> The second factor is economic independence. A study conducted in Leningrad a few years ago . . . showed that only in about 36 per cent of families are men the head. . . . For generations women had been accustomed to look up to men, the breadwinners. They

saw men from their vantage point in the kitchen. Today, women work with men. Their vantage point has changed. This has brought some disillusionment.

The third factor is public opinion. . . . (*Current Digest of the Soviet Press,* December 1968, p. 11).

The revolution in the relations between the sexes is apparently as characteristic of communistic as of capitalistic societies.

REFERENCES

Current Digest of the Soviet Press (December 1968), 11.

Lang, Gladys Engel and Kurt Lang, "Collective Dynamics: Process and Form," in Arnold M. Rose (ed.), *Human Behavior and Social Processes, An Interactionalist Approach* (Boston: Houghton Mifflin, 1962), pp. 353–354.

VI

The Pursuit of Happiness: Adjusting the Establishment to the Lives of Women

Although the ultimate aim of Movement Women is a humane society where no one oppresses anyone else, they think, no more than their male counterparts, in terms of the public interest as it is conceived by those now concerned with making policy. Looking around them, they do not find the kind of public implied by the term public interest nor the kind of consensus. The concept implies a fundamental common welfare, basic common interests, however much dissensus there may also be. They see conflict instead, a status quo or Establishment in which a variety of oppressors exploit the rest of society: whites oppressing blacks, rich oppressing poor; and everyone oppressing women. To recognize a public interest would mean overlooking all this, accepting the status quo; it would lead to co-optation or assimilation or reform rather than to revolution. They view the concept of a public interest, therefore, as a kind of fascistic gimmick, demanding sacrifice of the individual for the sake of the state or the system or the Establishment, and hence as oppressive rather than as concerned for the general welfare. Since they do not think in terms

233

of such an overriding public interest, their major emphasis is on the self-actualization aspects of policy as it affects women. The hope among some is that ultimately the liberation of women will lead in the direction of a better society and hence will be in the public interest.

12

The Gut Issue:
Functions Not Jobs

A Revolution of Their Own

The original pioneers of the women's movement shared with their male counterparts opposition to capitalism, to racism, to war, to the system or the Establishment or the status quo. To the extent that they did, they were not differentiated from the New Left in general.

But they found that in addition to the usual grievances of the New Left they had others peculiar to their status as women. Their scenario for revolution therefore became different from that of the men, for the revolution they were seeking—Revolution 1— was not the same as the one the men were fomenting—Revolution 2. It was far more radical.

The grievances of women were unique, peculiar, and characteristic whatever the regime; they predated capitalism and survived its demise in the U.S.S.R. Thus, since their declaration of independence from SDS and the consequent influx of other women, the "politicos" who emphasize the political-revolutionary aspects of the Movement (Revolution 2) have been less characteristic than the "feminists" (proponents of Revolution 1) who highlight the issues peculiar to their status as women.

The Real Roadblock: Jobs Versus Functions

Although job discrimination was the original issue that propelled Movement Women out of SDS, there is remarkably little emphasis in their writings on jobs or careers or the traditional feministic grievances about discrimination.[1] With few exceptions, they are hardly concerned with them at all. The gut issue is far deeper than sex-typing of jobs or job discrimination: it is the sexual specialization of functions and the sexism on which it rests.

Job discrimination as an issue is by now old-hat and can be relegated to the more conventional reform-oriented women's organizations. The emphasis of Movement Women is on what they see as deeper, more revolutionary changes. They "aim their attack on the subtler rights denied them not by law or administrative rules, but by mores, custom, tradition, and convention. . . . This relative emphasis on rights in the area of crescive norms, especially the mores, as compared with enacted norms, characterizes the status issues at the present time" (Bernard, 1970). Not only change in official policy, but change also and primarily in the sexism on which the sexual assignment of functions rests. They do not systematically lobby in Congress, but challenge the "eternal verities," seek to stimulate paradigm shifts, and, by personal example, provide models for new ways to structure the relationships between the sexes. Their "demands can only be

---

1. A major exception is Joan Jordan. A mother of three, automated out of a job after 20 years in the labor force, she is a returnee to the campus. Her social demands are remarkably mild: free public nurseries and child-care centers; widely available planned parenthood centers; legal abortions; summer camps for all children; mass production methods for home industry; equal economic, social, and intellectual opportunities; parents on four-hour work days or shortened work weeks so fathers may regain closer relations with children; payment of wages to mothers for bearing and rearing children. See "The Place of American Women, Economic Exploitation of Women," *Revolutionary Age*, 1 (1968), reproduced by New England Free Press; present citation, pp. 20–21.

met by over-turning most of the existing structures of society."
And nothing less. They are less outraged by the sexual division
of labor—which, in any event, is derivative—than they are by the
sexual specialization of functions from which such division is
derived.

> Previously women . . . fought for equal access to high-status
> jobs and equal pay on all jobs. They felt . . . that since we live in a
> society in which a person is defined by the job he holds, women
> should have equal access to all jobs, and thus, equal chance at the
> definition of "human," "high status," or "worthwhile." . . . Women
> in the movement today have come from a very different political
> tradition. . . . The old jobs that women fought to hold—corporation
> executive, lawyer, doctor, banker, etc.—have very low status within
> our own peer group. . . . *We are seeking new life styles,* and there-
> fore place great emphasis not on job opportunities, but on social
> relationships in building a new political society.

As we noted earlier, Murdock showed a long time ago that
there are few kinds of labor that are universally sex-typed as male
and none as female. What women do in our society men do in
another, and vice versa. So long as work is sex-typed at all, to be
sure, whatever men do has more prestige than what women do.
But what disturbs the Movement Women most is that regardless
of the name of the work they do, they "end up in service positions or servant roles, no matter what class of job they hold—
factory work, technician, secretary, research assistant." Since
whatever the sexual division of labor might be, women still performed the supportive or stroking function, were still the re-
storers, the healers, the builder-up-ers, what difference did it
make? They were automatically and ipso facto disqualified for
the top positions which demanded the aggression forbidden to
them by their functional assignment as women.

The ultimate anomaly, in brief, lay in the fact that there was
a fundamental incompatibility between some kinds of jobs and
some kinds of functions. Superordinate jobs in any organization
depended on an ability to fight, to compete, to take chances, to
be aggressive. Subordinate jobs were more consonant with the
stroking function. If people were programmed to fill subordinate
jobs, they would not perform well in jobs that required aggres-

sion. Men were programmed by the system to be aggressive, women to be unaggressive. There were, therefore, functional roadblocks to equal chances for the achievement of top positions. The best attack was not a superficial one on job discrimination per se but a more fundamental one on functional specialization and the sexism on which it rested.

Sexism as Target

"Sexism" versus "Male Chauvinism"

It is always difficult for an outsider to understand how much blood and tears are involved in any internecine struggle. A good deal of the writing of Movement Women in the early months was devoted to a turbulent attack on radical men. The bitterness of some was so great that "man-hating" itself became an issue. Once secession had been successfully completed and the women had achieved their own definition and identity, the virulence, though not the conviction of the attack subsided or at least became muted.

For, basically, the analysis on which the movement rested could not permit a personalistic point of view. Some members might hate men, some might blame them individually for the oppression of women, but the only acceptable stance had to be that it was the system or social structure or capitalism or the Establishment that was at fault. Men, like women themselves, were victims of the system. Not men, but the structure of capitalism or of the status quo or of the Establishment that imposes oppressive roles on them is the real enemy. Still, for whatever reason, the system is in the control of men. Every lever of power —money, police, guns, law—is in their hands. They may be programmed to fight for power, but once they achieve it, they use it to program the rest of us—men as well as women—to serve them. Thus, "however unwilling he may be in theory to play that role . . . the most immediate oppressor [of women] is 'the man.' " So "even if we prefer to view him as merely a pawn

in the game, he's still the foreman on the big plantation of males-
ville," used by the "plantation bosses" to oppress women. Women
must therefore "recognize man as the enemy if we are to start
freeing ourselves."

In addition, there were secondary gains from sexism for even
the oppressed men: "They reap many psychological and economic advantages from the power they wield." Sexism is far more
than merely a structurally imposed weapon of oppression; it has
functional bases also. In terms of the Bales schema, it may be
viewed as the payoff for men of the prescribed stroking function
of women. It is the male counterpart of whatever female role a
woman is engaged in, regardless of what it may be. By showing
solidarity, raising the status of others, giving help, rewarding,
agreeing, concurring, complying, understanding, passively accepting—as specified in the Bales schema—women create the appropriate assumption of superiority in men. Men accept the status
thus conferred upon them as a matter of course, in fact, assume
it.

Sometimes sexism, an impersonal phenomenon, becomes male
chauvinism, an insistence on "my sex, right or wrong." This term
was first used in the female manifesto of the 1967 SDS convention, where chauvinism was defined as the "surname of Nicolas
Chauvin, soldier of Napoleon I, notorious for his bellicose attachment to the lost imperial cause: militant, unreasoning devotion
to one's race, sex, etc., with contempt for other races, the opposite
sex, etc.: as, male chauvinism." (It might be added that
Chauvin's exaggerated patriotism became the butt of ridicule by
his comrades).

The discussions among Movement Women included both
terms, the more emotional term *male chauvinism* tending to
characterize the earlier months more than the later. More colorful and intriguing than the term *sexism,* it was taken over by
the outside world, and young men would gleefully and playfully
confess to being male chauvinists. But the more serious work of
the Movement Women relied on the soberer concept of sexism.
The onus was removed from men as individuals, but since they
were the ones who enforced it, they were legitimate targets of

action. Male chauvinism performed an important function in that no matter how low a man's status might be, there were always others—women—who were lower still.

Sexism, even in its male-chauvinism form, is viewed as beyond structural explanations. Not capitalism or any other special kind of social or economic or political structure is responsible for it. It exists under communism as well as under capitalism. It performs the same functions in any kind of structure. It depends ultimately on the oppression of women.

The term *oppression* as used by Movement Women is puzzling to many, to women as well as men. The definition of *oppress* given by the Oxford Dictionary is as good as any to illuminate its nature in both the interpersonal, or functional, aspect and the political, or structural, aspect: "(1) to press injuriously upon or against; to press down by force; to crush, trample down, smother, crowd. . . . (2) to lie heavy on, weight down, crush (the feelings, mind, spirits, etc.); to put down, suppress; to crush, overwhelm (a person). . . . (4) to keep under by tyrannical exercise of power; to load or burden with cruel or unjust impositions or restraints; to tyrannize over. . . . (6) . . . to force, ravish. . . ." Different women feel themselves oppressed in different ways. Few may ever have been ravished or felt themselves burdened with cruel or unjust impositions or restraints, but, conversely, few have never felt overwhelmed, put down, or never had their feelings, minds, or spirits crushed by men.

Movement Women have carried out their analyses of sexism as it manifests itself in a variety of life areas including science, interpersonal relationships, sexual relationships, and power relationships.

Sexism in Science and Scholarship

The most devastating assault on sexism is on its manifestation in science. The original basis on which sexism rested was revelation; male superiority and female subservience had been established in Genesis. This rationale was later supplemented or supplanted by natural law. It was a law of nature that men should rule over women; they were superior. Any challenge to this order of things was unnatural. But for the last hundred years the basis for sexism had rested primarily on scientific research. It was to science that its defenders appealed. Impugn that support, and the foundation on which sexism rested was shattered.

Naomi Weisstein, a psychologist at Loyola University, did precisely that (Weisstein, 1969). Since so much of the received wisdom about female psychology was based on clinical psychology and psychiatry, these were among her prime targets. She showed how lacking in evidence the once-influential Freudian theory was; and how even "years of intensive clinical experience is not the same thing as empirical evidence." Since even the instruments used in clinical research do not pass the tests of consistency, efficacy, agreement, and reliability, "we can safely conclude that theories of a clinical nature advanced about women are also worse than useless."

The rigorously empirical psychologists came off no better. It is not so much any inner dynamic or a set of fixed personality traits, but the social context in which behavior takes place that determines how people will act. Dr. Weisstein reviewed a brace of research projects on both animals and human beings, which show that the expectations of the experimenter himself influence the results he gets and that the social setting of any experiment will determine how subjects will respond to stimuli. Applying this knowledge to the intellectual development of women, Dr. Weisstein was surprised that it takes girls so long to learn that they must not be bright. Not until they get to high school do they get the message.

Dr. Weisstein did not conclude that there are no relevant mental, moral, or social differences between the sexes; she just says they have not been proved:

> Until psychologists realize that it is they who are limiting discovering of human potential by their refusal to accept evidence if they are clinical psychologists or, if they are rigorous, by their assumption that people move in a context-free ether, with only their innate dispositions and their individual traits determining what they will do, then psychology will have nothing of substance to offer in this task. I don't know what immutable differences exist between men and women apart from differences in their genitals; perhaps there are

some other unchangeable differences; probably there are a number of irrelevant differences. But it is clear that until social expectations for men and women are equal, until we provide equal respect for both men and women, our answers to this question will simply reflect our prejudices.

In connection with the "data" elicited by psychiatrists, Dr. Weisstein asks whether women's "psychiatrists could cow them into reporting something that was not true?" Even if psychiatrists do not cow women patients into reporting something that is not true, there is evidence that they elicit the kind of data that is congenial to them. Thus, for example, a nurse comes to a psychiatrist in a disturbed, distraught, disorganized state. Her husband is an alcoholic, he has no sexual relations with her, he is abusive. . . . The psychiatrist is unresponsive. He is bored. He pays only cursory attention. Later in the interview the woman mentions the fact that she was pregnant with another man's child when she married her husband. Ah, immediately the psychiatrist snaps to attention. This is the kind of thing he has been waiting for. His attention rewards the woman and she responds as she now knows he wants her to. In the end she is convinced that her marital misery is her fault (Scheff, 1968). It is on evidence derived under such circumstances that an indeterminate amount of theorizing about women depends.

It is curious to note that "psychologists' ideas of women's nature fit so remarkably the common prejudice and serve industry and commerce so well." Psychiatrists find "normal" in women precisely what to them is useful and desirable to be normal in women.

The subversion of the authority of even the most prestigious psychiatrists by such attacks on the foundations of their beliefs is drastic. When one psychiatrist makes the attainment of "the goal of a good life and a secure world in which to live it" rest on women's growing up "without dread of their biological functions and without subversion by feminist doctrine, and therefore . . . [their entering] motherhood with a sense of fulfillment and altruistic sentiment," his female listener can say, "Yeah? Prove it!" or "That may be the way it looks to you but it looks different to me. And my way is just as valid as yours. More so, maybe."

Sexism, it has been noted, has also permeated the other social sciences. It has determined the topics that sociologists, for example, have judged to be worth studying (Bernard, 1970). Research on marriage and the family has tended to prove that sexist ideologies were best (Bernard, 1971). Betty Friedan (1963) accused the social scientists of shoring up old prejudices: "Instead of destroying the old prejudices that restricted women's lives, social science in America merely gave them new authority. By a curious circular process, the insights of psychology and anthropology and sociology, which should have been powerful weapons to free women, somehow canceled each other out, trapping women in dead center." She was particularly critical of the structure-functionalists:

> Functionalism began as an attempt to make social science more "scientific" by borrowing from biology the idea of studying institutions as if they were muscles or bones, in terms of their "structure" and "function" in the social body. By studying an institution only in terms of its function within its own society, the social scientists intended to avert unscientific value judgments. In practice, functionalism was less a scientific movement than a scientific word-game. "The function is" was often translated "the function should be"; the social scientists did not recognize their own prejudices in functional disguise any more than the analysts recognized theirs in Freudian disguise.

Sexism has also, Movement Women note, greatly restricted the work of scholarship as well as of science, especially in the field of history. Imagine, for example, what it would be like if we had as good a record of the history of women as we have of the history of men in the literature, music, and art of the West. What if the great crises in the lives of women had been as well documented in fiction and theater as the father-son conflict, the sexual awakening of boys, the chase, the battle, which have been the major themes? Think how thin the corresponding literature dealing with women has been, how few women have told us what female experience has been. How much poorer we are for having no artists tell us about the great female "identity crises." Men, great men, have had insights. But it would have been illuminating to have female Shakespeares too. How did it feel to be a queen, a woman and therefore presumably the weaker vessel, married to a king whose "achievement motivation" did not match your own? Who had to be egged on? Who was so far from your own (in this case, sinister) level of competence? Who sent a woman to do a man's (again, in this case, sinister) work? Shakespeare did it superbly. But imagine it from a woman's pen.

Sexism in Interpersonal Relations

Although it was the male chauvinism of the members of SDS that originally precipitated the Women's Liberation Movement, its all-pervasive penetration among all men preoccupies Movement Women. An academic woman, author of a successful novel, notes that she is a "woman writer," that all her literary critiques are discounted as reflecting a woman's point of view; at a university debate in which one woman and two men participated, the woman's "point of view was never assailed or refuted. It was overlooked." Another woman, an economist, notes that "I get many 'fan' letters saying my work is 'superb,' 'magnificent'—both of these adjectives last week—but in public I am merely a 'competent' economist or an outstanding 'woman' economist." It is the unquestioning assumption of male superiority that infuriates Movement Women, as the same assumption of white superiority infuriates the black man.

An archetypical example of what Movement Women mean by male chauvinism was an interview that a famous television personality, David Frost, held with Golda Meir, Prime Minister of Israel. There she sat, a veritable Deborah in repose, majestic, imperturbable, beautiful, serene, answering his trivial questions with tolerant good humor. Known for his probing style, his technique of bringing out interesting facets of his subjects' personalities, Frost nevertheless asked, with the naive aplomb of his sexist point of view: "A few days ago your President said you thought like a man and were, in fact, the best man in his cabinet. Weren't you flattered by this encomium?" Too self-assured, too wise to be flabbergasted—as surely every woman in the audience must have been to hear the question—she replied simply with a laugh, "You men!"

The sexism of the liberal man is as obnoxious to Movement Women as the ill-mannered and even brutal chauvinism of the radical man. He is accepting of only as much of their position as will serve his own wishes. But he cannot really tolerate equality in interpersonal relations. He is in the forefront of those advocating more rights for women, but only because enlightened women are more useful than stupid ones. An unhappy woman will not be a good wife. A flighty empty-headed devotee of *True Confessions* will be a boring companion. But equality? Perish the thought:

> Talk to them about women . . . and they insist that they are with you 100 per cent. As long as they think you are putting women down for being what they are, a product of the pressures of society, they're two steps ahead of you. But when they catch on that it's the [male] pressures you are condemning, they come to a screeching halt, begin to frown and squirm and back-track.
>
> Before you know it you're being accused of being a snob . . . anti-man . . . and not knowing what you're talking about. . . . The liberal man cannot admit it is society's pressures, as exemplified by his attitude, that produce the artificial women he so smugly dismisses. . . . You will never find a liberal man who isn't very big on womanly charm. Take womanly charm out of his life and you are taking away the sun. Life would be a desert without it . . . [i.e., listening admiringly so as to draw out his ideas]. Liberal men are very big on rights for women, within limits.

No one should be misled by such men, "who do not appear to be the vicious oppressors of women." For "any man who is not working consciously to change the unequal relationship of men and women is opposing the interests of women. He is just as guilty as the more blatantly violent men and is actually a great deal more insidious."

Movement Women will not settle for the sexist's "different but equally good" ideology any more than black people would settle for separate but equally good schools.

> Inevitably it [a friendship] explodes. . . . This man—so admiring, so affectionate, so full of high regard for her—is shocked, reels backward, cannot believe his eyes and ears. . . . Yes, her worth is great, but not this great! She is still, after all, a girl: a great help,

but only supportive; friendly and energetic, but not a leader; bright and clever, but not a thinker, not an innovator. That's what she's asking to be treated as, as a man! I *did* respect her intelligence, so evidently she wants something more than respect. Equality. But that's impossible, surely she cannot imagine. . . . I'm a man, she's only a girl. . . . Surely it must be obvious to her that we aren't equal, we're different! Being a woman is just as good as being a man, every bit as good, better, in its own way. But she wants to be a man! . . . It cuts me to the quick!

This vignette is an illustration of being oppressed in the dictionary sense of "being put down." Men are reduced to confusion when women do not confer superiority on them, as anyone is when a role relationship does not proceed according to the social script. They fight back by denigrating the challenger.

Movement Women rebel against the passivity and receptivity that sexism imposes on them, the implication that their lives must be scheduled to accommodate men's, to be ready when men choose, invisible when they do not, that her time is less valuable than his. The cliche "Don't call me, I'll call you" is one of the most painful formulas for anguish ever concocted. The agony of waiting for the call can be excruciating. It can be inflicted on anyone of either sex. But since sexism arrogates the initiative to men, it is almost the destiny of women. Men are not to be distracted from their work, but women must always be available. "The arrogant male strolls in, sprawls himself down without inquiring whether she is busy, or about to leave, or enjoying a bit of solitude to think, assuming with total confidence that nothing could be as important as his attention, that he is doing her a favor by taking her away from whatever he interrupted."

Sexism in Sexual Relations

For those concerned with the interpersonal aspects of sexism, its expression even in sexual relations became a major preoccupation.[2] Its oppressive nature—in the dictionary sense not only of

2. In the area of sex, Movement Women were becoming truly liberated, not in the early twentieth-century sense, but in a quite modern sense. They were now free, for example, to admit that sexual relations were not so enjoyable to them when they were not, when, in fact, they were often revolting and nauseating. No generation of young for many years had

"pressing down by force" or "lying heavy on" or "ravishing," but also of "imposing cruel and unjust restraints"—is among the most bitterly resented grievances. The use of the concept of the vaginal orgasm by men, for example, is seen as a ploy to keep women sexually subservient, for recognition by women of the clitoral nature of sexual stimulability would render them sexually independent of men and deprive men of the use of the vagina for their own gratification.

> If woman's pleasure was obtained through the vagina, then she was totally dependent on the man's erect penis to achieve orgasm; she would receive her satisfaction only as a concomitant of man's seeking his. With the clitoral orgasm, woman's sexual pleasure was independent of the male's, and she could seek her satisfaction as aggressively as the man sought his, a prospect which didn't appeal to too many men. The definition of feminine sexuality as normally vaginal, in other words, was a part of keeping women down, of making them sexually as well as economically, socially, and politically subservient.

Although recent research requires some updating of this argument,[3] it does not controvert it.

Other Movement Women resent the power that the need to please men sexually confers on men. One of the most powerful polemicists among Movement Women makes a trenchant criticism of the use by men even of female liberation itself, finding that often such liberation merely means that young women become more available to them as sexual partners. She insists on the power aspects of sex: "Masculine sexuality has had to do with

---

been unintimidated enough ("frigid!" "Lesbian!") to say that. Being a "sex maniac" had become about as compulsive in the twentieth century as being frigid had been in the nineteenth. However, they were also learning how to take the initiative in a direct rather than a circuitous manner.

3. We are now told, for example, that "it is possible to have the clitoris completely removed without losing erotic sensations, pleasure and orgasm. . . . Evidently the nerve supply for erotic sensation is so lavishly supplied that large amounts of sexual tissue can be missing without destruction of sexual gratification." See John Money, "Clitoral Size and Erotic Sensation," *Medical Aspects of Human Sexuality*, 4 (March 1970), 95. William Masters reports (personal correspondence) women who achieve orgasm entirely by way of breast stimulation.

power, and until power relations are changed, no correction of the symptoms is going to do much more than make the rich richer and the poor poorer, *i.e.,* allow men to oppress women more openly and freely."

Sexism as Power Relationships: The Physical Bases of Female Subordination

To say that it is the stroking or supportive or expressive function assigned to women rather than any special social or economic structure that explains or accounts for sexism does not really account for this functional specialization itself. Since we know that men can perform the stroking function as well as women, why was it not written into their role scripts as well as into women's? Why is it optional for men, prescribed for women? Paid for, it might be added, in the case of professional counselors and therapists, expected free of charge as part of all feminine roles? Why not optional for everyone? or required of everyone? or allocated on the basis of spontaneous preference and suitability rather than sex? Seeking answers to these questions has led Movement Women to a closer examination of the structural nature of power. For interesting and important as the interpersonal manifestations of sexism undoubtedly are, there seems to be little that policy can do about them.

We have already touched on some of the structural aspects of sexism in Chapter 1, in attempting to interpret sex differences in personality and character. The point there was that the structure of the sphere of women, their status as subordinates, their status as a minority group, had to be invoked to explain why they were the way they were. The reverse emphasis is invoked here; what is it about women that accounts for their subordinate position?

The classical Marxists had made a distinction between exploitation, which was an economic phenomenon, and coercion, which was a political, power-based one. Both have been important in the case of women and both have rested on such gross physical sex differences as size and kinetic strength. Marxists have tended to explain the inferior status of women in terms of the first: women were exploited because they were physically less capable of productive work. Movement Women, while they do not reject the economic point of view, discount it or at least subordinate it to a power emphasis.

It has been woman's lesser capacity for violence as well as for work that has determined her subordination. In most societies woman has not only been less able than man to perform arduous kinds of work, she has also been less able to fight. Man not only has the strength to assert himself against nature, but also against his fellows. *Social coercion* has interplayed with the straightforward division of labor, based on biological capacity, to a much greater extent than generally admitted.

When hunting was a major economic activity, they admit, physical factors may have been enough to assign it to men, and coercion was not required. But with the coming of agriculture, the arduous work of tilling and cultivation was imposed on women not because they were especially suited to it but because of socially instituted coercion. With early industrialization and urbanization, as the importance of gross physical differences became attenuated, coercion became pre-eminent; thus "physical deficiency [in the sense of inability to perform work] is not now, any more than in the past, a sufficient explanation of women's relegation to inferior status."

Movement Women minimize the economic argument based on a sexually determined division of labor because it leads, they believe, to an overly optimistic conclusion, namely, that technology, by supplying physical strength and speed to women, will finally bring about their liberation. An interpretation that rests exclusively on the physical capacity to perform productive work is not, they believe, adequate to explain the low status of women vis-à-vis men. Certainly not in this day and age.

Coercion is the true basis of women's inferior status, and coercion rests on power and hence, ultimately, on physical force. Thus "male supremacy rests finally on force, physical power, rape, assault and the threat to assault. As a final resource when all else has failed, the male resorts to attack. But the fear of force is before every woman always as a deterrent—dismissal, divorce, violence—personal, sexual, or economic."

It is quite amazing how liberating is the mere ability to defend themselves physically:

Women are attacked, beaten and raped every day. By men! Women are afraid to walk certain streets after dark, and even afraid to walk into buildings where they live. It's about time that we as Women get strong in order to defend ourselves! Two of us (ages 29 and 43) . . . decided to learn Karate. . . . The trouble is, even now, after actually learning how to punch, we don't really want to punch at men. The first thing we think about is: "But I don't want to hurt him." Then we realize that this is really a traditional feminine cover-up for the truth which is that we are afraid of men. Women have always known that to hit a man seriously means risking getting killed. . . . As a result of Karate, we are gaining confidence in our bodies and are going through some fantastic changes in terms of our feelings of self-worth. Our confidence has increased not only in confrontations with "dirty-old-men" in the streets, but also in nonphysical confrontations with our own men and society in general. We do feel as though we have more control over our own lives because of our new potential physical power.

The frequency with which violence and physical force appear in the writings of Movement Women, and their resort to karate for self-protection, remind an academic sociologist of the gaping lacunae in the professional literature on the relations between the sexes. Have the sociological researchers been victimized the same way as the psychologists have? Have they overlooked whole areas of behavior because there was no room for them in their own middle-class frame of reference? We know that in some ethnic groups women are only a generation or so away from the sanctioned use of physical force by men. Why does it take a Movement Woman to remind us that the threat of it is still operating in marriage?

. . . the threat of force itself . . . begins by a man's paling or flushing, clenching his fists at his sides or gritting his teeth, perhaps making lurching but controlled motions or wild threatening ones while he states his case. In this circumstance it is difficult for a woman to pursue the argument which is bringing about the reaction, usually an argument for more freedom, respect, or equality in the marital situation. And of course, the conciliation of this scene, even if he has beaten her, may require his apology, but also hers, for provoking him. After a while the conditioning becomes so strong that a slight change of color on his part, or a slight stiffening of stance . . . suffices to quiet her or keep her in line.

The part played by force or violence in the relations of the sexes is remarkably underplayed in the research literature. There used to be discussion of the use of physical force in the rearing of children; "spare the rod and spoil the child" was once an accepted aphorism. And an old folk saying advised that the more you whipped dogs, donkeys, and women the better they were. But little serious research. Sadism, yes, and cruelty as a ground for divorce—but almost nothing on wife-beating, on marital rape.

Still, physical variables—height, weight, kinetic or muscular strength, aggression-stimulating hormones—are not trivial or ignorable in explaining socially relevant variables. The average man is taller, heavier, muscularly stronger, and physically more aggressive than the average woman. The cliché of the cave man dragging home a female by the hair need have no anthropological basis in fact but it represents an archetypical truth. In a crunch—and I am amazed to learn from the writings of Movement Women how common such crunches can be—the average man can enforce his will by sheer brute strength. Women may be as motivated to violence as men are, but since their physical equipment for violence is less effective in actual use, they are at a great disadvantage in a physical encounter. It is true that here, as elsewhere, technology modifies "natural" relationships. Guns, bombs, and poisons are great equalizers between men and women as well as among men.[4]

There was a time when, at least in middle-class circles, there were powerful moral constraints on the use of physical force by men on women.[5] In the 1930's there was a spate of moving pictures (which the public lapped up) in which men struck women. But the pleasure was vicarious; striking a woman was not countenanced.

Violence is always contrary to the interests of women, not only because they cannot hold their own in a bona fide fight with a

4. Otto Pollak notes that "the woman who kills uses poison more often than any other means." See *The Criminality of Women* (Philadelphia: University of Pennsylvania Press, 1950), p. 16. Among the 13 Weathermen indicted for planning terrorist bombings, 7 were women (*Washington Post,* July 24, 1970).

5. The moral development of boys had come to depend on the sheer propinquity of the mother. See Travis Herschi, *Causes of Delinquency* (Berkeley: University of California Press, 1969), pp. 237–239.

man, but also because they must call upon men for protection against other men. They are literally protegées, hence in a subordinate status almost by definition.

"Sex and violence" are often bracketed together today as major concerns. "Make love, not war," has been one of the prime imperatives of young radicals. Still I am led to ponder the use of violence by many of them. Has it ricocheted against women?

From a long historical perspective, it is probably true that physical sex differences played a larger part in all social structures when almost everyone was young, for it is especially in the earlier years that differences between the sexes are most salient. And what looks like a recrudescence of salience may be a concomitant of the very large cohort of young people on the scene today. In the later years, physical differences no longer favor men. After retirement, in fact, it is the men who are likely to become the protegés.

Having lived so many years in an ambience that forbade the use of physical force by men against women, in the absence of serious research guidance, I must confess that I cannot gauge the part played by sheer physical size and kinetic strength in determining the position of women. I am willing to go along with Movement Women in concluding that it may be greater than we have been led to believe.

To interpret sexism in terms of physical force does not imply that such force has to be invoked every day in order to guarantee male supremacy. The sexist ideology is absorbed in the socialization process, by women as well as by men, and requires no physical reinforcement thereafter. It is self-enforcing.

So much, then, for sexism and its many ramifications. It is, understandably, one of the major targets of Movement Women. But so also are marriage and the nuclear family.

Marriage as Target

Related to both sexism and the privatized nuclear family as a target of Movement Women is marriage as now institutionalized. We noted earlier that although marriage had a marked effect on work motivation among women, it had little effect on actual professional achievement. Once committed to a career, the married women showed achievement equal to that of unmarried women. So long as children were not involved, then, marriage as related to the careers of women has little relevance for the public interest. But it still has relevance for Movement Women concerned with self-actualization, not so much because of any effect it might have on careers as because of what sexism in marriage does to the personalities of women.

Although there is a formidable research basis for the charge that marriage as now structured in our society is not good for wives (Bernard, 1971), Movement Women do not rely on this research in their indictments. They rely on their own experiences and observations.

Movement Women feel that women have, in effect, been sold a bill of goods in marriage. Though it "is made to seem attractive and inevitable," marriage "is a trap." They have been programmed from childhood to think that not marrying is a fate worse than death: "Better dead than unwed." They are encouraged to put all their eggs in this one basket. It is their self-fulfillment. Actually it imposes subservience on women and ultimately deprives them of any identity of their own.

The attacks on marriage in the earlier polemics were part of the disillusionment the women experienced in the movement; it was a counterpart of the disillusionment they were experiencing at their exclusion from policy and leadership positions, and it reflected the same male chauvinism. "As [Movement Women] got married, they found that there were no models for a marriage in which both man and woman were politically active. Was the once-active woman now to assume a supportive role, stay home with the kids or get an unwanted job to support her activist husband? Were both partners' interests to have equal weight in determining what kind of work they would do, where they would live?" The answer to the first brace of questions was, apparently, "Yes" to both; to the second, "No, neither."

The picture of the marriages of women in the movement looks grim as depicted in the early polemics. The women "earn the money in the mundane jobs that our society pays people to do,

so the radical men can be at home and be political and creative.
. . . But in order to do this, these men need followers and main-
tainers. Thus, the workers of the movement . . . are the typists,
fund-raisers and community organizers." One is reminded of the
shtetl wife, except that she was more than happy to support her
learned husband in his studies. Or of the Old Testament wife
whose price was above jewels, who supported her husband so he
could sit at the town gates and engage in disputations. In the
communes described in Washington, the men were engaging in
their own thing, whether or not it was remunerative at all,
whereas the women, when they worked, had the commonplace
jobs—substitute teacher, secretary, telephone operator. In a large
proportion of communes, it was the women, doing the work society would pay for, who supplied the stable, on-going income.

One document, a kind of "Can-this-marriage-be-saved" manual,
analyzes the dynamics of husband-wife relations and tries to show
the wife how she can protect herself and liberate herself from her
husband's oppression. The way to achieve this goal includes
learning to call the shots as he fires them, that is, to learn to
"understand, identify, and explicitly state the many psychological
techniques of domination in and out of the home. . . . No woman
should feel befuddled and helpless in an argument with her husband. She ought to be able to identify his stratagems as he uses
them and thus to protect herself against them, to say, you're using
the two-cop routine, the premature apology, the purposeful mis-
understanding, etc." (We are reminded of the movement a generation ago to help the victims of propaganda disarm the manipu-
lators by giving them names for all the techniques used by them).

Still, most Movement Women marry. For "even when they
admit its [marriage's] many faults, they are convinced that it is the
only way to avoid loneliness and insecurity and even terror.
. . . [But] there is little reality in the human relations in this
society, and least of all in marriage."

Among Movement Women who do not marry, there is no feeling of failure. Some, in fact, positively advocate not getting married and having children, though not necessarily celibacy. For
some, living alone, "autonomously in control of her own life" was
the ideal solution. For some, female communes. "The commune

should be politically rather than socially oriented (liberation, not snagging men, should be the goal) and women should practice self-sufficiency individually and collectively. Possibilities for learning from each other should be exploited, while resisting temptation to fall back on each other for entertainment."

At least some nonmovement women have found communes the answer for a satisfying design for living. The February 1967 issue of *The Church Woman* devoted to the single woman included descriptions of two communities of religious lay women. In 1960 there were 141,141 women living in religious group quarters. Several groups of religious have disbanded as orders and reorganized as community workers, living in urban communes. The idea is not at all uncongenial.

Some Movement Women do advocate celibacy as a way of avoiding the slavery of marriage. ("He offers us marriage . . . and has his slave for life!") Or of achieving serenity. "Celibacy would be worthwhile in order to preserve the quietness—'be still and know that I am God'—needed for graceful loving." Or a way of escaping from male aggression. Or a way of depriving men of control over women.

Certainly not all of the Movement Women subscribe to these extreme views; but enough of them do to make an impact. In a large number of cases the husbands, if not enthusiastic about their wives' views, are open to being convinced. And many, in time, do become convinced. Recently male liberation groups have even begun to form (*Newsweek,* July 20, 1970, 75–76).[6]

Quite aside from the destructive effects on women of marriage as now institutionalized, Movement Women also charge it with performing anti-revolutionary functions for industry and the Establishment. By absorbing the shocks that the world inflicts on men, wives deflect any revolutionary rage the men might otherwise feel.

---

6. Some husbands willingly babysit so that their wives may attend Movement meetings. One young husband was won over to his wife's point of view when she convinced him of the servility of traditional female role prescriptions. *He* did not want an inferior wife. Another young man, when asked why he preferred the company of Movement Women, replied as though the answer were self-evident: they were more interesting and they contributed more to the relationship than more dependent girls did.

Women serve as "lightning rods" for men's frustration at other factors in their environment. This can be especially serviceable for the ruling class. Often it is the man of the family who experiences most directly the real power relationships in the society. . . . When wives play their traditional role as takers of shit, they often absorb their husbands' legitimate anger and frustration at their own powerlessness and oppression. With every worker provided with a sponge to soak up his possibly revolutionary ire, the bosses rest more secure. Chauvinist attitudes help to maintain this asocial system of tension-release.

The Nuclear Family as Target

The birth of children transforms a marriage into a family. It ushers in a panoply of new relationships that have a profound effect on the position of women. For it is the erroneous insistence that the functions of "reproduction, sexuality, and the socialization of children . . . are . . . intrinsically related to each other" that is the key to the subordinate position of women. The path is "maternity, family, absence from production and public life, sexual inequality." Historically valid, perhaps, but not intrinsically so. For the nuclear family as we now know it is only one way to organize these functions. They could be structured in other ways. They could, in brief, "tomorrow be de-composed into a new pattern." And many in addition to Movement Women believe they should be.

Much as Movement Women might like to see the development of the surrogate womb, they do not count on it for the present. The reproductive function is accepted as intrinsically female; and not much can be done to liberate women from it, except to play down its importance.

Although not among their major goals, it may turn out that this under-emphasis on reproduction may constitute a major contribution of the revolution the Movement Women are bringing about. One hears more and more often from young women the following model for their own lives:

We think one should avoid pregnancy (by abortion if necessary) at this time. If one has a talent for dealing with children, she (or he) can work in a nursery school or an orphanage or even set up a child-care center. If one has an overpowering need to possess a child of one's own, there are many homeless children and unwanted children soon to be born; there is no need, where the world problem is overpopulation and not underpopulation, to bring still more into the world.

For the child-rearing or socialization function is not the same as the reproductive function; and there is no inherent reason, say the Movement Women, why child rearing should be relegated exclusively to women. "They [reproduction and socialization] are [only] historically, not intrinsically, related to each other in the present modern family." They can be separated and structured differently (Bernard, 1966). Movement Women do not accept the psychiatrists' declaration that some "inner space" in women's "somatic design" for the bearing of children also carries with it "a biological, psychological, and ethical commitment to take care of human infancy." They take seriously W. J. Goode's conclusion that real equality between the sexes will require a radical re-organization of society, a reorganization that relieves women of the exclusive responsibility of child rearing. They are ready for it.

We noted earlier that all the thinking and research embodied in this book presupposed the persistence of the status quo, of present "social arrangements," the current way of structuring not only work but also family functions. In Chapter 8 we looked at plans, suggestions, and ideas for somehow or other integrating the "two roles of women," which characterize the present sexual specialization of functions. There has been near unanimity about the necessity for providing help with child care—by industry, the community, private co-operatives, whoever—for women who want it. Part-time work programs, interrupted careers and retool-ing programs, counseling—some proposals have been more hu-manitarian than others, and some more hard-boiled. Whatever form they took, all were designed to make participation in the labor force easier, all presupposed the existing institutional struc-ture. All took for granted the present sexual differentiation of functions. Whatever else might or might not be "woman's work," at least child care and child rearing were peculiarly, intrinsically, eternally, unchangeably women's functions.

But once the legal proscription of the sexual division of labor is achieved, there is no longer a *logical* ground for the sexual specialization of functions (other than reproduction) either. Movement Women challenge the old assumptions. Merely helping women bear the load of child care and child rearing is viewed as inadequate. More, much more, is needed. They zero in on the basic problem as they see it: the nuclear family itself. They are not opposed to the nuclear family per se; they accept the father-mother-child constellation. They are not looking for an amorphous, unstructured, impersonal, irresponsible pattern of parent-child relationship. What they reject is the way this group is supposed to live, the privatized household it is expected to maintain, and the division of labor it is supposed to conform to. They protest the way it is now structured as the basic agency of their exploitation by society. As now set up, "the family . . . is the primary agent of sexual repression in this society. . . . By defining woman primarily within the family . . . . it has deprived her of her humanity. . . . If women are to liberate themselves they must come squarely to grips with the reality of the family."

The diagnosis of the family as the major roadblock to the full emancipation of women is very old. It has been monotonously documented ever since the first industrial revolution. Even before Marx it was recognized as wasteful to the economy as well as limiting to women.

As a unit of consumption independent homes are uneconomical, not to say wasteful, according to rationalistically-minded reformers who have made the modern home a target of their criticisms for over a century. The pre-Marxist socialist, Charles Fourier, was one of the first to point out the defects of the system, and throughout the 19th and 20th centuries socialists and feminists repeated essentially the same arguments as those he used. The spectacle of millions of separate heating systems, kitchens, and laundries, of millions of women marketing individually and cooking individually and thus missing the advantages of a division of labor and specialization and machine technology, seemed to violate most of the canons of efficiency that were being evolved by business and industry. Fourier himself proposed as a remedy that groups of families combine to live cooperatively in phalansteries or apartment houses with common kitchens which would permit a division of labor. Although the actual experiments with phalanxes were not too encouraging when tried out, the ideal of cooperative living arrangements has persisted, doubtless because it represents a real solution to a pressing problem (Bernard, 1942).

I have already commented on the deteriorating effects of domesticity on the mentality of women.

But no one seemed able to do much about it, although some did try, in communities of one kind or another throughout the nineteenth century. In the current ambience of challenge to all authority, to all collective representations, to all taken-for-granted norms inherited from the past, more and more women are challenging those which have defined their functions in ways that inevitably lead to role conflict and deprive them of opportunities to achieve self-actualization. Movement Women are quick to point out the fatal flaw in the classical analysis: it failed to distinguish between the reproductive and the child-rearing or socializing functions. Such a defect of analysis renders any solution all but impossible.

If the nuclear family as structured were performing well the socializing function assigned to it, an argument might be made for its indispensability, regardless of its costs to the economy as a whole or to individual women themselves. But it was not. Barrington Moore was therefore willing to examine the idea that the family might not even survive as an institution. His concern was not only for women but for everyone, men and children as well as women. The family as now structured was contrary to the public interest.

Following Bertrand Russell, Moore argued that there are conditions now that "make it possible for the advanced industrial societies of the world to do away with the family and substitute other social arrangements that impose fewer unnecessary and painful restrictions on humanity" (Moore, 1958, p. 162). He felt that obligatory affection among kin was "a true relic of barbarism." The demands made on a modern wife and mother were becoming impossible to meet; children were a burden and their care often degrading and demeaning. (Some Movement Women call it "shit-work.") Nor, contrary to all the clichés, did it even do a good job in child rearing to compensate for its defects. Even in 1958, years before Movement Women arrived on the scene, Moore noted, as many have increasingly done since then, that the troubles of adolescence constituted evidence of the "inadequacy" of the family "in stabilizing the human personality." Like Movement Women, he accused modern students of the family of doing little more than "projecting certain middle-class hopes on to a refractory reality." He called for new and creative ways to rear children that would supply the love and affection we know they require but which the modern family by no means guarantees them. Movement Women concurred: "Ask the children what they think of the institution which supposedly exists for their upbringing, their benefit. All the love between 'man and woman' in the world will not make that tiny unit any less lonely, and less perverted to the child who is raised within it." Moore's indictment took on added force in the 1960's, when the public began to feel an enormous bafflement at the alleged outcomes of the child-rearing practices of the 1940's and 1950's. The behavior of the radical young seemed to document Moore's charges. A young woman with the kind of home and family life that was almost archetypically a model of correct child rearing was blown to bits in a bomb factory; young men from the "best" families turned up in jails on narcotics charges. Alienated youth became stereotypes. "The family" that middle-class people were so assiduously protecting against its critics was, indeed, foundering on a "refractory reality." W. J. Goode (1963), like Moore, agreed that conditions now made possible a radical restructuring of family relations, but he noted that "the family bases upon which all societies rest at present [still] required that much of the daily work of the house and children be handed over to women."

If there were indeed something intrinsic in human beings that made the nuclear family as now structured inevitable, the situation would, of course, be hopeless. But there is not. Kinship groups are very old, as, of course, are units of parents-and-offspring. But families are culturally and especially psychologically defined groups. And the extremely privatized nuclear family as we know it today is, historically speaking, not very ancient.

Philippe Aries asks if we are not "unconsciously overly impressed by the part the family has played in our society for several centuries, and therefore . . . tempted to exaggerate its scope and even attribute to it an almost absolute sort of historical authority?" He thinks so. He argues, in fact, that the concept of the family as we think of it is new.

> In the Middle Ages . . . the family existed in silence; it did not awaken feeling strong enough to inspire poet or artist. We must recognize the importance of this silence; not much value was placed on the family. Similarly we must admit the significance of the iconographic blossoming which after the 15th and especially the 16th century followed this long period of obscurity; the birth and development of the concept of the family.
> This powerful concept was formed around the conjugal family, that of the parents and children. This concept is closely linked to that of childhood. It has less and less to do with problems such as the honour of a line, the integrity of an inheritance, or the age and permanence of a name; it springs simply from the unique relationship between the parents and their children (Aries, 1962, p. 364).

Aries' emphasis on the affectional aspects of the family, it might be noted in passing, was in direct contradiction to the Marx-Engels emphasis on the property aspects, a model on which Movement Women tended to rely. Aries traced the diastolic-systolic pattern of conjugal and consanguineal emphases in the family back to the Frankish state, noting the impact each had on the relative power of wives. He did not disregard property aspects, but he did not emphasize them either.

In Chapter 4 we noted the increasing privatization of the home after the fifteenth century. It paralleled and reflected the increasing privatization of the family.

> In the 18th century, the family began to hold society at a distance, to push it back beyond a steadily extending zone of private life. . . . The modern family . . . cuts itself off from the world and opposes to society the isolated group of parents and children. All the energy of the group is expended on helping the children to rise in the world, individually and without any collective ambi-

tion; the children rather than the family [constitute the core]. . . .
The family has become an exclusive society (Aries, 1962, pp. 398,
404).

This privatization and isolation of the child-centered family
reached almost absurd proportions in the twentieth century—
with baneful results. Young people were leaving it as soon as they
could (Bernard, 1972). And at least part of the motivation that
led women to enter the labor force had to do with escape from
the family. For our purposes here, the major relevance lies in the
fact that the burden of maintaining this privatized, isolated, and
probably unwholesome family fell chiefly on the shoulders of
women. They had to be at the service of the children, (if not
as chauffeur, then as symbolic anchor) not only when they were
infants and preschoolers but also when they were teenagers and
even young adults. More and more of them were coming to feel
that they'd had it.

We referred in Chapter 8 to evidence from a long-time follow-
up study of 400 marriages showing that marriages in which there
was a high degree of role differentiation—the wife specializing
almost exclusively in domestic roles and the husband in the provider role—tended to deteriorate into "empty shell" marriages.
The author of the same study questioned "the extent to which
children are well served in a highly differentiated family. . . . In
families where the wife also works, it is clear that role differentiation is retarded, with the husband assuming some of the household—i.e., specifically family—tasks. Although direct evidence
on this is wanting, it seems reasonable to suggest that the father
also continues to share at least some active responsibility for the
socialization of all children, not just the first-born. Thus, although
the child's interaction with the mother is reduced when she
works, his interactions with his parents may not be greatly reduced at all. In other words, the child may have a more balanced
set of relationships with his parents in cases where both mother
and father work" (Dizard, 1968, p. 74).

Enough of diagnosis, Movement Women were saying. So they,
as well as others, translated academic discussion into action. They
proposed no longer to just stand there, but to do something. An

amorphous set of experiments, proposals, and trials-and-errors began to flood the idea hopper. They have not as yet jelled enough to tell us what is happening or is likely to happen. It will take several years before we fully understand what is happening, but it is quite clear that some kind of revolution is taking place. Whether or not it will conform entirely to the ideals of Movement Women, it is certainly later than most conventional people think, as some of the proposed solutions indicate.

REFERENCES

Aries, Philippe, *Centuries of Childhood* (New York: Knopf, 1962).

Bernard, Jessie, *American Family Behavior* (New York: Harper, 1942), p. 519.

———, "The Fourth Revolution," *Jour. Soc. Issues,* 22 (April 1966), pp. 76–87.

———, "The Status of Women in Modern Patterns of Culture," Annals Amer. Acad. Pol. & Soc. Sci., 375 (Jan. 1968), 3–14.

———, "Sexism and Discrimination," *American Sociologist,* 5 (Nov. 1970).

———, *The Future of Marriage* (New York: Macmillan, 1971), Chapter 3.

Dizard, Jan, *Social Change in the Family* (Chicago: Community and Family Study Center, University of Chicago, 1968), p. 74.

Friedan, Betty, *The Feminine Mystique* (New York: Norton, 1963).

Goode, William Josiah, *World Revolution and Family Patterns* (New York: Free Press, 1963), p. 373.

Moore, Barrington, "Thoughts on the Future of the Family," in *Political Power and Social Theory* (Cambridge: Harvard University Press, 1958), p. 162.

Newsweek (July 20, 1970), 75–76.

Scheff, Thomas J., "Negotiating Reality: Notes on Power in the Assessment of Responsibility," *Social Problems,* 16 (Summer 1968), 7–10.

Weisstein, Naomi, "Kinder, Kuche, Kirche as Scientific Law: Psychology Constructs the Female," *Motive,* 29 (March-April 1969), 78–85.

13

Some Proposed Ways Out

Communes

Some Movement Women would like to experiment with rearing children communally. "It's just not honest to talk about freedom for women unless you get the child rearing off their backs. We may not be ready for [rearing children communally] but if we're going to be honest, we've got to talk about it. Face it, raise the questions." Some do more than advocate merely talking about it, raising questions. They are experimenting with "communal" child rearing, and in at least some cases, they are succeeding, even if only temporarily.

Because so many communes and collectives are transitory, ephemeral, here-today-and-gone-tomorrow, and because few, if any, keep records, we may never have a complete or accurate account of them as they functioned in the 1960's and 1970's. In 1969, the journal of the commune movement, *Modern Utopia,* listed almost 200 "intentional" communities, and it was estimated that there must be four to six times that number (Otto, 1970). Most of what we know about them derives from journalistic accounts, very few of which tell us about child-rearing practices, even though at least one community was established along the lines laid down by B. F. Skinner in *Walden Two* in which strict conditioning procedures were to be practiced (Todd, 1970).

264

In the summer of 1969 there were between 300 and 400 individuals living in an estimated 40 to 60 communes in Washington, D.C., with an average membership of about nine. Some were organized around common vocational interests: leather-working, film-making, guerrilla theater, rock music, light shows, puppetry, and what-have-you. Some were religious or ideological: Catholic, antiwar activist, Christian Renewal. Some were drug-oriented. There was a loose confederation among the communes; the Washington Free Community, Inc., a sort of nonprofit "Urban Coalition" for radicals, operated a food-buying cooperative. Plans were under consideration to establish a nonprofit restaurant.

The communes varied widely in morale, organization, and success. Some achieved true communitarianism; others remained mere crash pads, their members "chillingly apart," not even seeing one another for weeks. A few tried group marriage but most observed marital bonds. Some were stable; others had rapid turnover. Almost all commune residents were in their twenties or late teens (Bernstein, 1969).

The following account is of one of the more successful communes and is one of the few accounts that describe the effects on children of such a design for living.

"She's not a housewife any more," says John of his 29-year-old wife, Nina. [These are not their real names.] "This is the first time we've been able to be together like human beings since we've had the kids. Now, one person cooks every 11 days and cleans the house."

John . . . is a principal figure in what is widely regarded as one of the city's most successful communes. . . . John and Nina live in serenity with 13 other people, among them their 3-year-old daughter, Mary, and her brother, Philip, 2. Two other children live in the house, Barry, age 6, and Paul, 3, the sons of the home's other principals, Dave and Myra.

The remaining seven adults in the house of 15 are two unmarried couples, two single men and one single girl, all in their late teens and early 20's. . . .

John, Nina and their two children live on . . . $45 a week . . . and a small stipend. . . . "Before we moved here we were always scrounging on $200 a week," John says. "You can't make it on $45 a week in the real world, but in this world you can, with four people. And there's been no drop in quality. In fact there's a richness that was never there before. . . ."

Adds Nina . . . "I've never felt so free. I wanted more kids. Now, with the other two children here, who are like our own, we don't need any more. John and I have complete freedom to go off. We don't need baby-sitters. We can walk off and just take a 10-minute stroll together. We couldn't do that before. . . . I was . . . bad-tempered and bitchy . . . because I was so tied to the apartment and the kids. . . . We . . . live conventional lives. . . . We don't have a group marriage or anything like it. We have a tribal family in which we're all very close and center things around the children."

The house is demonstrably oriented toward the children. . . . Last week when Dave and Myra were touring Canada, their sons stayed behind with their other "parents" and the remaining seven adults who roughly fill the role of aunts and uncles in a large, closely tied family.

For the two small boys, the situation presented few unusual difficulties because, after only three months of communal living, they seem acclimated to their unusual family structure. . . . "In conventional families," says John, "kids get the attention of just two people—their parents. Here the authority structure involves a wide variety of people. It removes all the Freudian germs. Their attachment to their parents is not neurotic. They don't always worry about what Mommy and Daddy do. They're not watching them every moment because there are others to be concerned with who are also concerned with them."

Since coming to the commune "there has been a tremendous change in our kids," according to him. . . . "They're more secure, because of the other people around and because I have more time to spend with them now that I have fewer household duties. . . ."

John regards the organization structure of the commune as "optional," noting that "there's just one list in this house: for cooking and cleaning once every 11 days. . . . A really communal situation doesn't come from lists. What's important is integration. That's the word that flows through everything here: integration of education, of interpersonal relationships, of responsibility. Straight society is fragmented, everybody is in boxes and there is no integration, no flow. Every time I see a co-op or commune go down, it's because of overimmersion of the self on the part of the members—like in straight society. Marriage and children guard against that. Communes work if you understand what marriage and family are—

not in the legal sense, but in the spiritual sense. This place works because we have love and trust" (Bernstein, 1969).[1]

Others, not in the radical movement, are thinking in terms of a more sophisticated, large-scale analogue, "child-care communities" built in to conventional apartment houses, a cross between child-care centers and co-operatives:

> Can we devise some new self-maintaining social institution, especially for the central city, that would help out families with working mothers or overburdened mothers by performing many of the needed child care and domestic services that are performed by the home-making mother in the conventional family or by a paid housekeeper in a well-to-do professional family?
>
> The answer is that it might be surprisingly easy to create institutions of this sort, when we consider how close to them we are already. What is most needed for professional families, broken families, or slum families is evidently group child care, supplemented by group dining arrangements to reduce the burden of shopping, cooking, and cleaning up. If facilities for those could be built into new residential or urban renewal developments or into large new apartment buildings, it might take only a relatively small organizational effort to make "child care communities" based on such services. These would meet the needs of a special housing and rental market, they could improve life greatly for both mothers and children, and yet with their group economies they might cost little more than is already being spent by the families and by society on care and preschool arrangements for many. . . .

1. For an account of a rural commune, See *Life*, July 18, 1969; and for related rural experiments, Sara Davidson, "Open Land: Getting Back to the Communal Garden," *Harper's* (June 1970), 91–102. It is difficult to know precisely the current status of communes. Many are versions of co-operatives. Some distinguish themselves as collectives or, in technical terms, task-oriented groups. Some of the more stable ones may show up in census reports as "households of unrelated individuals," which were increasing far more rapidly than husband-wife households in the 1960's. For a brief statistical overview of such households, see Jessie Bernard, "Present Demographic Trends and Structural Outcomes in Family Life Today," in James A. Peterson (ed.), *Marriage and Family Counseling: Perspective and Prospect* (New York: Association Press, 1968), pp. 60–80. Census figures doubtless vastly underenumerate households of unrelated individuals, since so many of them are of very short duration.

Concerning the acceptability and stability of such a social institution as the community described here, it may be worth noting that group dining and group child care were common in the "extended families" in the poor agricultural households of Eastern Europe in the last century. Some 15 to 30 people of several generations lived under one roof. . . . Like-wise in the hard life of the early Israeli kibbutzim or collective farms, the women needed to and wished to contribute their labor equally with the men, and this was made possible only by group dining and group child care. . . .

Such examples may seem alien to the American tradition and situation. But they show that group dining and group child care may be a useful and stable response to situations where women must work, not only at high income levels but in hard poverty situations, whenever a large group can be brought together by one means or another for the organization of such service. The United States today may be becoming more receptive to such ideas than in the past. The addition of such services in new housing projects would provide a functional integration of the community unit, a "systems" approach to family and neighborhood problems that would not be out of line with current thinking (Platt, 1969, pp. 17–18).

It is an interesting illustration of Moore's charge that modern students do little more than project "certain middle-class hopes on to a refractory reality" that the editors of the journal that published this article felt called upon to note the fact that child-care communities were controversial. They quoted Jerome Kagan on the dangers that may befall children reared in them, such as seriously diluted ties with their parents, weakened emotional involvement of the mother with her own child, and so on, precisely the outcomes that John and Nina judged to be among the benefits for children of communal living, and that Movement Women believe to be far preferable to the results of present family living.

In Sweden, experiments with "megahouseholds" and "megafamilies" were also in process, cooperative or communal in structure according to the preferences of their members, and also greatly concerned with the welfare of children. Such arrangements made possible a more flexible assignment of roles.

Fine, say Movement Women about these ideas, fine so far as they go. But they do not go far enough. They are only a step or two ahead of the standard proposals such as, for instance, that industry, academia, and business help bear the costs of child rearing exacted from women in terms of professional careers by providing maternity leave and part-time work and even child-care centers. There is nothing truly revolutionary in this approach. Alva Myrdal and Viola Klein have been promoting that solution for a long time; it is also, essentially, the approach of conventional women's organizations. But it is not good enough. It answers one part of the Movement Women's charge against the nuclear family as a child-rearing agency, but not another, for it still recognizes that child rearing basically is exclusively a woman's function. This Movement Women reject. The rearing of children is too important to leave to one sex; both should participate in it.

Child rearing is the most important function in any society, as important as defense, and there is no intrinsic reason why it should be allocated to one sex alone. "Housework and child care, like other socially useful, but denigrated labor, fall unevenly on the shoulders of the most oppressed groups. Such work should be equally distributed among all who benefit from it."

Men and the Child-Rearing Function

Movement Women attacked the specialization of women in child rearing from two angles: that of women themselves and that of the children. Their own case could be simply stated: so long as child rearing is an exclusive female function, equality in any other area remains impossible. And the evidence is convincing, as derived from the discussion of the two-role pattern of living and the difficulty of reconciling the two roles under present social arrangements.

But in addition, Movement Women argued for less rigid role specialization from the point of view of the children's welfare.

They wanted the kind of "marriage that has the potential for giving children the love and concern of two parents rather than one." They accuse our society, despite its insistence that it is child-centered, of being really antichild. (One commented on the hostile glances she elicited as she nursed her infant in the park.) It is argued that children have a right to more attention from men, not only from fathers, but also from teachers and others in their world. Diatribes against momism and the good Jewish mother have long since become standard fare in the media and in cocktail-party chatter. The femininization in our society not only of infant care but also of child rearing and socialization has been characterized as dysfunctional for children, especially as having a demasculinizing effect on boys (Sexton, 1969).

Although there is a fair degree of consensus among Movement Women that the isolated nuclear family with its rigidly specialized functions is not a suitable agency for rearing children ("the private home as it now exists will appear a torture chamber to post-revolutionary people") nor the allocating of the entire responsibility for child rearing to women fair, still there is not as yet agreement on suitable substitutes.

Some suggest that "care of children . . . be delegated to those who have the talents and interest in [it] and [that] they be rewarded for their work in the same way as bridge builders or teachers." Others propose that instead of specializing certain people for the many jobs required for performing the child-rearing function, everyone be called upon to contribute. Let everyone be required to spend a year or two (or whatever period of time is necessary) in some form of child-rearing service. Thus, instead of women having to take at least ten years from their professional careers for child rearing, everyone would take out at least one year from his or her career for this service. If everyone were so drafted, far more services than now would be available for more children in the form of, say, tutoring, recreation leadership, scouting, or what-have-you. Still others have no specific plan in mind, but they know that, whatever form child rearing and socialization take, they are not the sole responsibility of women; they are everyone's, "society's."

Parenthetical Aside: Role Specialization from
the Husband-Father's Angle

Since this essay is about women, we have been looking at the effects of the sexual specialization of functions from their point of view. But, societies being all of a piece, these effects could just as well be viewed from the point of view of men. Erik Grønseth, the Norwegian sociologist, has done precisely that. He has shown how all the dysfunctionalites we have been examining from the point of view of women "may fruitfully and strategically be seen . . . as consequences of the common, underlying husband-as-economic-provider role phenomenon" (Grønseth, 1970). Thus he notes the disastrous consequences that resulted when capitalism for the first time in history made one man alone responsible for the economic provision of his children and their caretakers. Among them were economic discrimination against women; complete economic dependence of children and wives on the father-husband; the consequent subjugation of women and concomitant sex-role inequalities in both the family and the outside world; a neurotically symbiotic character in marital and parent-child relations; lack of autonomy of the nuclear family and its subjection to capitalistic economic and political systems; sexual oppression and repression; elitist authoritarianism and fascist political tendencies; alienation, apathy, destructiveness. . . .

It should be pointed out, however, that even under the inauspicious conditions currently prevailing, wives are already eroding the exclusive responsibility of husbands and fathers for the economic support of families, especially in middle-income brackets. "Wives' earnings accounted for 30 per cent or more of the income in almost half of the families with incomes between $10,000 and $15,000. They accounted for 20 per cent or more in almost three-fifths of the families with incomes of $15,000 or more" in 1967 (Women's Bureau, *1969 Handbook on Women Workers*). Unfortunately, while wives were sharing the provider role, husbands were not equally willing to share the domestic role. It was a situation analogous to that in the world of work where women were "sharing" their professions with men whereas men were not "sharing" theirs with women.

Implementing the Shared-Role Ideology

As yet ways for fully implementing the shared-role ideology remain in the realm of discussion and debate with, here and there, attempts at practical experiments. Still, it is surprising how rapidly an idea, once its time has come, begins to challenge the Establishment.

One of the ways proposed for implementing the shared-roles ideology within marriage as now structured is part-time work. As early as the first edition of *Women's Two Roles* in 1956, Alva Myrdal and Viola Klein had discussed part-time work as a solution for the problems of the married woman worker, but, as we noted in Chapter 8, had concluded that it was "neither practicable nor desirable" (Myrdal, 1956, p. 163). The arguments against it were too strong. Although women themselves, and even some employers, were satisfied with it, most employers and unions were opposed to it. Alice Rossi had granted part-time work partial approval but did not see much opportunity to find such work for women as industry is now structured (Rossi, 1965, pp. 112–113). The Professional and Executive Corps for part-time work at HEW had been established by John Gardner and had proved feasible there. But the concept was still of part-time work as a boon to women; the new concept was quite different.

In 1953, Ashley Montague had proposed that husbands and wives each work only half a day, thus making it possible for them to share both the provider and the domestic roles. The idea was not taken seriously. Others proposed that the rotation be on a semiannual basis, each spouse working half a year and remaining home the other half. Or on an annual basis, no matter.

Bruno Betteleheim had adumbrated the shared-role idea. Like Movement Women, though to a lesser degree, he had challenged our acceptance of the two-role split in the lives of women. He objected to any solution that accepted the division of their lives into separate periods: "I do not believe that the solution suggested by some of dividing woman's life into three parts—before marriage, the time when the children grow up, and the period after they have reached adolescence—offers a solution to woman's problems." He did not deny that varying degrees of investment in family and work did characterize different periods in the lives of women, but he hoped that neither would have to be completely sacrificed to the other. Ideally, as he saw it, work and family would be integrated for the sake not only of women but also of men, and for some fortunate few the work of both husband and wife would be integrated as well: ". . . a most important first step to permit both men and women to find more satisfaction in their own life, and their lives with each other, would be to organize society so that this split can be undone" (Bettelheim, 1965).

Bettelheim recognized the difficulties involved in making such arrangements for the total labor force. Still he rebuked us for accepting the industrial point of view that motherhood must adjust to the job rather than vice versa, that self-actualization in one sphere must cost the other. He implied, as many others have, that it is not fair to demand that the entire burden of adjusting to the multiple demands made on women in modern society be borne by them alone. It was once argued that workers whose jobs were eliminated by technology should not have to pay the entire price for such progress; in that case, we now accept that argument and make provision for severance pay or for provision for retraining. The same logic, Bettelheim implied, may be said to apply in the case of women. Their services are needed; they should not have to bear the entire brunt of making them available. Actually, the idea had not even occurred to most employers.[2]

Bettelheim stopped just short of the Movement Women's position, namely that roles should be shared. His specific remedies included "shorter working hours for mothers of young children, work close to their home, excellent professional care for their chil-

2. A study of twenty employers in a small city in 1959 reported that in answer to the question, "In the conflict between employee and family roles, are *all* adjustments made by the family?" most employers did, in fact, "expect the modifications to occur in family roles—not in the employer role." See James E. Conyers, "Employers' Attitudes toward Working Mothers," in Ivan Nye and Lois W. Hoffman (eds.), *The Employed Mother in America* (Chicago: Rand McNally, 1963), pp. 382–383).

dren during the first four and later six hours these women spend at work away from home, ready availability of the mother to her children in case of emergency, etc." Avant garde as some of these proposals may sound, they still presuppose the current sexual differentiation of function. They constitute, essentially, a recommendation of the double-track uninterrupted career pattern, with provisions for making it feasible for more women.

It is hard to remain avant garde very long in this fast-moving age. The shared-role idea sounded far out when Movement Women first began to advocate it; it was already beginning to be taken seriously in the 1970's. In June 1970, for example, a television program was devoted to a debate on the question whether union contracts should include clauses that made part-time work optional for both men and women. Almost half of the studio audience (46 per cent) agreed and 75 per cent of the television audience (WGBV-TV release, 1970). Neither the studio nor the television audience was a cross-section of the American public, but they might well have been a good sample of a prophetic minority. Once an issue becomes a topic for a television program, it can be taken for granted that more general debate is not too far behind.

Equally prophetic was the conclusion of Esther Peterson, a veteran of labor battles past and present, who was the judge of the debate. She was not likely to be too visionary. Her verdict was positive. Cautious, but positive:

> The formulation of the question made difficult a thorough discussion of a problem which merited better treatment. The question is far too complex for a simple "for" or "against." Unions have not been able to achieve voluntary over-time, let alone voluntary part-time. The thrust of unions' efforts has been for full-time jobs with adequate pay. When a crucial problem for the great majority of families is how to get sufficient income to make ends meet, how practical is it to expect families to manage on two part-time incomes? Or how likely is it that they should wish to do so? One is sympathetic to the basic situation which the question reflects: the under-utilization of women's ability and the unremitting routine of household tasks.
>
> However, my vote goes to those who are working for a society where no one is forced into a pre-determined role on account of sex; a society where men and women have the option to plan and

pattern their lives as they themselves choose. This society will require many things: a new climate of opinion which accepts equality of the sexes while still recognizing human and biological differences; a society which provides day care and supplementary home services which make choice possible; a society where non-merit factors in employment such as sex do not count; a society which provides a new concept of training for both young men and women with an eye to employment and social usefulness along with active parenthood. And most important, a society that provides a shortened work day and work week with adequate pay for all workers—thus permitting time for families to be together, for fathers to participate in family activities (including the care and raising of children) where both parents can develop to their fullest as human beings. It's a long way down the road, but it's coming (WGBV-TV release, July 24, 1970).

It may not be too long before we catch up with Sweden, which has already arrived at a policy of shared parenthood roles. In 1968 it had become government policy there, as noted in Chapter 8, to change "the division of functions as between the sexes . . . in such a way that both the man and the woman in a family are afforded the same practical opportunities of participating in both active parenthood and gainful employment" (Government of Sweden, 1968).

Even with men sharing the child-rearing and socialization functions, the problem is not licked. Research on child rearing, approached without preconceptions, is, in my opinion, the major research frontier of this day and age. We will have to know a great deal more to be able to do a better job of providing the ambience required to raise the kind of men and women needed to wrestle with the modern world. The insights of Movement Women should help.

The Tote Board

The evaluation of results of a pursuit-of-happiness orientation is far more difficult than the evaluation of results of a general-welfare orientation. There is nothing to serve as a standard analogous to the gross national product. In Chapter 6, the elimination of the sex-typing of work could be judged in the public interest because it would, by putting the best person in any job and utilizing workers at their highest potential, maximize the gross national product. But, in terms of the pursuit of happiness, how can one evaluate functional specialization as expressed in "one role," "two roles," and "shared roles"? Admittedly a hazardous effort, even with research support, the evaluation in the accompanying tote board is offered as a start.

The highly differentiated one-role pattern is given an across-the-board negative on the basis primarily of Jan Dizard's report on 400 families. The negative for *C* women might be modified for the younger ages, but beyond that, the negative evaluation seems correct. The two-role pattern, in which wives share the provider role, is evaluated positively for all except "nestlings" and other domestic women who do not wish to participate in the labor force and willingly pay the "empty shell" costs. The shared-role pattern would facilitate the pursuit of happiness except for two categories. For men with high achievement motivation (*A*), who thrive on professional competition, who derive a great deal of

The Tote Board

Degree of Sexual Specialization of Roles	Pursuit of Happiness						Children
	Women			Men			
	A	B	C	A'	B'	C'	
"One Role" (Maximum role differentiation)	−	−	−	−	−	−	−
"Two Roles" (Wife shares provider role)	+	+	−	+	+	+	+
"Shared roles" (Men and women share many roles)	+	+	+	−	+	+	+
No sex-typing of work	+	+	+	+	+	−	+

This chart is based on research cited in Chapter 5 under "Work, Marriage, and the Pursuit of Happiness."
Legend:
+ means pursuit of happiness is enchanced; − means pursuit of happiness is retarded.
A refers to pioneer-type women; *B* to traditional women; *C* to housewife types or "nestlings."
A' refers to men with high achievement and/or power motivation; *B'* to average men; *C'* to men who are low in achievement or power motivation.

satisfaction from driving to the top, any diversion from this life style would be a negative; they do not wish to invest time and energy in other than their professional roles. Nor, again, would "nestlings" and other domestic women wish to share the provider role.

The elimination of sex-typing of work, evaluated positively on the general-welfare criterion in Chapter 6 is here evaluated positively on the pursuit-of-happiness criterion also for all except one category. Men who need the advantage of sex in order to compete successfully would suffer a loss; they would no longer be favored simply because they were men; their maleness alone would not be an asset.

Medium and Message

The message of the angry young women we have been describing here does not need decoding. It is not occult. In an age when we must underplay rather than emphasize the maternal function, we have to stop thinking of women in such narrow terms. We must get used to the idea that reproduction is going to play only a minor part in their lives; we must become accustomed to them as human beings quite aside from their reproductive functions. We have to reconceptualize sex and sexuality; we have to rethink masculinity and femininity; we have to redefine maleness and femaleness. Changing men and women will not make them alike, but only different from one another in different ways.

We need a sexuality and a kind of concept of sex that are suitable for the kind of life we lead in this day and age, a life that demands all the talents the human species can muster from its genetic pool, whatever the sex of the body which harbors them. We cannot afford to disqualify a large segment of the population for high achievement by the mental or spiritual analogues of traditional Chinese foot-binding.

Hostile critics of Movement Women, once the flurry of faddish media coverage had somewhat subsided, leaned back and breathed more easily. Now that the fad was over, they could relax and forget it. Not so. Women's revolutions, unlike men's, are not apocalyptic. Women do not expect Armageddon. They are accustomed to a relatively slow pace. These women have already succeeded. It has already begun to seem odd that it has been men who defined female sexuality, men who defined female orgasm, men who were setting the norms for female mental health, men who were making the decisions about abortion, men who were making most of the policy decisions affecting women. *Very* odd.

Men are so accustomed to being the center of all analyses and discussions of the human condition that they cannot bear to be excluded from women's, or at least to be viewed as merely peripheral, not the main characters. "Us, too!" they invariably shout. We need to be liberated too! Of course they do. . . .

This facetiousness on my part is unwarranted. Men do, indeed, have grievances. It is destructive to them to be specialized in the provider role, as the discussion of the whole concept of the career in Chapter 9 indicated. The costs of the achievement it exacts are heavy to men, to marriage, and to children. Movement Women do see that both they and men are creatures of this demanding system. They want men as well as women to be liberated from its destructive effects.

Movement Women are carrying off a revolution in (perhaps malgré elles) a very womanly way, but in behalf of all of us.

> We want to create a world where men and women can relate to each other and to children as sharing, loving equals. Men, you have nothing to lose but your chains. . . . There will . . . be thousands of millions of women people to discover, touch and become with, who will say with a Vietnamese girl, 'Let us now emulate each other,' who will understand you when you say we must make a new world in which we do not meet each other as exploiters and used objects. Where we love one another and into which a new kind of human being can be born. We want a different world, not a share in this one, and we demand that all people be a part of it.

This revolution is the most universal, most humane, and most human revolution of all. Who can be opposed to a revolution that asks, "How do we live with others? How do we bring up our kids? How is family life and work shared? How can we all be human?" A revolution that reminds us, "We must get busy to eliminate what are not properly humane or even human ideas —the warrior, the killer, the hero as homicide"? That urges us to begin the revolution with love since "all of us, black, white, and gold, male and female, have it within our power to create a world we could bear, out of the desert we inhabit, for we hold our very fate in our hands"?

This is truly a case where self-actualization and the public interest do in fact coincide, where the success of women means success for everyone. Whether or not revolution is a proper function for women to perform, this revolution is for all of us.

Is there any better use for women?

REFERENCES

Bernard, Jessie, "One Role, Two Roles, Shared Roles," *Issues in Industrial Society*, 2 (1), (1971), 21–28.

———, *The Future of Marriage* (New York: World Book, 1972), Chapter 3.

Bernstein, Carl, "Communes, A New Way of Life in District," *Washington Post*, July 6, 1969.

Bettelheim, Bruno, "The Commitment Required of a Woman Entering a Scientific Profession in Present-Day American Society," in Jacqueline A. Mattfeld and Carol G. Van Aken (eds.), *Women and the Scientific Professions* (Cambridge: M.I.T. Press, 1965).

Grønseth Erik, "The Dysfunctionality of the Husband Provider Role in Industrialized Societies," paper prepared for the 7th World Congress of Sociology, Varna, 1970.

Myrdal, Alva, *Women's Two Roles* (London: Routledge and Kegan Paul, 1956), p. 163.

Otto, Herbert, "Has Monogamy Failed?" *Saturday Review* (April 25, 1970), 24.

Platt, John R., "Child Care Communities: Units for Better Urban Living," *The Urban Review*, 3 (April 1969), 17–18.

Rossi, Alice, "Who Wants Women in the Scientific Professions?" in Mattfeld and Van Aken (eds.), *op. cit.*, pp. 112–113.

Sexton, Patricia Cayo, *The Feminized Male: Classrooms, White Collars and the Decline of Manliness* (New York: Random House, 1969).

Sweden, Government of, *The Status of Women in Sweden*, report to the United Nations, 1968.

Todd, Richard, " 'Walden Two': Three? Many More?" *New York Times Magazine* (Mar. 15, 1970), 24–25, 114 ff.

WGBV-TV release, July 24, 1970, "The Nation Responds to The Advocates on Women's Liberation."

Women's Bureau, *1969 Handbook on Women Workers* (Washington, D.C.: Department of Labor, 1969), p. 34.

Name Index

281

Subject Index